NEVER SUBDUED

A True Story about the Philippine-American War
1898-1902 and how it led to the Moro Campaigns
against radical Islam 1902-1913

FRANKLIN HOOK

ISBN-10: 0615457010
EAN-13: 9780615457017
Library of Congress Control Number: 2011903481

HIS000000 HISTORY / General
HIS036000 HISTORY / United States / General
HIS027000 HISTORY / Military / General
HIS027110 HISTORY / Military / United States
HIS048000 HISTORY / Asia / Southeast Asia
HIS036060 HISTORY / United States / 20th Century
HIS037070 HISTORY / Modern / 20th Century
HIS037060 HISTORY / Modern / 19th Century
HIS036040 HISTORY / United States / 19th Century
COVER ART BY ARTIST RICK REEVES ENTITLED *I WOULD RATHER DIE AT THE FRONT*
REPRINTED WITH PERMISSION.

DEDICATION

For my son Christopher Power Hook and my niece Elizabeth Ann Karlgaard Keith, two souls that left this life too early. May God keep you in peace.

CONTENTS

CONTENTS

FOREWORD

You are about to read a tale of what it was like for a large number of young American men when they "went soljering" more than a century ago, in the steamy tropics of the Philippine Islands during the opening years of the 20th Century. What may surprise you is how uncannily alike "soljering" was then to that of their spiritual military heirs (perhaps including a few of their great and even great-great grandsons or granddaughters) in the cold mountain fastnesses of Afghanistan in the early 21st Century.

The context of the story is the period now referred to by most historians as the "Philippine-American War" or "Philippine War, which officially lasted three and one-half years, from February 1899 to July 1902. Until quite recently in the United States it was known as the "Philippine Insurrection" (the American supposition being that it was an armed insurgency of subject peoples against the legitimate sovereignty of the United States) and by Filipino scholars as the "Philippine Revolution" (viewed as a several decades long struggle from the late 19th Century through the first half of the 20th Century to throw off the "yoke" of first Spanish and then American Imperial rule). In recent years military historians, journalists, and politicians have often cited it as a prime example of a major American "victory" in a counterinsurgency. However this observation holds true only if the standard for success is narrowly defined as achieving military dominance and eliminating organized armed resistance in the short run. The real test is one of the outcomes over time. In the longer run did the investment of blood and treasure over a 47-year period end up benefiting the national interest or not? This is still a highly debatable point, and is complicated by the enormous impact on both the United States and the Philippines of the intervening Japanese invasion and occupation.

The origins of the Philippine-American War and the current war in Afghanistan bear no resemblance to one another. No one in the Philippine Islands had attacked the United States nor did they at any time pose an existential threat. Without going into the details of how it transpired, even President William McKinley's closest advisors and strongest supporters, such as Secretary of War Elihu Root and the American Governor General of the Philippines (and eventually President) William Howard Taft would later describe the path taken to unilaterally annex the islands, creating an unavoidable face-off between US occupiers and Filipino revolutionaries, as a "colossal blunder." Once American blood had been spilled, domestic politics permitted no way back.

Aside from the causes, the parallels between the two wars are eerily reminiscent. Deployment to the Philippines came as a surprise to the US Army, with little advance warning. It presented logistical nightmares of operating half way around the world with no established access points, friendly ports, or close by sources of supply. Intelligence was badly outdated, sparse and unreliable. Knowledge of the 75 languages of the Philippines was non-existent; other than Spanish which was only spoken by the elite and highly educated. Familiarity with the local cultures and customs was absent. This forced heavy dependence on often-unreliable third parties, in particular the "illustrados" or local autocrats created by the Spanish overlords who had their own separate agendas.

As it was, the burden of the war came to fall on a small sliver of the US populace of nearly 80 million (the population of the Philippines was between 7-8 million). The first year of the war there were no more than 20-25,000 boots on the ground, and at its peak about 70,000. One-year tours soon became two-year and officers spent even longer (for example, Captain John J. Pershing spent 4 ½ years in the islands without returning to the U.S.) At first it fell heaviest on the State Volunteer Regiments, drawn mostly from the National Guards and militias of the Western US (including North Dakota). Gradually the war effort came to be shouldered by US Army Regulars; a year earlier they had totaled less than 28,000 men. Few of the senior officers had experienced or been trained in the warfare that was required, with an attendant number of costly mistakes in judgment. Public support rapidly eroded after only a year or two and settled into apathy. In the meantime, anti-war sentiment became ever more vocal. The political problem was that a quick end had been promised; but the war dragged on and on, costs mounted, a steady stream of caskets came home, and the predicted end was always forecasted as being just around the corner. Is this beginning to sound familiar? Nevertheless, it is a tribute to the average "Doughboy" that they persevered.

So, settle in and let Colonel Hook take you back to an earlier, but not necessarily simpler, time and place.

ROBERT A. FULTON
Author of Moroland, the History of Uncle Sam and the Moros 1899-1920

PREFACE and ACKNOWLEDGEMENTS

This is a story about war, real war in real places. Since it involves military organization, I believe some explanation of units of the US Army in 1898 – 1902 would be helpful for those not familiar with some of the terms. I have attempted to do that, with apologies to my military comrades in advance for any obvious mistakes, and refer the reader to Appendix I for the results.

I was first intrigued about the subject matter for this book in February 1999 when I received my usual Veterans of Foreign Wars Magazine featuring a cover painting of the Philippines War and articles on the VFW founders. The year 1999 was the 100 year anniversary of the VFW. There were several interesting follow up articles in the months to follow. Then, in 2002, Richard Kolb, the editor of VFW, published a booklet called Blaze in the Boondocks, which included a feature about the 1st North Dakota Volunteer Infantry, and that ten of its members had been recipients of the Medal of Honor in that conflict. I was hooked (no pun intended). What followed was nearly ten years of intermittent research, collecting articles and photographs, and multiple visits to the North Dakota State Historical Society whenever I returned to Bismarck, my hometown and place of practice for more years than I care to count.

Along the way, I corresponded with experts on the history, dedicated archivists, fabulous researchers and authors, and numerous other enthusiasts. I was not surprised to learn in 2009, just as my research was beginning to gel that there was another researcher about to publish a story on the 1st North Dakota. He was John Durand, Elkhorn, WI, author of The Boys 1st North Dakota Volunteers in the Philippines. Durand was looking for help identifying members of Young's Scouts.

The photo is on page 71 of this manuscript and on the cover of Durand's book. I could not help John at that time, but later I identified Frank Anders by comparing his photos as a young man to the second from the left in the top row of the photo in question. Since then, John and I have corresponded. I find his work to be a superb body of research and thank him profusely for permission to quote some of it. We also share John Kinne's diary, available from the University of North Dakota Libraries, as a keystone in the story. Curt Hanson, head of the Elwyn B. Robinson Department of Special Collections at UND's Chester Fritz Library, was helpful in supplying that diary.

Thanks to John Hallberg of NDSU Institute for Regional Studies and Archives, Fargo, North Dakota; Sharon Silengo, photo archivist North Dakota Historical Society, Bismarck; and Carol Bohl of the Cass County, Missouri Historical Society, who provided data from Archie Galt's burial site and post war history.

Communications with Richard Kolb, editor of VFW, Balangniga Encounter experts and authors Bob Coutie and Prof. Rolando O. Borrinaga of the Philippine Islands, all of whom were kind enough to grant me permission to quote their works, are hereby recognized. Likewise, C. Douglas Sterner, recognized military historian, author and curator, Military Times Hall of Valor, sent his permission, as did Michael Patterson, Arlington Cemetery Webmaster.

Arnaldo Dumindin, who has the most prolific website with public domain and other photographs of the Philippine-American War, emailed me that he appreciated the fact that I was writing about it since his goal was "to draw interest on this war that even most Filipinos aren't aware ever took place."

The most helpful on the most difficult part of this true history has been Moroland author Robert A. Fulton of Bend, Oregon. Without his encouragement and help and his prolific writing and remarkable website, I would still be bogged down somewhere between the

Balangiga Encounter and the Battle of Bud Bagsak. I will be forever grateful, Bob. Thank you so much.

Rick Reeves of Tampa, FLA, is the talented artist whose work appears on the cover.

Finally, thanks to my son, Paul Hook, Mill City, Oregon, and grandson, Stephen Hook, APO Germany, for cartographic designs used in the text.

Franklin Hook, Spring 2011

A TRUE STORY
INTRODUCTION

Dear Reader,

This story is a narrative history, with imaginative but logical conversations amongst the principle participants and some of the individual movements and conversations in battle or elsewhere. Some of the conversations are documented in available records (for example, the conversation between Pvt. John Kinne and Major Frank White when Chief Scout "Dad" Killian was mortally wounded at Morong is documented in Kinne's diary). Another documented conversation (not written as such) was made by the Philippine Insurgent Leader's mother, Trinidad Famy y Aguinaldo, at the assassination of General Luna. One of the soldiers killed in action during Sterling Archibald Galt's heroic swim is given a fictitious name because his identity could not be found. Otherwise, with some minimal artistic embellishment by the author, this is a true story mostly told by those who were there.

Would you believe ten Medals of Honor, our nation's highest award for valor, were awarded to ten North Dakota soldiers in four battles in one war? It's true! Of the ten native North Dakotans, two were from Fargo, two from Valley City, and one each from Wahpeton,

Langdon, Mandan, Grafton, Devil's Lake, and Jamestown. Sterling A. Galt,* who was born in Maryland, has been listed in some records to have also enlisted from Maryland, which is credited (erroneously I believe) for his Medal of Honor. We will show research showing that he resided and enlisted in Valley City, ND, which his compatriots in the 1st North Dakota Volunteer Infantry accepted without a doubt. The war was the Philippine-American War 1899 – 1902, also called the Philippine Insurrection, a term criticized by liberal historians and activists as inaccurate.

There were eventually eighty-eight Medals of Honor awarded to all branches of service in this conflict. Of the ten awarded to North Dakotans, eight were awarded to members of Young's Scouts in two separate engagements in a three day period. Young's Scouts were a group of handpicked sharpshooters organized by a civilian, William H. Young. Young was a Vermont native, a Connecticut resident, a worldwide adventurer, and an ex-Dakota Territory Indian War's Scout who came to the attention of General Henry W. Lawton, one of two division officers in command in the northern Philippine campaign.

Young picked his initial twenty-five sharpshooters from three units known for their expertise. Sixteen came from the 1st North Dakota Volunteer Infantry, and, eventually, twenty-six North Dakotans would serve in the Scouts.[1] Others were recruited from the 2nd Oregon Volunteer Infantry (three were MOH recipients) and some from the 4th

---

* Medal of Honor recipient, Sterling A. Galt, born in Taneytown, Maryland, was a member of CO. G, of the 1st ND Vol. Infantry. Sterling Archibald Galt died in 1908 at the age of forty-three and is buried in Harrisonville, MO. Galt was awarded his medal for bravery at Bamban, Luzon, Nov 9, 1899. He was also a member of Young's Scouts. He is listed in the citation as a member of CO F, 36th US Volunteers, which was the unit he was assigned after his reenlistment. After his reenlistment, he stayed in the service long enough to achieve the highest enlisted rank of sergeant major. His birth date is given as 1866 on his headstone. The circumstances of Galt's death, described later in this text, tell a sad and poignant story of an unrecognized war casualty. The youngest person to receive the Medal of Honor was probably Willie Johnson who earned it during the civil war at age eleven, just before his twelfth birthday and actually received it just after his thirteenth

1 John B. Kinne, Diary 1898-1899 CO B First North Dakota Infantry (Original from the North Dakota Grand Lodge Library. University of North Dakota Elwyn B Robinson Dept. of Special Collections, Chester Fritz Library).

US Cavalry (dismounted). Captain William Birkhimer, who led the attack at San Miguel after Chief Scout Young was felled by a bullet in the knee, came from the 3rd US Artillery, and there was one other civilian besides Young, for a total of twenty-seven.

One may think that eighty-eight Medals of Honor are many for one small war, but it was the only award for valor at the time.* It does not diminish the heroic acts of the men involved, as will be seen in the descriptions provided in the citations of record, nor in other historic records available. What is remarkable is the relative percentage of native North Dakotans honored by the Medal compared to other states of origin of the combat troops. Perhaps the hunting/sharpshooter skills, harsh native environment, and sense of responsibility from these hard working lads had something to do with it.

The reader in the 21st century and beyond will come to appreciate the brutality of the conditions, the inhumanity of men in war, the unremitting courage and resolve of those Americans involved, and the realization that these engagements at the end of the 19th century and the beginning of the 20th would not be the last time our soldiers would be opposing elements of radical Islam. When the conflict expanded into the Moro Campaigns (Moro is a Spanish word for Islam) in the southern Philippines, the hostilities did not end until 1935, when the U.S. finally ceded authority to the newly created Philippine Commonwealth. The Moro's to this day have never been subdued.

"What is past is prologue".2

The following soldiers from North Dakota were awarded the Medal of Honor:

Anders, Franklin L Fargo CO B 1st ND VOL INF 5/13/1899
Boehler, Otto Wahpeton CO I 1st ND VOL INF 5/16/1899
Davis, Charles P Valley City CO G 1st ND VOL INF 5/16/1899
Downs Willis H Jamestown CO H 1st ND VOL INF 5/13/1899

---

* The Silver Star and the Distinguished Service Cross were first authorized in 1918 and authorized to Spanish American and Philippine American War Veterans at that time. Major (later Colonel) Frank Charles White from Valley City, a member deployed with the 1st ND Volunteers, who served two terms as Governor of ND, and was also United States Treasurer from 1921-28, was later awarded the Silver Star for bravery during combat in the Philippines
2 William Shakespeare. The Tempest.

Galt, Sterling A* Valley City CO G 1st ND VOL INF 11/9/1899
Jensen, Gotfred Devil's Lake CO D 1st ND VOL INF 5/13/1899
Kinne, John Fargo CO B 1st ND VOL INF 5/16/1899
Longfellow, Richard Mandan CO A 1st ND VOL INF 5/16/1899
Ross, Frank F Langdon CO H 1st ND VOL INF 5/16/1899
Sletteland, Thomas Grafton CO C 1st ND VOL INF 4/12/1899
Part I of this tale is their story. Part II tells the rest.

PART I

PROLOGUE

USS MAINE SUNK IN HAVANA CUBA HARBOR FEBRUARY 15, 1898
photo source: www.history.navy.mil

SETTING THE STAGE

The Philippine Insurrection was preceded by the U.S. war with Spain, which only lasted about four months in the spring and summer of 1898. The Spanish American War resulted in about four hundred U.S. casualties, but gained for the U.S. the former Spanish possessions of Puerto Rico, Guam, and the Philippines. The immediate causes of the Spanish American War were blamed by many historians on "outside forces," especially the sinking of the battleship Maine in a Cuban harbor in February 1898. Some speculate that yellow journalism led by William Randolph Hearst and possibly an act of sabotage on the Maine by someone promoting U.S. Imperialism were responsible. Two hundred sixty-six American lives were lost in that tragedy, and the outrage in the American press and in Congress resulted in a U.S.

demand that Spain leave Cuba, supported by a presidential order to use a naval blockade. Spain's response was to declare war on the United States on April 20th, and Congress returned the favor on April 25th.

America emerged as a world power after the U.S. Navy destroyed Spain's Pacific Fleet in Manila Bay on May 1, 1898, and later destroyed her Atlantic Fleet in subsequent engagements.

The Filipinos were initially happy that the Americans intervened to disrupt a stern Spanish rule until it became obvious that America had no intention of helping them gain their independence but instead apparently wanted to make the Philippines another American colony. A rebellion or insurgency resulted, headed by native leader Emilio Aguinaldo, whose insurgents returned initial American fire provoked by them crossing a no trespass zone near Manila on February 4, 1899. The fighting continued for over three years in the North, despite the capture of Aguinaldo in March 1901. The insurgents continued to battle, and it was not until July 4, 1902, that President Theodore Roosevelt declared the conflict officially over. Unfortunately, the Moro (Islamic) Fundamentalists, with a long history of piracy, rape, murder, kidnapping (for slavery), and thievery continued hostilities for years afterward. To this day, they remain a threat to peace in the area, especially the southern Islands.

Because most of the units fighting the Spanish American War in Cuba were regular Army units, the soldiers sent to the Philippines were mostly recruited from National Guard units from the western United States. The 1st North Dakota Volunteer Infantry was assembled in Fargo on May 8, 1898,[3] from various militias across the state. They departed for San Francisco shortly thereafter, and the good times and favorable enthusiastic public who greeted and cheered the troops as they journeyed west disappeared as soon as the troops embarked and set sail on old, decrepit cargo ships for the Philippine Islands. The journey, for some, turned into a nightmare as will be seen, but the survivors were in trenches and engaged in battle south of Manila by the morning of August 12, 1898.

---

3 http://www.spanamwar.com/1stnorthdakotalouden.html

CHAPTER ONE

May 26 - June 2, 1898

"You want to know something? We are still in the Dark Ages. The Dark Ages- they haven't ended yet." – Combat veteran and author Kurt Vonnegut (from Deadeye Dick)

Twenty-two-year-old Pvt. Franklin Lafayette Anders, son of a Union soldier and born on a US Military post at Fort Abraham Lincoln, Dakota Territory, stood on the brick landing platform at the Northern Pacific* railway station in Fargo, ND, along with 684 of his National Guard compatriots. The date was May 26, 1898, and the group was volunteers from various National Guard units from across the state.

Although the previous night had produced a steady rain, it was a typical North Dakota late May day, breezy with northwest wind at thirteen knots, scattered clouds, and an 11:00 am temperature approaching 70 degrees F.

Frank, who was reflecting on the events that brought him here as the noise of the crowd around the railroad station became more boisterous, snapped his attention back to the present when a number of Red River Valley bicycle enthusiasts pedaled up to join the event. He turned to his new friend John Kinne, a recently enlisted volunteer from the Fargo NDNG unit, and said, "If it gets any rowdier, John, we may have to join the party."

"I don't think that sergeant would approve," Kinne said, nodding at the khaki clad non-com patrolling the platform.

* Now the Burlington Northern railroad.

John Baxter Kinne, born in Beloit, Wisconsin, came to Fargo with his family from a farm in Sargent County near Lisbon, ND. Two years younger that Anders, Kinne shared the same rank, although Anders, on his 2nd enlistment, had more longevity and was due for promotion soon. Kinne was about to be a freshman student at Fargo College** *(just finishing as a senior in the Fargo College Prep School, later known as Fargo High School)* when the North Dakota governor called for volunteers. Anders, who worked for the railroad, had a seventh grade education *(later a college graduate engineer)*, but both shared an interest in people and history.

"But keep an eye on Shephard and Huntley," Kinne continued. He was referring to his preparatory college classmates Gail Shepherd and Howard Huntley, who joined with Kinne as volunteers in Fargo.[4] These rambunctious eighteen-year-old pre-college boys tickled Kinne's more conservative personality. Both Anders and Kinne had managed to pull them out of more than one potential scuffle in the past week, and both were now eying some of the pretty young bicyclists.

About that time, the National Guard band, which would return to Lisbon after the troops were off, started up with a rousing version of Frank W. Meacham's *American Patrol,* popularized by John Phillip Sousa. According to author John Durand,[5] referring to his grandfather Tom Stafne's notes *(Tom was a volunteer from Wahpeton's Company I)*, there were at least two other bands from Fargo- Moorhead present for the troop sendoff.

The music was enough to stimulate the non-com into ordering his troops to fall in just in time before the first of two troop trains appeared crossing the Red River from Moorhead, MN, four and a half blocks away to the east.

Anders and Kinne stood adjacent to one another in the pre-embarkation lineup, and the two stood behind other Company B volunteers. Other future medal recipients like Pvt. Otto Boehler, a sturdy

---

** *Fargo College was closed in 1922, and its Carnegie funded library raised in the 1960's*

4 *Kinne, Diary 1898-1899 CO B First North Dakota Infantry, 1.*

5 *John Durand, The Boys, 1st North Dakota Volunteers in the Philippines. (Puzzlebox Press, Elkhorn, 2010), 19.*

German immigrant from Wahpeton, ND, a Red River town forty-five miles south of Fargo; Pvt. Frank Ross from Langdon, ND, a farming community near the Canadian border; and Gotfred Jensen, a Danish immigrant from Devil's Lake were scattered amongst the other companies. Ross was born in Illinois, but had moved with his family to North Dakota.

The train, its coal fired steam engine belching a cloud of black smoke, screeched to a halt. The noise from the boisterous crowd increased as the regiment came to attention, followed by parade rest. Homemade signs of "Remember the Maine" and "God Bless America" amongst others not so reverent like "To Hell with Spain" waved above the crowd. The cheers got louder.

The top kick, Sergeant Major John E. Mattison from Jamestown's Company H, brought the troops back to attention with a sharp command, turned on his heels crisply, saluted his company/battalion commander, who in turn saluted the acting (but soon to be permanent) regimental commander, Lieutenant Colonel William C. Treumann, and said, "They're all yours, Colonel."

"Company Commanders, front and center," Treumann barked with a trace of a German accent. "Regiment...PAA-RAADE REST! Now listen, gentlemen. "I want this embarkation to go smoothly, and you are in front of me to make that happen, so I don't have to shout. We will board the second battalion first, Companies A, G, H, and K on this NP train. I want at least two commissioned officers in each car, no smoking while you are under way, and maintain order. Is that clear?"

"Yes, sir!" chorused the commanders.

"The rest of you will march to the Great Northern Depot and wait for the next train. Now get it done. Commanders atten-hut! Dismissed."

As the seven company commanders herded their charges along the new cobblestone brick platform, the train's brakeman descended the cupola of the caboose gripping a large red flag in one hand and a smoke flare in the other and proceeded east along the tracks. He was checking to make sure no other railroad traffic was coming. In railroad parlance this action by the brakeman was called "chasing the red."[6]. His

---

6 "Train Wreck Disasters 1898," http://search.aol.com/aol/ search?s_it=wscreen-aolexperience-w&q=train+wrecks+1898.

action assured the safety of the departing troops. Lack of such pro-
cedure resulted in a horrible troop train accident one month later in
Tupelo, Mississippi, in which five soldiers were killed and fifteen were
seriously injured, when a following train plowed into one stopped for
troop loading.[7]

The Northern Pacific Depot was brand new replacing the old
building that was destroyed in the spring flood a year earlier. Since
the second troop train was a Great Northern Train, and its depot and
separate Red River Bridge were only a few blocks away it was easy to
manage the departure from two locations.

The designated companies boarded the first chartered train, as
ordered by the regimental commander, and the troops departed on
the southern route through the state, which took them through Valley
City, Jamestown, Bismarck, Dickinson, and points west. The specific
companies were split up as indicated, so the departing troops could
pass through their hometowns as they headed west.

At about noon, the remaining troops now repositioned, Treumann
noted the second train crossing the GN railway bridge further north
from the NP's bridge and ordered the remaining companies aboard
the Great Northern. At 12:30 it departed *"amid much noise and confusion, many handshakes and farewells"* north to Grand Forks, where *"the
1st Battalion was served dinner."*[8]

After traveling all night, they had breakfast in Glasgow, Montana.

---

7 *Ibid.*
8 *Kinne, Diary 1898-1899 CO B First North Dakota Infantry, 1.*

What is particularly interesting in this picture is the material in the lower right (sic).[9] During the 1890s, Fargo paved many streets with wooden blocks. When the flood of 1897 occurred, the blocks simply floated away in the water and can be clearly seen piling up in the photograph above. Wooden blocks were not used again as pavers. http://digitalhorizonsonline.org/u?/uw,/108 Photo credit NDSU Institute for Regional Studies.

---

9 North Dakota State University, "Fargo, North Dakota, 1897 Red River Flood, "http://www.fargo-history.com/floods/fargo-floods-1890s-3.htm.

This photograph of the 1897 flood looks southwest. The building on the far left is Jones Hall at Fargo College. The building on the far right is the Cass County Courthouse. Photo credit NDSU Institute for Regional Studies.

The NP Railroad Bridge. Note that the railroad has parked a train on the bridge to add weight during the flood of 1897.- Photo credit NDSU Institute for Regional Studies.

The photo below taken circa 1930's still shows a cobblestone brick platform at Fargo's Great Northern Depot. It was originally called the St. Paul, Minneapolis & Manitoba Railway Depot, but the name was changed on September 18, 1889, and a new depot built in 1906. The Great Northern Railroad was preceded in Fargo by the Northern Pacific and ran a route north of the NP to Seattle. The Great Northern, together with the Northern Pacific, the Chicago, Burlington and Quincy Railroad and the Spokane, Portland and Seattle Railway merged to form the Burlington Northern. Photo credit NDSU Institute for Regional Studies.

Great Northern Depot, Fargo, ND, 1906 was built on the site of the old St. Paul, Minneapolis & Manitoba Railway Depot. Photo credit NDSU Institute for Regional Studies.

Kinne's and most of the others' first look at the Rocky Mountains came on the second day of travel, and all of the new recruits were dazzled by antelope racing the train as they approached the mountains. Before they got there, the train passed through a Blackfoot Indian Reservation, with its teepees and log with mud encased homes. Strings of meat hanging to dry on poles surrounded Native Americans who waved blankets at the passing soldiers in response to their shouts. Once into the mountains, spectacular scenery greeted the soldiers as they crossed over a 220 foot high bridge over the Midvale River, through a tunnel and emerged into a canyon *"with steep towering walls of rock on either side, through the center of which was a madly rushing torrent."*[10]

As evening descended, the men noticed green grass and pine trees covering the mountains to the tree lines, and despite the late May mountain cold, marveled at the intensity of the colors. With darkness came the scattered glow of a few forest fires seen at a distance. They awoke to the delights of more spectacular and ever changing

10 *Kinne Diary, 2.*

scenery in Idaho, where the first travel delay occurred because of a washout at Kootenai Falls.[11]

At Bonner's Ferry, ID, Quartermaster Sergeant Charles S. Foster[12] took pictures of Native American Indians shaking hands with some of the soldiers, who left them with small gifts of tobacco, *"leaving them in good humor."*[13]

At Spokane, the conductor said that the first troop train on the Northern Pacific Route had preceded them by two hours, and, although it could not be proven in a court of law, the Great Northern train they were on suddenly picked up speed as if to make a race of it to Portland. Sure enough, while traveling at *"an unusual rate of speed there was a terrible crash and jar."*[14] Most of the soldiers were thrown from their seats. Although there were no serious injuries, subsequent investigation revealed that the front trucks (railway wheel units) of the tender had derailed, which resulted in a six hour delay.

In Walla Walla, Portland and Salem troops were greeted by cheering people and crowds of girls with roses and lunch baskets for every soldier.. Similar crowds followed the Northern Pacific train at stops across the country, as depicted on the next page at a troop train stop in Bismarck on Thursday, May 26, 1898.

---

11 Ibid.

12 Durand, John, "A Roster of the 1st North Dakota Volunteer Infantry," *Spanish American War Centennial Website,* http://www.spanamwar.com/1stnorthdakotaroster.html.

13 Kinne.

14 Ibid.

National Guard leaving for the Philippines Bismarck. May 26, 1898. Photo credit State Historical Society of North Dakota.

After Salem, the first Great Northern train proceeded to Ashland, OR, the home of Lt. J. E. Thornton, an officer from the 2nd Oregon Volunteer Infantry, *"with whom some were to have some very interesting experiences later on the Islands."*[15] The half hour stop resulted in more flowers and lunches given by the patriotic crowds.

In San Francisco on June 1, the troops debarked the Oakland ferry and marched into a new glass-roofed ferry building preceded by an army band and the 2nd battalion of the North Dakota Volunteer Infantry, which had greeted them at the pier. After dumping their baggage and eating a meal courtesy of the Red Cross, the regiment marched about three miles in the rain to a campground surrounded by an old Chinese cemetery. The march through the streets of San Francisco elicited the usual noise, cheers, and whoop-DE-do seen throughout the country as they traveled west and was only dampened the next day by derisive accounts from the local press who labeled the volunteers farmers and criticized their clothes and lack of drilling.[16]

---

15 Kinne, *Diary 1898-1899 CO B First North Dakota Infantry,* 3.
16 *Ibid.*

After pitching their tent and digging a sink trench supervised by Corporal Gilbert Griffin, tent mates Kinne, Anders, Huntley, and Shepherd were allowed some free time and promptly headed for a tour of Chinatown.

"Been an interesting four days," Anders said, "especially the trip through the Shasta Route."

"That was OK," Huntley replied, "but not as much fun as we just had digging that trench."

"Ya, well, maybe you should have more respect for the dead! If that had been an Indian burial ground, you would likely be without a scalp right now," said Anders.

Anders was referring to his experience in western Dakota. He had to quit school at age fifteen when his father, a veteran Union soldier, died from his Civil War wounds. Frank Anders then worked various jobs to help support his family, including work with Indians on the Standing Rock Reservation. He acquired respect for the Native Americans and their beliefs. He was upset with some of his tent mates, who, while digging the sink around their tent, uncovered buried Chinese remains, some with hair queues still attached, which incited a game with the young recruits.[17]

Properly chastised, the pre-college boys offered apologies. The group then spent the rest of the evening quietly walking through Chinatown.

---

17 Ibid.

CHAPTER TWO

June 2 – July 31, 1898

"The wonder is always new that any sane man can be a sailor." –Ralph Waldo Emerson

Lieutenant Colonel Will Treumann[*] had a daily orderly appointed from the ranks. This position was termed a "dog robber" in Army parlance and was a coveted position. The lucky appointee escaped guard duty and was usually assured a good night's sleep. If the designated dog robber had brownnosed his way to the appointment, by taking extra care with his personal appearance, he was subject to harassment and derision by the rest of the troops. On Sunday, June 5, 1898, Pvt. John Kinne achieved dog robber duty, escaping guard duty.[18]

The next day, the regiment turned in their old Springfield rifles, most of which were Civil War "trapdoor" (old muzzle loaders converted to breach loaders by Allin Conversions) models for newer Model 1889's. Later, the best shooters would get a few Krag-Jorgensen models 1896, magazine-loaded weapons also manufactured by Springfield. This new model had the advantage of shooting lighter .30 caliber ammunition, which was smokeless, compared to the old .45 and .40 caliber ammo. Soldiers using the old ammo often had to wait

---

Treumann had assumed command of the regiment when the Colonel commanding was rejected, likely because he would not take a reduction in rank for the reduced size regiment, and had returned to Lisbon along with the 4-F Chaplain and the band for which the Army felt no need.

18 Kinne, Diary 1898-1899 CO B First North Dakota Infantry

for the smoke to clear before they could shoot again. Smokeless firing did not give away positions to the enemy. In spite of US Army policy of insisting on single shot firing during engagements, the magazines allowed much faster repeats when needed.

The soldiers also got paid to the end of the month in spite of it being only June 10, the privates drawing $26.52. A week later, the whole outfit was vaccinated, resulting in inflamed, swollen, and sore arms. Howard Huntley, John Kinne, and Al Davis, another Company B grunt, got into trouble when they returned late from attending an exhibition of military drills followed by a banquet put on by the 13th Minnesota Infantry at the Presidio. The guards would not let the late-comers in the gate, and they had to resort to sneaking over the fence, during which Al Davis was caught by a guard. He later escaped when an alarm went off, causing noise and confusion. The men felt relieved that their escapade did not result in punishment.

As overseas departure drew near, troops continued to drill and sharpen their shooting skills. Sgt. Alexander Louden, from Bathgate, ND, and who served as a prison guard before being deployed, had a marvelous record as a sharpshooter. *"In the army rifle matches he shot down all regiments, regular and volunteer, at the Presidio, near San Francisco, Calif. He was requested to join the National Rifle association, which he did and has competed with all teams at the association from Bangor, ME, to Pasedena (sic), Calif. He says, 'Our team, known as the Dickinson, North Dakota Team took second place. Individually, I was beaten once.'"[19]* Other sharpshooters, like Thomas Sletteland from Grafton, ND, who was the first North Dakota recipient of the Medal of Honor, and Richard (Mose) Longfellow from Mandan, would prove their mettle after honing their shooting skills at the Presidio. Occasional episodes of questionable conduct continued to occur while the troops were garrisoned, like when an enlisted man from Montana returned to camp inebriated, failed to salute an officer when ordered to do so, and insulted the "gentleman," who then struck him with a saber. The drunk was laid out prostrate, and, when the Colonel

---

19 *"Alexander Louden Recalls His Service with the 1st North Dakota Volunteer Infantry," Spanish American War Centennial Website, http://www.spanamwar. com/1stnorthdakotalouden.html.*

was informed, he was so angry that he snatched the officer's shoulder straps and confined him to quarters.

Gambling continued to be a universal method of income redistribution amongst the troops which is nothing new since biblical times. Common games included coin pitching, chuck-a-luck (a three dice game), craps, and of course poker.

Al Davis, whose first name was Jesse, and John Kinne along with others continued to hone their sharpshooting skills at the Presidio. Drills became physically tougher. On June 28, the regiment received orders to break camp and board the Valencia,* an old transport ship.

A large enthusiastic crowd lined the streets and the dock as the troops marched to the ship, and they were again given lunch baskets by the Red Cross as they boarded. Most of these lunches later spoiled and were thrown overboard due to seasickness.

John Kinne and Pvt. Harry Cramer were assigned upper bunks, which meant you wouldn't get covered in vomit from seasick soldiers. Between the seasickness and sore arms, it was an unpleasant start, and it got worse.

Seven soldiers died during the month-long trip to the Philippines. *"As each death occurred it would be proclaimed by a flag being placed at half-mast."*[20] Most of the deaths were attributed to typhoid fever with dehydration present, and there was one accidental death.

The first part of the trip, the eight day voyage to the Hawaiian Islands, had been relatively benign, and only one other vessel, a windjammer, was seen during that period, and that was the day after the Fourth of July. Harry Cramer proved to be an exceptional forager, even managing to steal a freshly baked pie, but burned himself on the arm while smuggling the tasty dessert back to his buddies. Otherwise, the days were taken up with exercise drills, policing their "quarters," inspections of personnel and equipment, et cetera.

* Spelled Valentia in John Kinne's diary. The SS Valencia came to a tragic end in January 1906, when she became the center of a famous Canadian shipwreck, at night, when the vessel rammed ashore in the fog and scores clung to her rigging until the surf pounded her to bits and drowned 117 men, women, and children on the shore where Pacific Rim National Park (near Vancouver) is today. The famous hiking trail there was laid out specifically as a result of the Valencia tragedy

20 Kinne, Diary 1898-1899 CO B First North Dakota Infantry, 10.

The first sight of the Hawaiian Islands was the leper island of Molokai, on the sixth of July. It was reported that Father Damain, after serving the outcast lepers for twelve years, finally contracted the disease and died. His successor, Brother Dutton, also contracted the illness in 1912. Currently, when the North Dakotans aboard the Valencia passed Molokai in 1898, it was said that Brother Dutton was *"awaiting his fate"* among the inhabitants.[21]

CIVILIAN TROOPSHIP SS VALENCIA 1898[22]

Toward evening of July 6th, the Valencia approached Honolulu. Anchored in "Wai Momi" ("Water of Pearl" or "Pu'uloa") were a number

21 Ibid, 7.
22 Anglo Boer War Museum, http://www.goldiproductions.com/ angloboerwarmuseum/Boer94a_game_ships.

of US Naval vessels, including transport and warships. Among these was the monitor* USS Monadnock. See US Navy photo below.[23]

*Members of the 1ˢᵗ North Dakota Volunteer Infantry watched a drunken sailor jump from the Monadnock into shark infested water and attempt to swim back to the Wai Momi (called Pearl Harbor after 12/7/1941) shore from where he had just returned. He was subsequently rescued and taken back to the monitor.[24] Other ships surrounding the Valencia in Pearl Harbor included the USS Newport with General Merritt,** [25] the Astor Battery, and two*

A monitor was a warship designed to operate in shallow waters and could thus support combat troops ashore. The very first ship thus designed was the USS Monitor which did battle against another ironclad vessel, a Confederate ship, the Merrimack, March 9, 1862.

23 Robert Hurst, U.S. Naval Historical Center Photograph # NH 70502.

24 Kinne, Diary 1898-1899 CO B First North Dakota Infantry, 7.

*** Major General Wesley Merritt, an 1860 graduate of West Point, was on a fast track to senior command during the Civil War when he skipped three ranks and went from Captain in 1863 to Brigadier General. This highly decorated old Indian Fighter and Civil War hero commanded the first Philippine Expedition*

25 James E. Kelly, "A Portrait of General Merritt," http://www.gdg.org/Research/OOB/Union/July1-3/wmerit.html.

other Batteries of the 3rd Artillery aboard. Besides the Newport, the troops awoke on July 7th to see the Morgan City, The City of Para Ohio, and the Indiana all nearby. These vessels would all be part of a convoy to the Philippine Islands.

USS Newport (above in dry dock[26]) carried General Merritt, the Astor Battery*** and Batteries H & K of the 3rd Artillery.[27]

---

26 Wikipedia, the free encyclopedia File, Newport.pg12.JPG

*** In April, 1898, following the declaration of war on Spain, millionaire patriot John Jacob Astor offered money to the government to fund a light artillery battery in exchange for a colonel's commission. provided it was commanded by a regular artillery officer. The job landed in the lap of a young 2nd lieutenant, Peyton C. March, who later became Army Chief of Staff, but who also became famous for commanding the "Astor Battery" during the Battle of Manila.

27 Kinne, Diary 1898-1899 CO B First North Dakota Infantry, 8.

City of Para[28] below was a chartered troopship from the Pacific Mail Steamship CO. She carried the 13th Volunteer Minnesota Infantry and was part of the convoy from Hawaii to the Philippines. A poignant excerpt from one of the soldiers aboard, Lynden K. Emory is quoted below.

28 Lynden Emory, "King of Company B of the 13th Minnesota Volunteer Infantry," Unpublished memoirs, http://www.spanamwar.com/cityofpara.htm.

"After leaving <u>Hawaii</u>, we were in a hot climate and the holds got so well warmed up that our nights were not restful. Also our food, what little of it there was, had not been properly cooked, and we had to drink distilled sea water. Trouble was that the distilling plant wasn't large enough, so we lined up at the water tap with our canteens, filled them with hot water, and had to wait until it cooled enough to drink. But the officers still had ice water, good food, and had brought along six cows which were placed in stalls in an upper hold, were well fed (even got fresh carrots which we stole every time the guard turned his head). The cows were killed one by one to provide the officers with fresh meat. Our meat was canned, and so tough and greasy that we named it 'slumgullion'.

"One of the Co. E men died and had a typical burial at sea – sewn in the blanket, a heavy piece of iron tied to his feet, carried to the ship's rail, and after a brief service, 'taps' was blown, the stretcher was lifted and he slid over the rail. Otherwise one day was about like another, until we got near the China Sea where we passed an active volcano, which had erupted at the sea bottom, and had built up enough so that it was just visible above the waves. A strange sight as we passed it at dusk."[29]

After four days at sea, the Morgan City, a vessel chartered from the Southern Pacific Company from May 12 to August 31, 1898, at the rate of $400 per day, fell behind the convoy. It was later learned that a fire had broken out aboard ship. The crew had fought the fire day and night, and the coal bunkers were still burning when the vessel arrived in Manila. Troops aboard were ignorant of the peril they were in, but they arrived without injury or loss of life from the blaze.

The Valencia had slowed to accompany the lagging Morgan City with lots of wig-wag, or semaphore, signaling that the troops could not interpret well. On the morning of the 29th, the Valencia found herself in the Philippine Islands, with Morgan City still lagging behind. On July 31st, the North Dakota Volunteers sighted the rest of the fleet, which had preceded them into Manila Bay. The Newport, which had started out with them, had arrived six days earlier. The convoy got separated because the USS Charleston, their major escort vessel and thus the "mother hen" of the group, opened her sealed orders

29 Ibid.

directing the cruiser to capture the Island of Guam in the Mariana Islands, so it left the transports unescorted.

At about 11:00 am, the Valencia pulled into Manila Bay led by the Indiana. She passed Corregidor Island, passed a line of battleships and recently sunken Spanish ships, and took her place with the other transports. That night, the troops saw and heard, for the first time, shots fired in anger.

CHAPTER THREE

July 31 – August 12, 1898

"I've seen my share of war zones and heard enough shots fired in anger to last a lifetime." –William J. Drummond, Journalist

The night of July 31, 1898, in Manila Bay was damp with misty rain. Everything seemed peaceful and quiet. Most of the troops were asleep. John Kinne recalled what happened:

"–nearly all were sleeping except those of us on guard, (when) we were startled by the report of infantry and rapid fire guns and the boom and flash of cannon, followed almost instantly by volley firing at a little distance from the first line of fire. We watched this spectacle for about four hours with considerable anxiety, but it gradually diminished and finally ceased entirely."[30]

Most of the American volunteers that had preceded the 1st North Dakota into the combat zone were already in trenches in front of the city of Manila. These included the 10th Pennsylvania, the 1st California, and the 1st Colorado Volunteer regiments. These units were supported by the independence seeking rebels led by Emilio Aguinaldo. The 1st Pennsylvania was the first American unit to come under fire from the Spaniards and although the reason was never quite solved for the start of it, it was likely the presence of the native rebels that triggered hostilities.

---

30 Kinne, Diary 1898-1899 CO B First North Dakota Infantry,11.

This is a rare photograph of Filipino Guerrillas posted outside of Manila circa July-August 1898.[31]

On August 3, the 1st North Dakota got orders to prepare for landing. The troops were issued a quart of water each, and the Valencia moved her anchorage closer to shore. In true army tradition, it was a "hurry up and wait" process and the soldiers did not actually land until the next afternoon. There were plenty of rumors to go around fueled by a trip ashore by the regimental surgeon, Dr. Black, the purser, and the ship's chief engineer. They reported that a Utah artillery battery had been captured without a shot being fired, and hundreds more outrageous tales, including that of a Pennsylvania company that disappeared. Most of the tales proved to be false.[32]

---

31 Skutatos, Militaryphotos.net, May 18, 2008, http://www.militaryphotos.net/forums/showthread.php?134380-Philippine-Insurrection-Philippine-American-War-SOME-CONTENT-MAY-BE-NSFW.

32 Kinne, Diary 1898-1899 CO B First North Dakota Infantry,11.

August 4th proved to be the most eventful day for the American fleet and for the 1st North Dakota. As the USS Monterey approached, a salute was fired from Commodore* Dewey's flagship, the Olympia. The Monterey was a gunship that would add considerable firepower to Dewey's fleet. She drew up and anchored with the line of other gunboats beyond Dewey's flagship.

Photo # NR&L(O) 18336 Battle of Manila Bay

USS Olympia[33] *Battle of Manila Bay, 1 May 1898.*

Contemporary photograph of a painting by Hong Kong artist Pun Woo, showing USS Olympia in the foreground, leading the U.S. Asiatic Squadron during the battle. The original painting appears to have been

---

* The rank of commodore in the US Navy was equivalent to a one star brigadier general of the army. Today, the term is reserved for senior captains who command a squadron. The rank of one star admiral or Rear Admiral (lower half) was restored to the navy in 1984 after many years of controversy. Dewey was given a special promotion and rank of Admiral of the Navy following his victory in Manila Bay.

33 www.history.navy.mil/photos/events/spanam/events/man.

copied from an engraving published in Harpers' Pictorial History of the
War with Spain. U.S. Naval Historical Center Photograph.

At about 5:30 pm of August 4th, the regiment boarded junks and were taken ashore to the province of Cavite.

The next day, Kinne saw Harry Cramer bearing down on him waving two slips of paper. "John, John!" Cramer yelled.

"Are those what I think they are?" Kinne asked.

"Yup. Two passes to the town!"

"How did you finagle that?"

"Must be my good behavior."

"Riiiiight," replied Kinne. "Well, let's go!"

Inside the wall, the pals found about 600 Spaniards guarded by native Filipinos. They were told there were about 1000 more prisoners on the mainland. They spent the next couple of hours browsing the town, found more shell holes in the walls, saw some native art, and had some native coconut drinks. They also were approached by natives speaking Pidgin English. The most common phrases confirmed the Filipino's delight that the Americans were there to help. The native guards would also use gestures using both index fingers to show how they would "fight together." This attitude was a reflection of their leader, Emilio Aguinaldo, who was quoted as follows: *"Divine Providence is about to place Independence within our reach. The Americans have extended their protective mantle to our beloved country, now that they have severed relations with Spain; owing to the tyranny that nation is exercising in Cuba. The American fleet will prevent any reinforcements coming from Spain. There, where you see the American flag flying, assemble in numbers; they are our redeemers!"*[34]

---

34 *National Center for History in the Schools, UCLA, and the Organization of American Historians, "The Philippine-American War," http://www.learner.org/courses/amerhistory/pdf/Philippine-War_L-One.pdf.*

***Emilio Aguinaldo, Rebel Leader Courtesy Dover Publications
Dictionary of American Portraits 1967.***

The National Center for History in Schools, UCLA and the Organization of American Historians in preparing teaching material for
history instructors indicates this about Aguinaldo:

*"The Filipino Revolution, therefore, began in 1896 when, under the
flag of the Katipunan, or 'Society of the Sons of the People,' some 20,000
Filipinos staged an uprising against their Spanish overlords. Twenty-
seven-year-old Emilio Aguinaldo, the son of a wealthy aristocrat,
rose quickly to the top of the revolutionary movement, and became
president of the Katipunan in the spring of 1897. 'Filipino citizens!' he
declared. 'Let us follow the example of European and American
nations. Let us march under the Flag of Liberty, Equality, and Fraternity!'*

*With 200,000 Spanish troops tied down in Cuba, Madrid could ill
afford a war in the Philippines. Spanish authorities offered Aguinaldo
a declaration of peace in exchange for his promise to move the*

revolutionary leadership to Hong Kong. The Spanish sweetened the peace overture with an undisclosed amount of cash and a commitment to grant certain reforms to the Filipinos. Though Aguinaldo did not believe the Spanish would deliver on their guarantees of political, land, and economic reforms, he desperately needed the money for food and supplies. Aguinaldo thus agreed to resettle in Hong Kong, where he could then buy guns to smuggle back to freedom fighters in the Philippines."[35]

In responding to Aguinaldo's appeal to *"gather where the American flag was flying,"* about 1000 natives appeared outside the walls of Cavite on the night of August 6. Completely ignorant of the cause, a commander of a volunteer Colorado outfit ordered a company out to disperse the crowd, which they did.

On August 9, the regiment got orders to move again and had to abandon their comfortable barracks for two-man pup tents. Harry Cramer and John Kinne were paired, but Kinne was much shorter than Cramer, whose legs protruded outside of the tent unless he lay down at an angle. In order for Cramer to stay dry without Kinne having to share his space, it was necessary for Kinne to cover Cramer's feet with Kinne's own poncho. The first wet night, Kinne came back from guard duty late when Harry was already asleep at an angle and had to wrap his legs over Harry's. As a result, he didn't get much sleep. The poncho loaner solved the problem when it was Harry's turn to come back late.

---

35 *Ibid.*

Emilio Aguinaldo is seated 2nd from the right in this photo of the Hong Kong exiles taken in early 1898 before his return to the Philippines.[36]

On the morning of 12 August, Company B was ordered into the trenches, which they approached five at a time by wading in knee high mud. Their mission was to prevent any flanking movement or advance by the Spanish troops. They could see Spanish soldiers and sentries across the marsh. No heavy firing occurred during the day, with only an occasional gunshot heard. The next morning, a single cannon was fired, apparently as a signal, and the whole front line of Spaniards opened fire, with lead shot falling all around Company B. Twenty men under Lieutenant Matthias Hildreth[37] saw the most action as they were closest to the front line.

---

36 Dumindin, "Philippine-American War, 1899-1902."
37 Durand, "The Boys" 96-7.

Shortly after the intense firefight began, the 1st ND was ordered to the rear. Later, Dewey's flagship opened an artillery barrage supported by the Astor Battery.

After an hour and twenty minutes, the Spaniards hoisted a white flag in Manila, but the word of Spanish surrender did not reach the embattled troops on the line. A charge by Aguinaldo's guerrillas breached the Spanish trenches about 200 yards away and drove the enemy troops into the woods toward Manila. A counter charge by the Spaniards resulted in a retreat by both the native rebels and the Americans. John Kinne described what happened:

"Just as we got to (the third line of) these trenches we could see the rear of the line crossing after the Astor Battery and we proceeded in single file up the road about half way and lay in a ditch beside the road waiting for orders. Word was brought that the Astor Battery was all cut to pieces and we were ordered to advance in a very hail of bullets. We had to jump a ditch and were halted again alongside the road.

"About this time the natives began to rush back in droves, one carrying a native officer shot through the jaw, and we saw some of the Astor Battery coming in our direction and we thought they were retreating. We then had orders to retreat and most of us were mighty glad to do so."[38]

Kinne also observed Pvt. Frank E. Berg (of Bismarck-Mandan's Company A), the only North Dakota man wounded in the battle of Manila, take a bullet through the leg. As the Americans retreated, they saw many wounded soldiers and others drop from exhaustion. The Astor Battery's men returned and drove the Spanish away using their pistols. They told the North Dakotans that their 1st and 2nd Sergeants were both killed in the pistol charge.

Newly promoted Admiral Dewey, while waiting for General Wesley Merritt's force to arrive from the States, had sent a ship to Hong Kong to retrieve the exiled rebel leader Aguinaldo. Aguinaldo's insurgents were a significant force in the defeat of the Spanish in Manila, and the Spanish were deathly afraid of being captured by them. The first American troops to arrive in the Philippines were elements of the 1st California Volunteer Infantry.

---

38 Kinne, Diary 1898-1899 CO B First North Dakota Infantry, 14.

They arrived on June 30, 1898, and were quartered in Fort San Felipe Neri in Cavite Province and assigned to the arsenal there with full approval of Aguinaldo. Other regiments followed. By the end of July, 470 officers and 10,464 infantry troops had been stationed in the country.[39]

Maj Gen Wesley Merritt   Brig Gen Thomas Anderson   Brig Gen Arthur MacArthur   Brig gen Francis Greene

photos[40]

With Spanish Forces in Manila on the verge of defeat and an American flag flying over a large building, the North Dakotans and others were given orders not to let any of the insurgents into the city. An agreement had been reached by the Americans (primarily Admiral Dewey) with the surrendering Spanish, who were afraid of the rebels and of pillaging, looting, and atrocities taken in revenge. Several companies of armed insurgents were turned away by U.S. guards that evening.[41] The guards obeyed their orders, and their action, together with the rejection of insurgents outside the walls of Cavite on August 6th, provided the first real chink in US relations with Aguinaldo's guerillas.

---

39 Arnaldo Dumindin, "Philippine-American War, 1899-1902," http://philippineamericanwar.webs.com/background.htm.

40 Ibid.

41 Kinne, Diary 1898-1899 CO B First North Dakota Infantry,15.

CHAPTER FOUR

August 13, 1898

"To appreciate where you are now, you should know where you came from." –Ang Pungsod

The Spanish troops and leaders had good reason to fear the insurgents. Historian Arnaldo Dumindin put it this way:

"For centuries the Spanish had ruled the Philippines with a heavy–often deadly–hand. They considered the Filipino people to be ruthless, uncivilized, and sub-human. There was great fear that if the city fell to Aguinaldo and his revolutionary forces, there would be hell to pay."[42]

Dumindin also indicated General Merritt and Admiral Dewey purposely left Aguinaldo out of their plans to take Manila. It apparently happened that way, but Aguinaldo did not believe it and quoted in his memoirs that Dewey promised to support the revolution; up to the battle on August 13, Aguinaldo felt he had the confidence of both American commanders.

If there was any intention of a mock battle, the men of the 1st North Dakota and their officers were unaware of it. Likewise, the men of the Astor Battery, who lost two of their own that morning, were unaware of a staged battle, nor was Pvt. Frank Berg of Bismarck's Company A who was shot in the leg.

Dumindin continues with this statement in reference to events of August 13th:

---

42 Dumindin, *"Philippine-American War, 1899-1902."*

"As the naval bombardment ended and the American forces continued north in two columns, the Filipinos — who had not been apprised of the script —raced to join the battle. They thought there was a real battle going on that would liberate their capitol and they did not want to be left out."[43]

Dumindin's last quotation has validity. If there was a "script," no one in the firefight was aware of it. What had happened is likely as follows:

General Fermin Jaudenes, the Spanish Military Governor, convinced the Belgian diplomat, Edouard Andre, to negotiate a peaceful surrender with the Americans. Andre's first contact with Dewey apparently had been days before, but, on the day of the battle, was after 11:45 am on August 13, long after Dewey's barrage and after Dewey had raised the "Do you surrender?" international flag aboard his flagship.

However, other sources quoting Dewey in a cable to Secretary of the Navy John D. Long six weeks earlier suggest that there indeed were other political agendas going on.

"Consistently I have refrained from assisting him (Aguinaldo) in any way with the force under my command, and on several occasions I have declined requests that I should do so, telling him the squadron could not act until the arrival of the United States troops. At the same time I have given him to understand that I consider insurgents as friends, being opposed to a common enemy...My relations with him are cordial, but I am not in his confidence. The United States has not been bound in any way to assist insurgents by any act or promises, and he is not, to my knowledge, committed to assist us. I believe he expects to capture Manila without my assistance, but (I) doubt (the insurgent's) ability, they not yet having many guns."[44]

In addition to Dewey, General Merritt had no intention of getting too involved with Aguinaldo, as indicated by this quote on his instructions from President McKinley:

"My instructions from the President fully contemplated the occupation of the islands by the American land forces, and stated that

---

43 Ibid.

44 C. Douglas Sterner, "Home of Heroes Victory in the Philip," pineshttp://www.homeofheroes.com/wallofhonor/spanish_am/16_trouble.html.

'the powers of the military occupant (American Army) are absolute and supreme and immediately operate upon the political conditions of the inhabitants.' I did not consider it wise to hold any direct communication with the insurgent leader (Aguinaldo) until I should be in possession of the city of Manila, especially as I would not until then be in a position to issue a proclamation to enforce my authority, in event that his pretensions should clash with my designs. For these reasons the preparations for the attack on the city were pressed and military operations conducted without reference to the situation of the insurgent forces." [45]

So the situation was that Aguinaldo and the insurgents were under the delusion that the Americans would fully support the revolution, and the American military leaders, although sympathetic to their cause, did not want to antagonize the rebels. Indeed, General Merritt's instructions revealed the American President's true intention of adding the Philippines as a US Territory. Here is another side of those events as described by C. Douglas Sterner, a well-regarded military historian and author:

"In the closing days of July, General Arthur (father of Douglas)) MacArthur's Brigade joined the rest of Merritt's force, bringing the total American troop strength to more than 10,000 soldiers, amassed only a few miles south of the Walled City of Manila at Camp Dewey. To the east, Aguinaldo waited impatiently with his force of 20,000 insurgents, eager to attack and claim the Philippine Capital. General Jaudenes and his 15,000 Spanish defenders were completely cut off, surrounded, and running out of food and supplies. It was reported that some in the city resorted to eating rats to fill their empty bellies. General Jaudenes knew that defeat was eminent, but the Spanish were proud traditionalists at warfare, and the beleaguered commander was determined NOT to surrender his city to the 'savage and uncivilized forces' under Aguinaldo.

"Between Manila and General Merritt's three brigades at Camp Dewey sat the seaside guardhouse of Fort San Antonio de Abad, just two miles south of the city. The Spanish trenches stretched eastward towards Blockhouse #4, with the insurgent forces in full command to the east. The arriving American soldiers moved into some of the insurgent positions between Camp Dewey and the Spanish lines in the closing days of July,

---

45 Ibid.

bringing them directly under the enemy guns. There was only sporadic fire from the Spanish artillery as the newly arrived American forces came ashore to dig trenches and prepare for the coming assault. On the night of July 31st, the American forces (author's note: or Rebels?) could restrain their fire no longer.

"The one-and-a-half hour battle that followed pitted the infantry and artillery fire of the two opposing forces against each other in what became the deadliest battle in the Pacific. When the Americans returned fire, their positions were exposed and the Spanish adjusted their fire, resulting in 10 Americans killed and 33 wounded. The following day, Admiral Dewey suggested that the Americans hold their fire in the coming days as General Merritt continued to deploy his forces for a final assault. '(It is) Better to have small losses, night after night, in the trenches, than to run the risk of greater losses by premature attack' he cautioned.

"In the days that followed, Merritt's forces continued to land and take up positions. The First Colorado Volunteer Infantry moved their own lines eastward to the Pasay Road approaching Manila from the east. Their work was arduous, fighting swamps, monsoon rains, and intermittent enemy fire. At night the Spanish guns continued to fire on American positions, resulting in 5 more deaths and 10 Americans wounded. On August 7th Admiral Dewey sent a message to General Jaudenes warning that unless he ordered his soldiers to stop firing on American positions, the U.S. Naval commander would turn the big guns of his ships on the city within 48 hours.

"General Jaudenes realized that the message from the American Admiral was tantamount to a demand for surrender. He also realized that defiance of Dewey's ultimatum would be suicide for himself and his forces. With Aguinaldo and his Filipino force arrayed to the east, Merritt and his 3 divisions to the south, and the U.S. Naval squadron in the harbor, time had run out for the Spanish empire in the Philippines. What followed was five days of negotiations creating an unusual scenario for surrender. It would pit allies against each other, create a strange alliance between enemies, script one of the strangest battles in military history, and set the stage for a sequel war. It would become known as the Mock Battle of Manila."[46]

---

46 Ibid.

The senior opposing commanders *did* script a battle that would save face for the Spaniards and protect them from insurgent reprisals. In their minds, the script would save lives on both sides, and perhaps it did. Unfortunately, it didn't have to happen, and lives were still lost and many were wounded.

The first reason that events spiraled out of control was that Admiral Dewey had earlier cut the undersea telegraph cable to Hong Kong in order to prevent Spain's Central Command and Control from learning of his victory over their fleet, and thus preventing Spain from sending reinforcements. As a result, the American commanders and probably the Spanish did not know that Spain had already signed a surrender agreement when the Battle of Manila took place. Dewey was apparently unaware of a second undersea telegraph cable extending from the Philippine Islands south to Borneo and thus to rest of the world.

The second reason was that when the Spaniards raised the white flag over Manila, the visibility was such that the flag blended in with the sky, and Dewey did not see it for some time. He thought the Spaniards might be contemplating a double cross because, according to the "script," they were supposed to respond to his international flag, asking, "Do you surrender?" The capitulation of Manila *(surrender was at the time a politically incorrect word)* would allow transfer of control to the Americans and save face for the Spaniards as well as protect them from the "savage Filipinos."

This delay in response by the Spaniards allowed the third and most significant reason for the downhill spiral of events: the entry of the insurgents into the battle. After the initial intense battle, fighting and sniping continued throughout the day as the Americans and the Spanish leaders carried out what was left of the "script." By the time the surrender was complete, six Americans had lost their lives along with ninety-two wounded. The Spanish had forty-nine KIA and 100 wounded. It is unknown how many native Filipino insurgents were casualties.

One can only imagine how Aguinaldo and his band felt having been barred from entering their own capital city, unable to celebrate a victory over the brutal Spaniards under whom they had suffered for years, and betrayed, in their minds, by the Americans.

US troops fighting in the woods near Manila[47]

American held Spanish POWs in Manila[48]

47 Dumindin, "Philippine-American War, 1899-1902."
48 Ibid.

Astor Battery headed for the front prior to the Battle of 8/13/98[49]

Graves of American soldiers killed in Manila. The "mock" Battle of Manila was not bloodless.[50]

_____

49 Ibid.
50 Ibid.

President McKinley[51]

On the American side, even President McKinley was uncertain what to do or how he felt.

"When I realized that the Philippines had dropped into our lap I confess I did not know what to do with them."[52] *After analyzing it further, McKinley came to the conclusion that "there was nothing left for us to do but take them all (the islands), educate the Filipinos, and civilize and Christianize them, (most of them were Roman Catholics) and by God's grace, do the best that we could by them."*[53]

---

51 Ibid.
52 Thomas Patterson and Dennis Merril, Major Problems in American Foreign Relations Vol. I, D.C. Heath, 1995, NY, 424.
53 Ibid.

CHAPTER FIVE

August 13, 1898 – February 5, 1899.

"Destiny' is not as manifest as it was a few weeks ago." –William Jennings Bryan, speaking at the start of the Philippine-American War

So now the situation is set for more trouble. Aguinaldo and his insurgents are unhappy, the Spanish are safe, protected by the Americans, most of whom just want to go home, and the American military leaders are unsure of what America's policy is going to be, as demonstrated by President McKinley's lack of direction. Under these circumstances, it was remarkable that hostilities remained as quiet as they did for as long as they did. Even when they eventually broke out, the Yanks had no stomach initially for killing their former friends, until, of course, the fight became personal, as it does when your buddies are killed or wounded.

John Kinne recalls the attitudes of his outfit:

"Up to the time we took Manila the Filipinos were our best friends, and their stock phrase when expressing their friendship for us was 'Americano Filipino equal' and place their forefingers side by side to demonstrate our equality....After August 13th these significant words were seldom repeated as they seem to think we had double crossed them."[54]

Sporadic incidents punctuated the hostility for the next few months. On one occasion, a company of soldiers left the city for something to eat, and the guerrillas would not let them back in without a fight. Cooler heads prevailed, and the Yanks simply took a detour via

---

54 Kinne, Diary 1898-1899 CO B First North Dakota Infantry, 16.

the beach to get back to camp. Two weeks after the battle of Manila, the situation was approaching a crisis, and the 1ˢᵗ North Dakota was ordered to sleep with their rifles. Things quieted down again so that by the end of the month the soldiers were back to routine patrols. As the fall months arrived, many native vendors needed to enter the city to sell their crops and goods, which resulted in searches of all personnel entering the city. Tensions started to rise again.

On September 10, six Spanish POWs escaped, and two of them were caught and killed by the insurgents outside of the city walls. The other four waded into the ocean to avoid capture and gave themselves up to the Americans.

The next few weeks were typical garrison duty type days with an occasional dress parade and leisure time spent gambling, watching cock fights, or playing baseball. Halloween, Thanksgiving, and the holidays came and went with little to break the routine. Some of the officers and men who had persistent typhoid symptoms or were otherwise incapacitated were sent home.

Tension among the natives was smoldering but masked. On one occasion, Aguinaldo's favorite musical group, the Magdalo Band,* held a concert in the city, which was well attended.

Although not recognized by any country, Aguinaldo's rebels had declared their independence from Spain on June 12, 1898. They had a draft of a constitution (approved in January 1899), a national anthem without words composed by Julian Felipe, and an election process. Aguinaldo was declared the first president.

As the US Senate was about to ratify the Treaty of Paris, agreed to the previous December, and which gave the entire Philippines to the USA for a sum of $20 million, violence erupted on February 4, 1899. An English immigrant soldier on guard challenged three insurgents who had advanced beyond the limits set by the Americans. Pvt. William Grayson of Company D, 1ˢᵗ Nebraska Volunteer Infantry, described the events:

"About eight o'clock, Miller (Pvt. Orville H. Miller also of Company D) and I were cautiously pacing our district. We came to a fence and were trying to see what the Filipinos were up to. Suddenly, near at hand, on our left, was

_____

* The original band of 1896, still gives concerts under that name at the Aguinaldo Shrine at Freedom Park, Kawit, Cavite, Philippines

a low but unmistakable Filipino outpost signal whistle. It was immediately answered by a similar whistle about twenty-five yards to the right. Then a red lantern flashed a signal from blockhouse number seven. We have never seen such a sign used before. In a moment, something rose up slowly in front of us. It was a Filipino. I yelled, 'Halt!' and made it pretty loud, for I was accustomed to challenging the officer of the guard in approved military style. I challenged him with another loud 'Halt!' Then he shouted 'Halto!' to me. Well, I thought the best thing to do was to shoot him. He dropped. If I didn't kill him, I guess he died of fright. Two Filipinos sprang out of the gateway about fifteen feet from us. I called 'Halt!' and Miller fired and dropped one. I saw that another was left. Well, I think I got my second Filipino that time."[55]

Pvt. William W. Grayson (1876-1941): The Englishman who fired the shot that ignited the Philippine-American War. He acquired U.S. citizenship only in 1900. Previous to serving in the Philippines, he was an immigrant and a hotel worker. Upon his return to the United States from the Philippines, Grayson settled in San Francisco, California, and got married in October 1899. He worked as a house painter or an undertaker.[56]

55 Edwin Wildman, Aguinaldo: A Narrative of Filipino Ambitions (Norwood, MA, Norwood Press, 1901), 195.

56 Dumindin, "Philippine-American War, 1899-1902."

Officially, however, war on the USA was not declared by the Filipinos until the Malolos Congress declared war on the United States (June 2, 1899). The Congress President, Pedro Paterno, issuing the Proclamation of War.[57]

The first shots by Grayson and Miller triggered a violent response by the insurgents, possibly intended, as suggested by the pre encounter signals from the rebel lines described by both Grayson and Miller. As they ran back to their posts following the initial encounter, the sentinels shouted for their comrades to line up. Historian Dumindin continues:

"Filipino troops at San Juan del Monte exchanged fire with the American line in the Santa Mesa district of Manila. The companies of the Morong Battalion under Captain Narvaez and Captain Vicente Ramos charged the American positions and pushed back Grayson's unit and even captured an American artillery piece. 'By 10 o'clock at night,' said American historian James LeRoy, 'the American troops were engaged for two miles from Pasig River north and west.'"[58]

1899: US troops battling Filipinos. Location not specified, possibly in the Santa Mesa district of Manila.[59]

57 Yahoo Answer, http://search.aol.com/aol/search?query=yahoo+answers&s_it=keyword_rollover.
58 Dumindin, "Philippine-American War, 1899-1902."
59 Ibid.

Tactically, the US had two divisions of about 21,000 men spread around the Islands, including a police force in Manila of some 3000. In a sixteen mile semi-circle north to south around Manila, the American lines included some of the fourteen blockhouses the Spaniards had constructed. They were not in control of all of them. The American sector was also divided by the Pasig River, which flowed through Manila and emptied into the bay. The river separated the Yanks into north and south sectors. The 1st North Dakota was part of the 2nd Brigade of the 1st Division, which, along with three regular Army units, controlled the southern sector. Because the lines were stretched thin, only about 11,000 American soldiers faced a Filipino Army of nearly 30,000 men.

The Yanks had the advantage of firepower, particularly artillery. The 2nd Division controlled the northern sector, and the 1st Brigade of the 2nd Division had a volunteer artillery unit from Utah, and the US Navy supplied firepower from the USS Charleston. In the south, the 1st ND and the three regular Army units had support from the 6th Artillery and the USS Monadnock as well as gunboats patrolling the river.

In addition, the regular Army units were equipped with the new Krag-Jorgensen repeating rifles and double action Colt .45 caliber revolvers.

Many Filipinos had superior German manufactured Mauser rifles they had gotten from the Spaniards, but there were not enough to make a difference, and the Americans were better trained and better shots than the insurgents. *"'From the way (they fired), they couldn't hit a balloon 10 feet in front of them' a Colorado volunteer said after the battle."*[60]

John Kinne also described the intense firefight the 1st North Dakota was involved in the night of February 4th and 5th. Kinne described a continual roar of firing mostly near the water works where the Tennessee, California, Nebraska, 4th Cavalry, 14th Infantry, and two companies, I & C, from Wahpeton and Grafton, of the 1st North Dakota were located. *"The 1st North Dakota began volley firing, which was terrific for about*

---

60 Richard Kolb, editor, VFW Magazine Publication, "Blaze in the Boondocks, 2002.Fighting on America's Imperial Frontier in the Philippines, 1899-1913," 9.

three hours. The natives charged the 14th Infantry coming right up to the trenches where they were just slaughtered."[61]

The intense firefight kept up until about 11:00 AM, and *"during this time we were throwing a continuous hail of lead into the graveyard at our front,"*[62] which resulted in numerous sore arms from the rifle recoils. After the insurgents' charge, Major White then led Company G in a counter charge along with "Spud" Murphy's 14th Infantry. The North Dakota boys were complimented and advised by this regular Army officer, Captain Murphy of the 14th Infantry, *"Ah you North Dakota boys are a brave lot of lads,"* he said, referring to their actions during the counter charge, *"but (you'd better) line up there or you'll be shooting one another, (because) you run like a bunch of sheep!"*[63]

Major White's Valley City based Company G returned to the front after their charge with three POWs, two of whom were wounded. About to be promoted to corporal, Frank Anders challenged Charley Davis *(a future MOH recipient)* after he returned from the field hospital where he and a couple of others had escorted the prisoners.

"Hey, Charlie," Anders said. "Is it true that you tried to burn down the hospital?"

"Get real, Frank," Charley replied. "It was one of the N—ers." *(The 'N' word was a common reference for the insurgents amongst the American troops.)*

"What happened to him?" Anders asked.

"The Colonel had him shot."

"No shit?"

"No shit and good riddance. The feisty little bastard tried to attack the doctor, too."

Because the US had to wait for reinforcements, they could not advance after securing the victory and had to settle for stabilizing Manila. In spite of this, the city was set ablaze on February 22nd, but the fires were quickly put out and riots quelled a day later. Manila remained *"relatively calm for the rest of the war."*[64]

61 Kinne, *Diary 1898-1899 CO B First North Dakota Infantry*, 27.
62 Ibid.
63 Ibid.
64 Kolb, *"Blaze in the Boondocks, 2002. Fighting on America's Imperial Frontier in the Philippines, 1899-1913,"* 10.

Feb. 5, 1899: Battery A of the Utah Volunteer Light Artillery on McCloud Hill, Santa Mesa district, Manila, shelling Filipino positions in the San Juan Bridge area (Santa Mesa and San Juan del Monte). A soldier was killed near this gun a few minutes after the photo was taken.[65]

When it was over, the 1st North Dakota again came out without any KIA, and only two uniforms were penetrated by bullets, without wounds. Troops in the southern sector encountered heavier resistance than the north. Overall, the 14th Infantry had fourteen KIA and fifty wounded. The Filipinos' body count was over 700.[66]

After the vicious fight, the territory between the Filipino and the US trenches in the southern sector became known as "*Bloody Lane*."[67] Total casualties for the Americans in more than two days of battle were fifty-nine KIA and 278 WIA. The Filipinos had an estimated 3000 casualties, including 612 actually buried by the Yanks.[68]

---

65 Dumindin, "Philippine-American War, 1899-1902."
66 Ibid.
67 Kolb, "Blaze in the Boondocks, 2002. Fighting on America's Imperial Frontier in the Philippines, 1899-1913."
68 Ibid.

CHAPTER SIX

February 7 – March 15, 1899

"War is worse than hell." –*Captain Elliott, of the Kansas Regiment, February 27th*
Soldier's Letters...part of an anti-imperialism website operated and edited by Jim Zwick.[69]

On February 7, Fargo's Company B Artificer,* Joe Schlanser, and Kinne were sent to town to get provisions using a captured horse they called "God." Because the American lines had by then expanded to a distance of twenty-eight miles, they had to pass previous positions held by the insurgents whose forces were now divided. Local natives had been sent out from the city to bury their own Filipino dead, but had not kept up with the task. Sitting on the buckboard together, the two reflected on what they saw.[70]

"Hey, Joe," John Kinne said, pointing to arms and legs protruding from the ground. "Look at that!"

"I guess they didn't have enough dirt," mused Joe.

"More likely not enough people to do the job."

While in town, the two youngsters noted the presence of the German cruiser, *Irene,* which it was said had been caught unloading

---

69 http://www.historyguy.com/PhilipineAmericanwar.html.

* An Artificer was an enlisted rank in charge of a company's maintenance of equipment.

70 Kinne, Diary 1898-1899 CO B First North Dakota Infantry, 29.

20,000 brand new German manufactured Swedish Mauser** bolt action rifles.[71] There was no doubt some of the insurgents were found with brand new weapons. Apparently, Imperialism or more likely capitalistic profit was not confined to the Americans.

German manufactured Mauser, 1898[72].

German Cruiser Irene 1898.[73]

For the next few days, members of the 1st North Dakota observed or heard sporadic firing from entrenched rebels, but experienced

---

**All Swedish Mausers were manufactured by one of three companies: Mauser, Oberndorf am Neckar, Germany; Carl Gustafs Gevärsfaktoriet, Eskskilstuna, Sweden (Carl Gustaf's City Rifle Factory) and Husqvarna Vapenfabriks AB, Husqvarna, Sweden. The German Mauser Company granted other countries the rights to manufacture the Mauser design.*

71 http://search.aol.com/aol/search?s_it=topsearchbox.search&q=mauser+rifles
72 Ibid.
73 http://upload.wikimedia.org/wikipedia/commons/thumb/0/08/Herta_German_ Cruiser_

no fighting. There were, however, significant battles involving other volunteer units. On February 8th and 9th, two battalions of the 51st Iowa Volunteers, the Wyoming Light Battery, and the Nevada Cavalry, with Batteries A and D of the California Heavy Artillery, were involved in the Battle of San Roque in Cavite Provence, which resulted in a victory for the Americans, but only after the city was razed by fire set by the guerrillas themselves.

San Roque burns "On February 9, at 7:30 am, a party of three, headed by the Mayor of San Roque, came over the American line and asked for further time (after Dewey demanded surrender). Commodore Dewey, who was ashore, refused, and the delegation immediately returned. A white flag was then hoisted over a Filipino blockhouse, but it was a bluff, intended to draw the advance of American troops into a trap. Shortly thereafter the town was set ablaze by the Filipinos."[74]

---

74 Dumindin, "Philippine-American War, 1899-1902."

***San Roque after the battle*[75]**

Also on February 10th, six miles north of Manila the 20th Kansas Volunteers, the 1st South Dakota Volunteers, the Montana Regiment, the Idaho Volunteers, and the 10th Pennsylvania Volunteers all supported by regular Army artillery and also by Utah's Volunteer Light Battery were involved in the Battle of Caloocan.

The Americans were under the commands of Brig. General Arthur MacArthur and Maj. Gen. Elwell S. Otis, who had replaced General Merritt. The city of Caloocan was defended by troops under command of General Antonio Luna who together with a Belgian-trained engineer, Jose Alejandrino, had constructed trenches to defend the town. It turned out to be the bloodiest, most traumatic battle of the young war to that point, especially after The Igorots who Dumindin described as *"mountaineers from the Cordilleras of northern Luzon Island -sent a contingent of men to*

75 Ibid.

fight the Americans at Caloocan. The warriors were armed only with spears, axes, and shields."[76]

US Artillery a section of a light battery behind entrenchments just before the battle of Caloocan[77]

After the battles of San Roque and Caloocan on 24 February, and while he was recovering from a bout of bronchitis, John Kinne reflected on General Otis's answer to Secretary of War Russell Alexander Alger's query of "When will you send the volunteers home?" The reported coded reply from Otis was *"Doomsday."*

Kinne's reflection from his diary: *"We were beginning to think that was about right, as we had been anxiously looking for orders to go home for months."*[78] He didn't know it at the time, but it would be several grueling months, and many battles and heartbreaks before he would see North Dakota again.

---

76 Ibid.
77 Ibid.
78 Kinne, Diary 1898-1899 CO B First North Dakota Infantry, 32.

1899 painting, by G.W. Peters, drawn from eyewitness accounts, Title: "The Battle Before Caloocan, February 10, 1899—View from the Chinese Church." Maj. Gen. Arthur C. MacArthur, Jr., is the khaki-clad officer with binoculars; the battery of Utah Artillery is on the middle foreground, while the 10th Pennsylvania Volunteers occupy the ground behind the wall. This print came from the book, "Harper's Pictorial History of the War with Spain," published in 1899.

By the end of February 1899, there had been multiple episodes of escalation. On 22 February, there was an attack by insurgents on MacArthur's left front again at Caloocan, with the USS Monadnock throwing ten inch (in diameter) shells over the American lines into the Rebel trenches. At 11:00 am, there was heavy fighting in the Chinese cemetery in San Pedro Macati and General Otis ordered a 7:00 pm curfew to prevent more arson by the insurgents, who had been devastating civilian property with fires. Sniping was continuous throughout the day on the American lines. Return fire by the Yanks resulted in fatal collateral damage to two prominent businessmen whose white suits were mistaken by the Yanks for the uniforms of the rebels.

John Kinne was visited on 25 February by Gail Shephard and Howard Huntley, his former schoolmates who had been transferred to the hospital and ambulance corps. They told of being harassed by sniper fire behind the lines when they were dressing enemy wounds.

Others from the 10th Pennsylvania told of episodes of friendly fire received and given by the 20th US Infantry. In WWII parlance it was SNAFU, Situation Normal All Fouled Up.

On 3 March, Harry Cramer was escorted to the city by his buddies. He was going home on a disability discharge but had to spend some time in the hospital on Corregidor first. The troops continued to experience random sniper fire, but without serious repercussions. Another Company B member, Harry Zimmerman was sent home with a disability discharge on the 9th. On the 13th of March action picked up as the division started a drive to clean the insurgents out of the trenches and advance from San Pedro, drive the guerrillas out of the Church at Guadalupe and advance and occupy the villages of Taguig, Cainti and Pasig.

The 1st North Dakota was ordered to a reserve status because they had been in the trenches and under sporadic fire for so long. They were, however able to watch the action, as described by John Kinne: "The insurgents near the church were just about to eat breakfast when the river gunboats and Scott's Battery* opened fire on them and they fled with their meals untouched on the tables.–The gunboats on the river were delayed by two sunken cascos (shallow boats) but these were later removed.—The 22nd had six wounded on the first advance. One guard –told us the Chinamen had buried two hundred insurgents up to that time."[79]

---

* So-called because the battery's commander was Lt. Ernest Scott.
79 Kinne, Diary 1898-1899 CO B First North Dakota Infantry, 36.

US gunboat Laguna de Bay bombards Guadalupe Convent. The side-wheeled steamer used to be a passenger boat that plied the Manila - Lake Laguna de Bay route; Maj. Gen. Elwell S. Otis purchased her from a Spanish firm. Capt. Frank A. Grant of the Utah Volunteer Light Artillery armored the boat and mounted eight guns upon her. The gunboat was about 125 feet long and thirty-seven and a half feet wide.[80]

In the afternoon of the 13th General Charles King, an 1866 graduate of West Point and popular author with more than eighteen worldwide publications to his credit by 1901 visited the 1st North Dakota in their trenches. Kinne noted that the general was *"now in charge of our division,"*[81] but actually Medal of Honor recipient General Henry Ware Lawton was the division commander, and General King was the 1st Brigade commander although he most likely was acting as the Division's deputy commander after General Anderson departed. Initially the 1st ND was under the 2nd brigade (Anderson) of the 1st Division. After Otis replaced Merritt and Lawton replaced Anderson, they came to the 1st Brigade (King).

After the troops occupied Taguig a battalion of the 1st Washington Volunteers commanded by Major John Weisenburger, swam and waded across a river channel and took the town of Pateros. The next day, Pasig fell to a force commanded by Brig. Gen. Lloyd Wheaton.

---

80 *Dumindin, "Philippine-American War, 1899-1902."*
81 *Kinne, Diary 1898-1899 CO B First North Dakota Infantry.*

The net result was a sweep of guerillas out of the area along the Pasig River. The 1st ND and the Volunteers from Idaho were disgusted that they had been left out of the drive to clear the Pasig River banks of insurgents and commiserated about the fact together. Kinne quoted one of the Idaho troops: *"Wheaton should have let loose the savage Idaho's and the long strawed North Dakotas at the N—ers and kept the regulars in the trenches."*[82] Kinne agreed with him. On the 10th Harry Cramer, who was still on ambulatory trial to go home, and John Kinne were headed for San Pedro Macati when they observed a Idaho boy take a bullet through his sleeve while drinking water. *"I am going home, things are getting too hot around here,"*[83] the Idahoan said. They agreed and turned back to camp.

2nd Oregon Volunteers lined up at Pasig, March 15, 1899.[84]

---

82 Kinne, Diary 1898-1899 CO B First North Dakota Infantry, 37.
83 Ibid.
84 Dumindin, "Philippine-American War, 1899-1902."

CHAPTER SEVEN

March 15 – April 30, 1899

"You can't say civilization isn't advancing; in every war they kill you in a new way." –Will Rogers

During the remaining days of March 1899, heavy losses were experienced by the Volunteers from Montana and the 4th Cavalry, but the towns of Polo, Novoletches, San Francisco Del Monte, and Mariquina were taken. Malabon was also captured with the assistance of the gunboats, but Colonel Harry C. Egbert, commander of the 22nd Infantry regiment, was killed. On 27 March, Company B went back into the trenches; on the next day, Adolph Koplin from Bismarck's Company A, drowned in the Pasig River. His twin brother Rudolph survived. Adolph's death was the eighth death of the regiment since the deployment.

On April Fool's Day, each company of the North Dakota regiment was issued twelve Krag-Jorgensen rifles. John Kinne was one of the lucky twelve of Company B to get one, but then he was one of the best shooters. He also spent some time in front of General King's quarters as a guard, no doubt because the brigade commander recognized his marksmanship.

Company B also experienced three wounded in the trenches that day, one of whom, Cpl. John Byron, later died from his wounds. General King also took some of the Company B sharpshooters on more than one occasion to a point of high ground and had them direct fire into the enemy's trenches to try to draw their fire.

April 12, 1899 was the first major fight of the North Dakota regiment to involve significant casualties. Otis had charged General Lawton, the 1st Division commander, with the capture of the city of Santa Cruz, a commercial center on the south side of Lake Laguna de Bay. The subsequent campaign was supposed to deliver Aguinaldo a significant blow by destroying the enemy telegraph line, capture his river and lake fleet of *cascos* (shallow boats with woven mats or canvas covered overheads) and subdue any pockets of rebel resistance.

The problem was that Lawton did not have enough troops to occupy or garrison the towns he took, so that immediately after a victory, the Americans would advance to the next town and the rebels would fill in and occupy the towns they had just left. It turned out to be a major divisive point of disagreement between Lawton and Otis, which bubbled over when Lawton told a reporter that at least three times the number of troops was needed than what Otis was telling President McKinley. The truth of Lawton's statements would become evident before long, but he would not live to see the resolution of the problem.

Part of the initial movements by Lawton in what came to be known as the Laguna de Bay Campaign was an amphibious landing southwest of Santa Cruz on April 10th. (*Laguna de Bay, the Philippines' largest lake southeast of Manila, was connected to Manila and Manila Bay by a series of rivers.*)

There, the 1st North Dakota encountered some resistance, but the 2nd battalion, under command of Major John Fraine, escaped without casualties. Meanwhile, the 4th US Cavalry had also landed, but northeast of Santa Cruz. By mid-morning, the two prongs of the attack had linked and the City of Santa Cruz was theirs, mostly because of supporting artillery by the gunboats *Oeste* and the *Laguna de Bay*.

On April 12th, after having taken the town of Pagsanjan and captured some of Aguinaldo's lake fleet the previous day, Fraine's battalion was advancing in a skirmish line on enemy positions near the town of Paete. Although it was difficult to provide flankers to the skirmish line because of the terrain, Fraine did send five of them from Grafton's Company C and had them ascending a hill, underneath the hilltop position of Fraine's sharpshooters on the left flank of the skirmish line. The flankers included Corporal Isadora (Izzy) Driscoll, Private Alfred (Al) Almen, Private William (Bill) Lamb, Wagoner Peter (Pete) Tompkins, and Private Thomas (Tom) Sletteland.

"Geez, Izzy," said Pete Tompkins, "slow down a little, will you, we're getting ahead of the skirmish line, and this going is tough."

"Okay," replied Driscoll, "who's bringing up our rear?" he asked, turning to Al Almen, the man behind Pete Tompkins.

"Bill Lamb is behind me, and Tom Sletteland is bringing up the rear."

Lieutenant Thom Tharalson, a real estate salesman from Grafton, ND, in charge of the sharpshooters, was watching the flankers and the skirmish line from a position on top of the hill. He saw and heard the first shots, which came in a volley and killed three of the flankers instantly. Four of the five flankers were down and Tharalson saw Sletteland, the last in line, dive under a bush. Killed outright were Driscoll, Almen, and Lamb. Mortally wounded was Pete Tompkins, still alive but riddled with bullets, which had been fired from ambush just ten yards away. What happened next was truly amazing.

First, Sletteland crawled into the open to aid the wounded Pete Tompkins. The minute he showed himself, the insurgents opened fire. Sletteland returned fire with his Krag and then got close enough to Tompkins to grab his Krag as well and returned fire up to the total of ten shots from both rifles in rapid succession. All this happened from close range. He hit at least two of the enemy, grabbed Tompkins by one boot, tossed Tompkins rifle into a nearby bush, and dragged the wounded man to safety.

Lieutenant Tharalson and his sharpshooters, who had been observing all this, could not fire on the insurgents because of the proximity of Sletteland and Tompkins to their targets. They watched as the insurgents came out of their ambush cover on at least two occasions that they could see, to try to capture the guns and ammo of the killed Americans. Sletteland drove them back each time, and because he fired on several more occasions, likely prevented more attempts to capture the American weapons.

In the meantime, General Lawton hearing the firefight asked Major Fraine what was going on. Fraine, who had deployed additional troops to aid the ambushed flankers, when he saw them go down, gave Lawton an update.

"Sir, my five flankers on the hill ran into an ambush. I was just going up to talk with my sharpshooters on the hill when I saw them go down. I sent a platoon from each of my four companies to help, but we could use some artillery support."

"Where do you want it?" asked Lawton.

"I've got my platoons going up that hill on the left in single file from the skirmish line on both sides of the road over there," he said pointing out the positions, "and my sharpshooters are on top of the hill. The ambush was about half way up."

"We'll put the shells over their heads, at right angles to the slope, and parallel to the left of the road," said Lawton. "I'll direct fire from the gunboat."

"That should work," said Fraine.

It did. Author John Durand describes the action this way: "*Within minutes, more sharpshooters and the mountain guns arrived, and also the Laguna de Bay (with Lawton aboard), its field pieces and machine guns blazing. The battle raged as the skirmishers on the hill advanced with volley fire, and the big guns on the Laguna de Bay poured explosive and shrapnel into the jungle. At some time during the action, North Dakota Privates Herbert Files (Company I) and August Hensel (Company K) were wounded.*"[85]

When the rescuers reached Sletteland and Tompkins, Sletteland helped evacuate his wounded buddy to the road where an ambulance took him to Longos, where a field hospital had been set up in a church and where he died. Also mortally wounded in the battle was bugler George Schneller from Wahpeton's Company I.

---

85 John Durand, *The Boys, 1st North Dakota Volunteers in the Philippines.* Puzzlebox Press, Elkhorn, 237.

Site of the ambush near Paete on the east shore of Laguna de Bay[86]

During and after the battle at Paete, back on the west shore of Lake Laguna de Bay, General King continued to use the sharpshooters for special assignments and allowed them an extra ten rounds a day for practice. On 8 May, as the troops were entering the town of San Pedro, as part of General Lawton's Santa Cruz expedition, Kinne noted the presence of *"a fine athletic looking individual in civilian clothes leaning on his rifle.—He reminded me of Leather Stocking, the hero of (James Fennimore) Cooper's Tales. —We afterward learned his name was William H. Young–."*[87]

Indeed! William H. Young turned out to be one of those historical heroes like Daniel Boone or Jim Bowie for whom it is hard to separate fact from fiction regarding his exploits. He had a reputation as an

---

86 *Map designed by Paul Hook, Mill City, Oregon.*
87 *Kinne, Diary 1898-1899 CO B First North Dakota Infantry, 42.*

Indian fighter and undoubtedly was familiar with the Dakotas and by his own admission had been a civilian scout for the Army in Montana and the Dakotas. According to Kinne's diary he had also prospected in Montana and California. An apparent worldwide adventurer he had gone to China and Korea and had been a captain of the King's Guards in Korea. He had also fought with the Chinese side of the Japanese-Chinese conflict.

At the time Kinne first saw him he had recently been fighting with the Americans in the trenches, and had proven himself to be an excellent marksman. Later on the 29th, General Lawton, himself, noted the tall, well-muscled man and had asked one of his aides to bring him to him with the intention of sending this civilian to the rear. When Lawton asked him who he was and what was he doing here, Young replied that he had come to the Islands to prospect, but when he arrived near Manila, he could not enter the city because the insurgents had it surrounded. He was staying at a hotel when the shooting started, so he took his Mauser, headed for the trenches and thought he would *"help the boys out a little."*[88]

According to John Durand[89] Kinne's diary is almost a word-for word copy of Karl Faust's Campaigning in the Philippines (Hicks-Judd, San Francisco 1899) version of Lawton's first encounter with William Young. Here is Kinne's version of General Lawton's recollection: *"Soon after leaving Manolis (on April 29th) I entered the enemy's country and was greatly annoyed by the enemy's sharpshooters. One morning I ordered a halt to make a reconnaissance. Sitting on a log some distance to the front of where my staff and I were, I saw a man in civilian clothes, coolly watching operations. I asked who he was and one of my staff officers replied that he did not know but he had seen him on the firing line several times and although he had been ordered several times to the rear, he had disobeyed that order. The lieutenant said 'he has been continuously in front of our lines under fire, but the men can't keep him away.'*

"Now if there is anything which angers me it is to see a brave man needlessly expose himself, so I ordered the stranger sent to me. He approached and I was much taken with his appearance and said, 'who

---

88 Kinne, Diary 1898-1899 CO B First North Dakota Infantry, 62.
89 Durand, The Boys, 1st North Dakota Volunteers in the Philippines.

*are you and what are you doing here?' and he said, 'I am an American cit-
izen and my name is Young. I have been a scout in the Indian campaigns
in Montana and the Dakotas, and I thought I would come out here and
try to help the boys a little.' I recalled his name as one who had done some
gallant work against the redskins and asked him if he could pick compe-
tent men like himself from the N.D.'s, the 4th Cavalry, and the 2nd Oregon's.
He said he could and I at once offered him the post as chief of Scouts at a
salary of $150 a month, which he accepted, and the next day was ready
for business."90*

**Major General Henry Lawton engraving used on Philippine
currency 1923. Lawton is the only one of flag rank Medal of Honor
recipients (civil war) to have been KIA. His Arlington Cemetery web
page includes the following:**

90 *Kinne diary, 62.*

"On December 1 (1899) he (Lawton) was at Tang and on the 16th left Manila for San Macho. Here, during an engagement on 19th, he was on the firing line. Being 6 feet 3 inches in height, and attired in full uniform, he was a conspicuous target for insurgent sharpshooters. Hardly had his staff officers warned him of his danger when he suddenly cried, "I am shot," and fell dead. In the early part of 1900 his remains were brought back to his native country and buried with distinguished official honors. The sympathies of the public were so strong for his widow and children that a movement was started to raise funds to provide for their future, and within a very few weeks about $100,000 was secured."[91]

Lawton is also revered by the Filipinos in spite of his leading the "enemy." A clue to this affection is found in this commentary from the Arlington website: *"Soon after his death an extract from private letter was published, in which appeared following sentence: 'If I am shot by a Filipino bullet, it might was well be from one of my own men.' The peculiar phrase attracted considerable attention, especially in the early part of the Presidential campaign of 1900. The letter was written in Manila October 6, 1899, to John Barrett, ex-minister to Siam, then in NYC. The following extract from the letter gives the full setting of the mysterious sentence above quoted, and affords evidence that the continuation of the insurrection was due to direct encouragement from the US."*

"'I agree with you that mistakes have been made here, but I would to God that the whole truth of this whole Philippine situation could be known by everyone in America. I wish the people could know it as I know it, and as you know it. I agree that if the real facts in connection with this story, inspiration and conditions of this insurrection and the hostile ruptures, local and eternal, such as the Katipunan revolutionary society and juntas that now encourage the enemy, as well as the actual possibilities of these Philippines and people and their relation to this great East, which you have set forth so ably, could be understood at home in America, we would hear no more political talk of unjust shooting of government into the Filipinos or of unwise threats of hauling down our flag in the Philippines. You are right. Some of us have modified our views since we first

91 http://www.arlingtoncemetery.net/hwlawton.htm.

came, and it these so-called anti-imperialists of Boston would honestly ascertain the truth on the ground here, and not in distant America, they, whom I dislike to believe to be other than honest men misinformed, would be convinced of the error of their exaggerated statements and conclusions and of the cruel and unfortunate effect on their publications here. It is kind of you to caution me about exposure under fire, but if I am shot by a Filipino bullet, it might as well come from one of my own men. These are strong words, and yet I say them because I know from my own observation, confirmed by stories of captured Filipino prisoners, that the continuance of fighting is chiefly due to reports that are sent out from America and circulated among those ignorant natives by the leaders who know better."[92]

William Young's middle name was Henry and most people called him that. He picked his initial twenty-five Scouts from the sources General Lawton recommended. Lawton liked and respected him a lot, not only because of his reputation and appearance but also because he recognized him as a kindred spirit and besides, his name was Henry! These two tall natural leaders, Lawton was 6'3" and Young was 6'2", made an impressive pair. They had what we now call *"command presence."*

"Well, Henry, how many Scouts do you think you might need to help me out with some special operations?" Lawton asked.

"Depends on what you have in mind, General," Young replied.

"I need sharpshooters to pick off some of these rebel snipers, who are really beginning to piss me off. I need a small group that can infiltrate enemy lines quietly, search out and destroy targets I deem vital, and I need men who are not afraid of a fight."

"I've been watching your operations, General Lawton sir, and you have the resources. Some of those 1st North Dakota boys are really sharp. Let me pick twenty-five men from the Dakotas, the Oregon's and the 4th Cavs, and together with myself and my engineer friend Murphy from the Grant [93] we will have enough to start. Give me twenty-four hours."

---

92 *Ibid.*
93 *http://www.theshipslist.com/Forms/marriagesatsea.html.*

On 30 April, Young did indeed have his roster picked. They included sixteen from the 1st North Dakota.[94][95] There are some differences in the original roster between Kinne's and Durand's rosters.

Initial Roster(s) of Young's Scouts:
Company A (Bismarck-Mandan) Pvts. Michael Glassley and Calvin Wilson[95] or Richard Longfellow[94]

Company B (Fargo) Cpl. Franklin Anders and Pvts. Otto Luther and Edward McBain

Company C (Grafton) Pvt. Thomas Sletteland[95] or Forest Warren[94]

Company D (Devil's Lake) Pvt. Gotfred Jensen

Company G (Valley City) Pvts. Neal Christianson and Chas. Davis and maybe Sterling Galt[94]

Company H (Jamestown) Pvts. John Killian and Edwin Pannell[95] or Willis Downs[94]

Company I (Wahpeton) Pvts. Otto Boehler and John Desmond

Company K (Dickinson) Pvts. Patrick Hussey, John C. Smith and W. F. Thomas[95] or Frank Summerfield[94]

Five from the 2nd Oregon:
Company B (Portland) Pvts. Ed E. Lyon and Marcus Robertson
Company G (not specified) Pvts. James Harrington and Frank High
Company K (Salem) Pvt. William B. Scott
Company L (not specified) Pvt. James B. O' Neil

From the 4th US Cavalry:
Troop C Pvt. Eli L. Watkins
Troop G Pvt. Simon Harris
Troop L Pvt. Peter Quinn

---

94 Kinne, Diary 1898-1899 CO B First North Dakota Infantry.
95 Durand, The Boys, 1st North Dakota Volunteers in the Philippines.

Photo of Young's Scouts taken at San Pedro Macati late May 1899.[96] John Durand notes in his excellent work, "The Boys,"[97] that there are several rosters of the original 27 Scouts, and his differs slightly from John Kinne's[98] as noted above. It makes little difference since at least 37 men not including Young or Murphy, served in the Scouts, 26 of them from the 1st North Dakota. Young and Harrington died of their wounds and several others were wounded or disabled before this photo was taken prior to General Lawton disbanding the group. Frank Anders is 2nd from the left top row. John Kinne is said to be kneeling far left 1st row.

Here is another description of Lawton's first encounter with William H, Young as described by the authors of *Campaigning in the Philippines:*[99]

"GALLANT BEHAVIOR OF WILLIAM H. YOUNG.

"At *daybreak, on the 29th, (of April 1899) the 1st North Dakotas, 3d U. S. Inf. and Scott's platoon, moved down the south bank of the river toward San Rafael. At the same time Col. Summers' command, to which was added*

96 Richard Kolb, ed., VFW Magazine Publication, "Blaze in the Boondocks, 2002. Fighting on America's Imperial Frontier in the Philippines, 1899-1913."

97 Durand, The Boys, 1st North Dakota Volunteers in the Philippines.

98 Kinne, Diary 1898-1899 CO B First North Dakota Infantry.

99 Karl Irving, et al. Campaigning in the Philippines, San Francisco, Hicks-Judd, 1899.

Hawthorne's Separate Mountain Battery, moved down the north bank of the river in the same direction. About noon Col. Treumann's command developed a force of the enemy, afterward estimated at 400, which they drove on down the river. Here an incident took place which Gen. Lawton says he shall not soon forget, in that it made him acquainted with that splendid and gallant man and scout, William H. Young. He, in citizen's clothing, was noticed walking well in front of the right flankers of the advance point. Gen. Lawton ordered him in, intending to reprimand and send him to the rear. Something in the man's bearing and appearance made the General change his mind, and he directed him to go to the front and bring in a citizen that the General might get definite information about the location of San Rafael. He cheerfully complied, and in less than five minutes Gen. Lawton heard three shots and Young appeared as cool and collected as ever, bearing a rifle and haversack with eighty-six rounds of ammunition, dripping with blood. He had run into an insurgent outpost of eight men, and had alone killed one and driven the others off. His action prevented a surprise to our advance guard which was soon under a rapid and hot fire."[100]

In reference to the differences of the above rosters, Durand's may be more accurate at least concerning Company C.

Grafton's Thomas Sletteland had already demonstrated his grit on April 12th before Young picked his first roster, and his heroism was well known amongst the troops, even John Kinne, who noted in his diary on April 13th that *"Sergeant Major Whitiker (sic) (listed as Whittaker, A. A., CO A, Sergeant, in the 1st North Dakota Volunteer Infantry Roster) had died in the hospital, making the 9th death of our regiment.—While we were on the ferry (Pasig River ferry that evening) we met a reporter for the New York World—and it was reported that the North Dakotas had been the heaviest loser in the Santa Cruz campaign. Five were killed, four in Company C and one in Company D."*

Later on April 17th, Kinne knew who was involved and after the war inserted this into his diary: *"Pvt. Thomas Sletteland only survivor of five after the first volley from the insurgents near Paete, of whom it is said (quoting the MOH citation) 'Single handed and alone defended his dead and wounded comrades against a greatly superior force of the enemy,' and was later awarded the Congressional Medal of Honor."*[101]

100 Ibid.
101 Kinne, Diary 1898-1899 CO B First North Dakota Infantry.

Sletteland was the first North Dakotan ever awarded the Medal of Honor. Historian Dumindin discussing the Santa Cruz Campaign recorded his feat this way:

"After the capture of Malolos, the U.S. 2nd (sic actually 1st) Division under Maj. Gen. Henry W. Lawton was sent by Maj. Gen. Elwell S. Otis to the south into Laguna province, via Lake Laguna de Bay, to take the Filipino stronghold located in Santa Cruz, 48 miles (80 km) from Manila.

"The next day, April 12, 1899, the Americans launched another expedition to capture the town of Paete. About 220 men began the march at 2:45 that afternoon. After about an hour, the Americans spotted Filipino breast works 150 yards in front of them, manned by 50 or so Filipino fighters.

"Major John Fraine, commander of the 1st North Dakota Volunteers, (sic Fraine was a battalion commander under Treumann) sent a small squad consisting of one corporal and four privates to flank the Filipino positions. Some Filipinos hiding in thick foliage flanking the road fired at close range on the small force, killing four. The sole survivor, Private Thomas Sletteland managed to drive back the nearest group of Filipinos, who repeatedly tried to seize the rifles of his fallen comrades. He was later awarded the Medal of Honor."[102]

Sletteland was a Norwegian immigrant born in Bergen in February 1874. He died in 1915 at age forty or forty-one and is buried in the Veterans Cemetery, Mandan, ND.

North Dakota's first Medal of Honor recipient, Grafton's Thomas Sletteland.[103]

102 Dumindin, "Philippine-American War, 1899-1902."
103 Wikipedia, WEB Free Encyclopedia, http://search.aol.com/aol/search?s_it=wscreen-searchboxhtml&q=Thomas+Sletteland.

April 13, 1st North Dakota Volunteers in camp at Paete, Laguna Province. April 13, 1899, one day after the battle in which Sletteland was involved, and several comrades perished.[104]

104 Dumindin, "Philippine-American War, 1899-1902."

CHAPTER EIGHT

(Eighteen day time overlap)
April 12 – May 3, 1899

"War is not a life: it is a situation, one which may neither be ignored nor accepted." –T. S. Eliot

Before Lawton's encounter with Scout Young, besides the relatively heavy 1st North Dakota losses at the start of the Santa Cruz campaign at Paete on April 12th, losses were also sustained by 14th Infantry and 4th Cavalry on the first day of fighting in Santa Cruz with one KIA each and an additional five WIA between them. The losses on the Insurgents' side were much more severe with sixty-eight buried by the Americans and thirty-three enemy wounded treated at the American field hospital. The fighting in the city was all but over by the 14th, and Lawton's expedition returned from Santa Cruz on the 17th.

4th Cavalry men resting in a banana grove.[105]

On the next day, April 18, the 1st North Dakota got orders to prepare for a fifteen-day march and on the 22nd found themselves headed north in columns of four, along with the 22nd Infantry and Scott's Battery.* They would march straight through Manila and head northeast toward Norzagaray. (See map page 80.)

They were preceded by The 7th Cavalry led by West Point graduate Capt. James F. Bell, the 1st Nebraska Volunteer Infantry and the 3rd US Infantry. Their mission was to take and occupy Norzagaray, reconnoiter San Miguel , and force or turn the enemy's flank into MacArthur's advancing 2nd Division on Lawton's left or drive them further north.

---

105 Dumindin, "Philippine-American War, 1899-1902."
* So called because the battery's commanding officer of the 6th US Artillery was Lt. Ernest D. Scott.

Four days later, recently promoted to captain of the 7th Cavalry in March 1899, James Franklin Bell, an 1878 graduate of West Point,[106] was the first to encounter enemy resistance on the 22nd. The battle began when the 7th Cavalry unit under his command while on reconnaissance, was attacked by a strong force of about 1000 Filipinos led by General Gregorio del Pilar.[107] Forced to retreat to a defensive position, Bell sent for help to the 1st Nebraska, which promptly responded.

Captain James Franklin Bell in 1899[108] *

---

106 http://www.history.army.mil/books/cg&csa/Bell-JF.htm.
107 Dumindin, "Philippine-American War, 1899-1902."
108 Ibid.

* Capt. Bell was later transferred to the 36th Infantry and awarded the MOH for gallantry near Porac, Luzon, Philippine Islands, September 9, 1899. A man with an interesting career, one of Bell's first posts after graduating from West Point was to the 7th Cavalry (Custer's old outfit massacred at the Little Big Horn, 1876) Fort Lincoln, Dakota Territory in 1878, where Cpl. Frank Anders was born. He most likely knew Frank Ander's dad who was stationed at Fort Lincoln in 1875 when Franklin Anders entered the world. After a few months in the Philippines, Bell was promoted from his commission of captain in the Regular Army to brigadier-general in the Regular Army, skipping three ranks and outranking many officers previously his senior. Bell later rose to the rank of Major General and served as Army Chief of Staff from April 1906 – April 1910. He was also accused of war crimes while in the Philippines: See alleged war crimes at the end of this chapter

The Nebraskans were led by Col. John Stotsenberg, who, having experienced the insurgents' poor marksmanship before, rushed into the fray and was promptly surprised by the intensity and accuracy of the Filipinos' response. A fierce firefight followed during which both sides sustained heavy casualties. Further back near Novaliches, the 1st North Dakotans were also under fire, with John Kinne observing General Lawton, "who in his light colored clothing and white helmet, on a big black horse, was a conspicuous target for the enemy."[109]

As bullets were snapping twigs all around him Kinne shouted to Fred Hansche, a Company B corporal. *"Get down, Fred!"* About then, Fred was hit in the chest. As he fell, he said to Leo Ryan, hunkered down beside him, *"Leo, I am shot!"* Hansche was shot through the right side of his chest puncturing his lung, but he survived. As the firefight continued, some of the soldiers were dropping out because of the heat.

Pvt. Howard Fell, from Jamestown's Company H, took a bullet in the leg and kept going. The battle extended to a ridge with an open area beyond. At the end of a downhill slope, there was a creek with fifteen foot high banks. Kinne recalls the action: *"Captain Geary (Edward C. Geary, from Fargo's Company B) shouted 'Make it Boys' and jumped in and reached the other side. Then several others followed, but some could not swim or did not try. I threw my haversack and blanket across and swam the stream with my gun above the water and returned to get McIntyre's (James W., a waiter from Fargo's Company B) gun as he could not swim with it."[110]*

The insurgents were driven into their own defensive position at which point American artillery under Brig. General Irving Hale solidified the win. The Yanks had fifteen KIA and forty-three WIA, and the Filipinos an estimated 100 casualties.

The 1st ND had six missing at roll call the next morning, one of whom was the wounded corporal Hansche and another one of his buddies who stayed with him to the hospital.

The advance started again early the next morning at 0300 but was slow all day due to continuous firing from retreating Filipinos and delays caused by heat exhaustion and loss of the pack animals,

109 Kinne, Diary 1898-1899 CO B First North Dakota Infantry, 46.
110 Ibid.

carabao *(pronounced care-i-bow rhymes with wow)* not to be confused with caribou a reindeer-like animal. Americans would call the beasts water buffalo. Many of these animals dropped from exhaustion, especially those pulling heavy artillery pieces. When the troops reached San Jose, sleep was a welcome respite. The 1st North Dakota had nine of their carabou die during the night but captured more to replace them. The next day, Kinne and Company B had more to add to the legend of William H. Young: *"While our company was waiting in a shady spot for the coolies to cut a road through the brush on the banks of a road we had to cross, Captain Geary started out to watch the work, and in crossing an opening about the size of a city block, Young–spied three insurgents dodging around trying to get a shot at Capt. Geary. Young dropped two of them but the third got away. We passed that way a short time afterward as Young sauntered up with two of the insurgent's guns and bloody belts and cartridge boxes, threw them on the ox-cart and added two more notches to his rifle."*[111]

Over the next few days as the division continued its northern sweep they experienced drenching downpours, watched skirmishes from hillside advantages, observed Young and some of his companions take on more of the insurgents successfully, caught "gumps" (chickens) for supper and scrounged fruit including papaya, mangoes, apples, and bananas. Scout Young added more notches to his rifle and had at least nine since Kinne first saw him. The towns of Norzagaray, and Angat, passed under their boots. And it was at Angat or just beyond when General Lawton first saw William Henry Young in action as the division approached San Rafael. No doubt Lawton recognized Young's value to his mission. Historians Faust and Irving *et al.* reviewed Lawton's mission this way: *"The purposes of the expedition or plan of campaign contemplated the advance of this column on what appeared on most maps to be a practicable road through Novaliches and San Jose to Norzagaray, where a large insurgent force was reported to have their headquarters. In front of Norzagaray, junction with another column, 1200 strong, marching from Bocaue through Santa Maria, was to be made. After the capture and occupation of Norzagaray, the road leading north from there to San Miguel was to be thoroughly reconnoitered,*

111 *Ibid.*

especially as to the practicability for this column. On the best credited map, this route is represented as a good road. San Miguel was supposed to be an insurgent stronghold, and the probable rendezvous of the forces to be defeated, but it was suggested that the 1st Division column, could move on San Miguel along the road east of the swamp, thus making a combined attack with the 2nd Division. This Novaliches-San Jose route would promise that this column would get over on the extreme right of the insurgents' left; would invade their country; engage the enemy's forces, and prevent a concentration of the forces in our front upon Ma-cArthur, if not at the same time turn the enemy's flank and disconcert his plans. The combined northern movement of both field divisions, if unable to secure a decisive action against the northern insurgent army, would at least drive the enemy out of the Tagalog provinces into northern ones, whose inhabitants were reported unfriendly to the insurrection. At five o'clock next morning, April 22d, the command commenced the march northward, the 3d Inf. joining the column at its formation."[112]

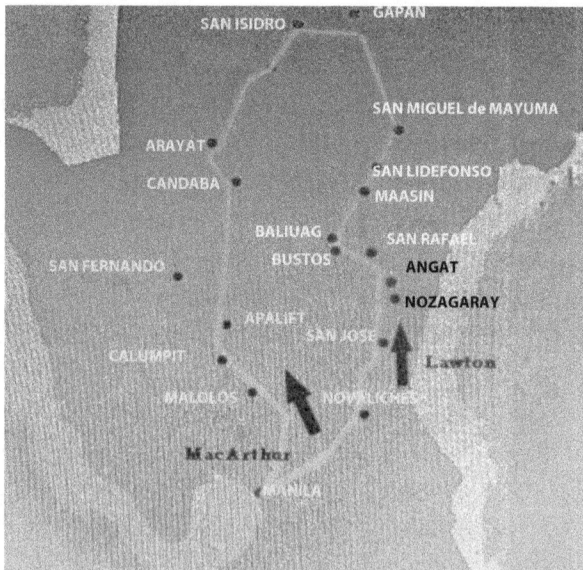

General Lawton's Route in the San Isidro Campaign[113]

---

112 Irving, *Campaigning in the Philippines.*
113 Map designed by Stephen Hook, Landstuhl, Germany.

General Lawton's 1st Division headed north flanking the right side of the insurgent's extreme left and hoping to turn the rebel forces into MacArthur 2nd Division also heading north on the rebel's right. At the very least, the two-pronged attack should drive the insurgents into the rebel unfriendly northern provinces.

On 30 April, Kinne and the others were made aware of the formation of "Young's Scouts" under the direction of General Lawton, and states in his diary "the three taken from our company were Corporal Anders, Luther and McBain."[114] At 1500 that same afternoon, the 1st North Dakota started an advance in front of the 22nd Infantry and engaged the enemy in a firefight in rock strewn jungle. At sunset they broke out of the jungle and could see Manila Bay from their high advantage point about thirty miles away. Since artillery had forced the insurgents to retreat, the North Dakotans camped for the night.

The next morning, Mayday, The Scouts split into two groups, one led by Young himself, and were out in front of elements of Treumann's 1st North Dakota Volunteers and headed west going down river on the south bank of the Angat. The other group of Scouts were led by Jim Harrington, the 2nd Oregon's most experienced veteran. They preceded a provisional group from 2nd Oregon led by Col. Owen Summers along the north bank. While Harrington's Scouts leading the 2nd Oregon ran into light resistance approaching San Rafael, heavier fighting broke out in front of Young's group on the south bank. John Durand quoting his grandfather's (Tom Stafney's) diary and Major Fraine, recorded the San Rafael victory this way: "'The enemy opened a heavy fire from across the river and to the front of our line'-Fraine . The firing came from near Titabon. Tom's (Stafney's) Company I (Wahpeton) had the point as they neared the bluffs near Titabon that looked down on the Americans in San Rafael. While one of the Astor Battery guns with Summers' Brigade began pounding the Filipinos on Tom's side of the river, Tom's battalion formed a skirmish line and advanced. 'Only two Co.'s of us did any shooting,' Tom said, because the enemy disappeared. 'One man from Company G (Valley*

---

114 Kinne, Diary 1898-1899 CO B First North Dakota Infantry, 51.

City) was slightly wounded in the leg,' Pvt. Charles Olstad, a Valley City blacksmith."[115]

On 2 May, having driven the insurgents out of San Rafael, the 22nd Infantry took the lead and Company B guarded the baggage train, which consisted of carts, some of them two wheeled, being pulled by mules, ponies, or carabao and which had been following the troops as they headed north.

That morning at "0 dark thirty" well before sunrise, Chief Scout William Henry Young, gathered up eight of his group who had been sleeping on their ponchos in a rice field on the south side of the river near San Rafael and headed out for the town of Bustos some three miles downstream. Their job was to reconnoiter the town, which had a population of between 6000 – 10,000, and which was on the way to Baliuag, Lawton's next objective.

Knowing their leader, however, the Scouts knew that that if they ran into any resistance, he would try to resolve it first before asking for any help from the troops behind them. Included in the group were Scouts Frank Anders, Mike Glassley, Charley Davis, Frank Ross, Will Downs, Archie Galt, Otto Boehler, and Fred Jensen.

"Okay, fellows, stay alert now," Young said, as they came over a ridge and Bustos came into view in dawn's early light. "Keep an eye on that church tower when we cross the road. We'll be in the open. Charley, you take the point. Archie and Will, right behind him. Cross over in threes. Go!"

Charley Davis scampered across the road with Downs and Galt right on his heels. They dived into the ditch on the other side. There was no reaction from the town. Young sent the next three over, which included Anders, Boehler, and Mike Glassley. Anders and Boehler made it without incident, but, as Glassley cleared the far side, all hell broke loose. Rifle slugs kicked up dust from the road as Glassley dived for cover.

Young turned to Fred Jensen and said, "Did you see where those shots came from?"

"Yep. See that shack by those bamboo trees to our right? There is one shooter in the trees, and two more in the shack."

---

115 Durand, *The Boys, 1st North Dakota Volunteers in the Philippines*, 263.

"I saw smoke from that clump of bushes on our left, too," said Frank Ross.

Young hollered across the road to his Scouts. "Fellas, there are shooters in the Church tower, and in the shack to our right, and in the bamboo trees next to the shack, too. There are more in those bushes to our left. You guys split up and take the ones on either side. We'll cover you from here. When you hear us ring the bell in the tower meet us there!"

"You three guys take the ones on the right," Anders said, pointing to Boehler, Downs, and Galt, "and we'll get the Gugus on the left." He then cupped his hands around his mouth and shouted back across the road. "We're on it, Chief!" With that, both groups headed out in running crouches, as the Scouts with Chief Young opened up with a withering cover fire.

As the firefight got more intense, insurgent groups could be seen on both sides and in front of Young's position, retreating into the town and beyond. When the Chief Scout heard the Krags open up both to the right and left of his position, he leaped to his feet and with a "let's go!" dashed across the road and headed into the town's center, followed by Jensen and Ross.

As they charged into town they were surprised by the number of insurgents running ahead of them. They were later told by one of the town's citizen *"amigos"* that there were approximately 400 insurgents that had been garrisoned in Bustos.

By the time Young, Jensen and Ross reached the church there was no one in the tower, and Young himself climbed the stairs to assure the safety of the other two. He rang the bell three times and by the time he got back downstairs, the other Scouts were already visible coming down the street from both directions. When they were all assembled Young asked for reports.

"Not much to tell," reported Cpl. Anders. "Charley here got a couple of Gugus and Mike got one that I saw. I winged one or two but we sure saw a lot of 'em runnin' to beat hell!"

"Same here," said Boehler, "Will and Archie nailed a couple and I winged a few, but mostly we watched them run."

"Knowing you, Otto," said Young, "you did more than wing a few."

Otto blushed and said, "Well, maybe," and then remained silent. Young patted him on the shoulder and then said, "Let's head back. We need to resupply, I'm nearly out of ammo, and we need to let the 22nd and Col. Treumann know what the situation is."

After they returned to camp, the Scouts had lunch and replenished their ammunition and supplies. It was already afternoon when John Kinne spotted Frank Anders with the Scouts before taking his place guarding the wagon supply train.

"Hey, Frank," he yelled. "What's this I hear about you guys taking Busto all by yourselves?"

"T'wairn't nuthin', John," Anders returned with a put on twang, "just a few of us 'long strawed' Dakotas doin' our job," he drawled, mimicking one of the Idaho soldiers who had previously commiserated with them about being used as reserves.

Kinne later recorded in his diary that the Scouts had routed "at least 400 armed natives"[116] out of the town of Busto, which was the largest town (about 10,000, Durand says population of 6000[117]) captured yet outside of Manila. They did it alone and without support and two hours before the main body of troops got there. They then returned to the encampment and baggage train to get re supplied before heading out to Baliuag, their next objective.

Lt. Col. Treumann's 1st North Dakota troops, minus the baggage train guards, and the 22nd US Infantry, led by Young's Scouts, were advancing on the left or south bank of the Angat River, which flowed from the mountains above Angat, west through Baliuag and Busto then south to Manila Bay.

They would have to cross to the north bank to get from Busto to Baliuag. Col. Summers commanding the 2nd Oregon Volunteers was advancing from San Rafael, which they had occupied without opposition, along the north bank. Summers also had half of Young's Scouts led by 2nd Oregon's Jim Harrington, the oldest and most experienced of Young's Scouts. While both commanders ran into opposition along the river, Young's Scouts on the south bank swam the river and infiltrated the town. With a few well-placed rifle shots they routed the

116 Kinne, Diary 1898-1899 CO B First North Dakota Infantry.
117 Durand, The Boys, 1st North Dakota Volunteers in the Philippines.

town's insurgents and then climbed the church's bell tower this time in Baliuag and rang a church bell for a second time that day to signal once again that a town was theirs.

On 3 May, the ND regiment moved across the river and occupied the town, and the day after that Wheaton's Brigade, which had been trailing the 2nd Oregon, left Baliuag and according to Kinne *"as their baggage train passed up our street it made about as good a parade as I ever saw. They had monkeys and goats, caribou (sic), cows with their calves, –parrots, –wooden wheeled carts, a fine coach with two pretty ponies driven by a clown–."*[118]

Shortly thereafter those left behind heard sounds of battle. The next day an ambulance came through carrying five wounded from Wheaton's brigade primarily from the 13th Minnesota.

* * *

"Alleged War crimes James Franklin Bell: (Posted by a writer for Wikipedia. For other opinions see soldiers', who fought with Bell, remarks in Chapter Fifteen)

"Bell elaborated on (his) orders and the accepted tactics of civilized warfare in a series of circulars, which specifically bestowed on his station commanders the right to retaliate. Brigadier General J. Franklin Bell told the New York Times on May 1, 1901 that: 'One-sixth of the natives of Luzon have either been killed or have died of the dengue fever in the last two years. The loss of life by killing alone has been great, but I think that not one man has been slain except were his death served the legitimate purposes of war. It has been necessary to adopt what other countries would probably be thought harsh measures, for the Filipino is tricky and crafty and has to be fought in his own way'

"A few months after the Balangiga Massacre *of September 1901, President* Theodore Roosevelt *ordered Bell's commander,* General Adna Chaffee *to adopt, 'in no unmistakable terms, the sternest measures to pacify* Samar.' (One of the Philippine islands).

"On December 7, 1901, Bell wrote a letter beginning with this introduction: 'the United States Government, disregarding many

---

118 Kinne, Diary 1898-1899 CO B First North Dakota Infantry, 52.

provocations to do otherwise, has for three years exercised an extraordinary forbearance and patiently adhered to a magnanimous and benevolent policy toward the inhabitants of the territory occupied by this brigade.'

"Bell followed this disclaimer with a long list of Filipino breaches against the laws of civilized warfare:

- *The Filipinos had broken General Order No. 100.*
- *The Filipinos had broken Article 63 by wearing civilian clothes with no special markings and returning home between battles and "divesting themselves of the character and appearance of soldiers... concealing their arms...posing as peaceful citizens...*
- *They have improvised and secreted in the vicinity of roads and trails rudely constructed infernal machines propelling poisoned arrows or darts.' (State of the art IED'S for 1899) Even the destruction of telegraph wires and bridges violated, in Bell's opinion, some section of Lincoln's General Orders.*

"The time had come to fight fire with fire Bell declared. America should 'severely punish, in the same or lesser degree, the commission of acts denounced in the aforementioned articles.' In other words, Bell went on record as planning to violate General Order No. 100 when an American was "murdered", soldiers were instructed to 'by lot select a P.O.W.–preferably one from the village in which the assassination took place–and execute him.'

"Another circular rationalized that 'it is an inevitable consequence of war that the innocent must generally suffer with the guilty" and that 'a short and severe war creates in the aggregate less loss and suffering than a benevolent war indefinitely prolonged.'

"Bell warned his commanders that young officers should not be restrained or discouraged without excellent reason. 'It is not necessary to seek or wait for authority from headquarters to do anything or take any action which will contribute to the end in view.'"[119]

---

119 http://en.wikipedia.org/wiki/J._Franklin_Bell.

Major General James Franklin Bell, Portrait by Adrian Lamb 1973
Photo Credit[120]

---

120 *http://en.wikipedia.org/wiki/J._Franklin_Bell.*

Gotfred Jensen, Devil's Lake, ND.
photo credit - C. Douglas Sterner, www.homeof heroes.com
Photo of Willis Downs, Jamestown, ND not available.

CHAPTER NINE

May 8 – 16, 1899

"Life is a box of chocolates, Forrest. You never know what you're gonna get." –Mrs. Gump.

General Lawton's communications with General Otis in Manila were dependent on the telegraph wire that was laid by the signal corps following the two divisions as they moved north. Otherwise, the field commanders would have to use couriers, which would be unreliable, hazardous, and delayed. On 8 May, one of the signal corps officers, Major Diggels was shot in the forehead and an enlisted man wounded when snipers attacked the men repairing a broken wire. Kinne's diary did not say whether the officer, who was from the 13th Minnesota, survived, but he along with Corporal Bill Allen from Manistee, MN and Private John Martin from Fargo, both Company B members, were on the detail that fetched the signal corps repairmen from San Rafael to repair the broken wire. Like Vietnam and the Middle East in the next two centuries, there was no safety anywhere in the country.

On 13 May, William H. Young and Private William R. Truelock of Grafton's Company C were wounded in an assault near San Miguel. During a charge on insurgent positions, Young was struck in the knee. When he was picked up by the medics some time later, he was surrounded by spent shell casings from his Mauser. He had bound his own wound. As he was carted off in the mule drawn ambulance, Young handed his rifle to Jim McIntyre, a Scout from Company B, and said, *"Keep it until I am out, and if I don't return you can have it."*[121] Sadly, Young never returned because he succumbed to sepsis or tetanus some days later.

When Young was felled by the rebel bullet, the lead of the charge was picked up by Captain William Birkhimer of the 3rd US Artillery, and sustained by other Scouts inspired by Corporal Frank Anders. Anders recalled the events and recorded them on wire, which is preserved by the North Dakota Historical Society. Here is his recollection in his own words: *"Try to picture this in your mind's eye if you can. A hot tropical sun beating down on us from above. Twelve of us crouching in a bamboo thicket. In front of us, an open wide field cris-crossed with irrigation dykes and entrenchments. Beyond that field, entrenched in a wooded hill about 150 yards from us, the Filipinos. The wind would break through a dyke in the open field frequently.*

"The Filipinos opened up a perfect fire. We began firing, and then dropped behind a group of fire ant hills to get organized. The Filipino officers were urging their men to charge when our gallant Chief of Scouts (William H. Young) stands out in the open waving his rifle and shouting 'c'mon boys, let's get at 'em'.

"Well the distance to the Filipino line was scarcely a city block. Before we covered half that distance the whole front line of the enemy rose up with a shout and leaped across the country in a counter charge. It certainly looked bad for us then, but luckily we were all crack shots and our bullets were beginning to take full effect.

"The horse of one of the Filipino officers was shot out from under him, the rider killed right after that. Men all along the line were beginning to fall. Then the native troop lines fell back in disorder and we went after them."[122]

The Medal of Honor is the highest military decoration awarded by the United States government. It is bestowed on a member of the armed forces who *"distinguishes himself by gallantry and intrepidity at risk of his life above and beyond the call of duty while engaged in an action against an enemy of the United States… Due to the nature of this medal, it is commonly presented posthumously."*[123]

---

121 Kinne, Diary 1898-1899 CO B First North Dakota Infantry, 53-54.

122 North Dakota State Historical Society, Capital Grounds, Bismarck, ND.

123 Wikipedia, WEB Free Encyclopedia, http://search.aol.com/aol/search?s_it=wscreen-searchboxhtml&q=Thomas+Sletteland.

All twelve men, all of whom were Young's Scouts, were recommended for the Medal for their actions that day and six were recipients. Their citations are almost identical: *"With eleven other scouts and without waiting for the supporting battalion to aid them or to get into position to do so, charged over a distance of about 150 yards and completely routed about 300 of the enemy who were in a line and in a position that could only be carried by a frontal attack."*

Had Young himself been mobile he would not have been awarded the medal because he was a civilian. There was no doubt amongst the Scouts, however, who the real inspiration of that charge was. Just imagine the odds, twenty-five to one and they routed them! The Filipinos were not cowards nor were they bad soldiers. They were fierce warriors who were not as good shots as the Americans, nor were they as well trained. They did not lack courage, as indicated by their fierce charge that worried the likes of Frank Anders. The Scouts had been in continuous combat and under stress for days and were exhausted, but the adrenaline was flowing and the fight or flight response was automatic for both sides. The rebels chose flight after experiencing the marksmanship of the Scouts.

Of the six medals awarded for the action, three of them went to North Dakota recipients. They were Corporal Anders from Fargo, Willis Downs from Jamestown, and Gotfred Jensen from Devil's Lake.

John Durand discussed the aftermath of the action of May 13th and points out with his excellent sources and research the discord amongst the remaining Scouts and their new self-appointed leader, Captain Birkhimer. The captain was a West Point graduate with the expected discipline that goes along with West Point, who expected the Scouts to hop to his orders like a Corps of West Point cadets. It wasn't going to happen. Birkhimer, although a hero in his own right, was not the natural born leader that William H. Young was and did not have his command presence. Besides, Young had handpicked his Scouts and they were proud of that and worshiped their leader. They were devastated at his loss due to the wound and were not about to accept Birkhimer as their new leader, especially after the captain criticized Young for leading an assault on San Miguel instead of just reconnoitering it like he was ordered. Things finally came to a head when Birkhimer took the two worst subordinate rascals, Frank Anders and Oregon's veteran Jim Harrington, to General Lawton intending to have them disciplined. Big mistake!

"General, sir," Captain Birkhimer addressed the Division Commander, "these men refuse to conform to military discipline and courtesy." Lawton stared at Birkhimer for what seemed like a full minute without saying a word. Finally, without taking his eyes from the Captain, he addressed the enlisted men in a barely audible soft voice.

"Would you gentlemen step outside for a moment while I talk to the Captain." It was not a question and the two Scouts immediately came to attention, saluted and exited the General's quarters, which had been temporarily set up in the newly captured town of San Miguel de Mayumo.

"Jesus, Frank," Jim Harrington said, "did you see the look on Lawton's face?"

"I saw it, Jim, and I don't think I would want to be in Birkhimer's shoes right now."

Anders, a non-commissioned officer, was especially antagonized since Birkhimer had dressed him down for a sloppy salute in front of the other enlisted men. General Lawton, on the other hand, exhibited good judgment in talking to the Captain in private, where Birkhimer's subordinates could neither hear nor observe.

After ten minutes, Captain Birkhimer appeared at the general's door and then left the room without saying a word to Anders or Harrington. That was the last they saw of him. They heard later that he had been reassigned. Unbeknownst to them, Birkhimer was also a distinguished lawyer and later that year served as an Associate Justice on the Supreme Court of the Philippines.

Besides the three North Dakotans, others who received the Medal of Honor for their actions on May 13, were Birkhimer from the 3rd US artillery, Edward E. Lyon and Peter H. Quinn, both from the 2nd Oregon Volunteers.

Cpl. Franklin Lafayette Anders[124]   *Anders the engineer/geologist*[125]

Frank Anders continued his education after the war. His biography in Wikipedia cites his post war service and death as follows:

"After returning to the United States in 1899, he worked for mining interests and in 1902 armed with only a seventh grade education and a few months at Dakota Business College (1895), he decided to attend Ripon College and after graduation in 1906 he became the first person awarded a scholarship by the University of Wisconsin-Madison, where he studied civil engineering and was initiated into Acacia Fraternity in 1907, and was chief engineer with Utah Smelting Corporation from 1909 until 1920. In 1918, he was commissioned a Captain in the Corps of Engineers and stationed in Fort Dodge, Iowa. In 1919 he was transferred to Fort Riley where he was in charge of hospitals and also served in Washington, D.C. and at the Henry Ford Hospital in Michigan. Major Anders died in 1966, and was the oldest surviving recipient of the Medal of Honor at his death."[126]

124 Daniel Tudor, Find a Grave member #46503178, http://www.findagrave.com/cgi-bin/fg.cgi?page=gr&GRid=6404100.

125 Wikipedia, Jan 2009, http://en,wikipedia.org/wikiFrank_L,_Anders.

126 Ibid.

Another biographical sketch of Anders is provided by the Elwyn B. Robinson Dept. of Special Collections, Chester Fritz Library, University of North Dakota:* *"Franklin LaFayette Anders was born November 10, 1875, at Fort Abraham Lincoln, Dakota Territory. His father, Franklin L. Anders, was born in October 1850 in Ohio, while his mother, Anna McLeod, was born in Scotland in 1846. At the time of his birth, Anders' father was stationed at Fort Abraham Lincoln. Upon the elder Anders' discharge, the family moved to Fargo. His father died in 1891 from wounds suffered in the Civil War, while his mother lived until 1946.*

"Anders attended public school in Fargo until 1890. Upon the death of his father, Anders supported the family by finding work with the Northern Pacific Railroad. In 1894, he enlisted in Company B, 1ˢᵗ Regiment of the North Dakota National Guard (After fighting in the Philippine Insurrection) He was discharged in September 1899, and moved to Salt Lake City, Utah, where he spent two years working in the mining industry. (While at Ripon College) he met Mary Hargrave; the couple was married on June 29, 1910 in Ripon. The couple had two children: Marion and Franklin."[127]

Here there appears to be some discrepancy in dates since the Anders papers indicate he served as City engineer in Fargo from 1910 to 1920, although called to active duty during WWI on September 12, 1918. I suspect the Anders' collection is accurate and Wikipedia is in error on the dates of service with the Utah Smelting Corp. Anders did die in 1966 after serving as general manager of the Lucky Strike Coal Company in Zap, ND, from 1920 to 1932 and as a consulting engineer for the ND Capital Commission (Bismarck) and other projects in ND in the 30's, 40's, and 50's.

On May 14, 1899, after Young's Scouts had been devastated by losses due to WIA's , exhaustion, illness, and other causes, some replacements were needed. Three more were chosen from the 1ˢᵗ North Dakota, including John Kinne, and one from the 4ᵗʰ Cavalry. Lawton had assigned a new leader of the Scouts. He was Lt. James

---

* For those interested there are extensive personal papers of Anders filed with the ND Historical Society.

127 Elwyn B Robinson, Dept. of Special Collections, Chester Fritz Library, University of North Dakota, Grand Forks, ND.

Thornton from the 2nd Oregon Volunteers.[128] The new Scouts started for San Miguel the next morning to join the originals. On the way, they passed San Ildefonso, where Truelock, of Grafton's Company C, had been wounded, and, a little further on just before entering San Miguel, they saw where Young had been shot in the knee during the assault on the city. There were still unburied insurgents and a horse lying in the field of battle.

After the new guys found the Scouts' quarters and had a meal, they joined some of the others going out to locate insurgents. It wasn't long before they found themselves in a firefight with the rebels. During the action Kinne and others observed a member of the 13th Minnesota shooting at a figure on a white horse. Then, Kinne heard his friend Frank Anders' voice: "Hey, Minnesota, that's one of ours!"

"Whoa. Sorry about that!"

"Well," Frank shouted, "at least you didn't hit him."

"Ya, it's good thing I don't know how to shoot!"

"Amen to that," Frank said to himself.

"Who's that on the horse, Frank?" asked Kinne, who was now in earshot of Anders.

"Well, well. Look who's here." Anders responded, then continued.

"Glad you came on board, John. I heard you were coming. To answer your question, that is Sterling Archibald Galt from Valley City. We call him Archie, and he stole that horse from the insurgents. He is a helluva rider and a good shot and I'm sure glad that Minnesota guy didn't hit him!"

During that little skirmish, the Scouts, who were leading the 2nd Oregon and the 13th Minnesota as they advanced, accounted for fourteen insurgents KIA and seven wounded.[129] The troops then halted for the night. Kinne had supper with Company K of the 2nd Oregon, and was informed by the new Scout Leader, Lt. Thornton, that Chief Scout Young was not doing well and was going to lose his leg. The next day, May 16, was going to be the most significant day in John Kinne's life. Here is the account of that day in Kinne's own words.

---

128 Durand, The Boys, 1st North Dakota Volunteers in the Philippines, 247.
129 Kinne, Diary 1898-1899 CO B First North Dakota Infantry.

Note the subdued description as opposed to that of his citation of valor described later.

"*We started early the next morning before daylight and soon after leaving the camp (we) passed an insurgent who had been wounded the day before. He waved his hand as we passed down the road and yelled 'Hospital'. We told him to crawl to the road and wait for the ambulance, which he did. We came to where the roads forked, and turned to the left and after advancing about a mile heard an insurgent bugle in a line of trees ahead. We deployed as skirmishers and passed through a line of trees and about a mile beyond without seeing any of the insurgents.*

"*About ten o'clock we heard several shots to our rear and an officer came up on horseback and gave us orders to go ahead and locate the enemy and then fall back, (because) they were strongly entrenched across the river about a half hour's walk ahead.*

"*We advanced cautiously and as we were crossing a rice field the insurgents opened fire on us from about 800 yards ahead. We advanced rapidly under heavy fire before we saw the insurgents in their trenches across the river, and the bridge all ablaze. We opened fire on them and advanced to the bank of the river. The native trenches were just on the opposite bank from us about 50 yards away. We got behind what little protection we could find and began picking off the insurgents as they would show their heads above the trench.*

"*There was a Spaniard fighting with the insurgents just about opposite where I was stationed, who was urging the Filipinos to rise and take aim. I emptied my rifle at this Spaniard but he seemed to have a charmed life. I could see my bullets hitting the ground in the field beyond. I called to Harris, (Pvt. Simon Harris from Troop G 4th US Cavalry, another Scout) who was at my right behind an ant hill which was about seven feet high, and told him about the Spaniard-about my inability to hit him. Harris told me to load my gun again, keep cool and take good aim. While loading my gun a bullet cut off a dead twig in front of my face which blinded me for a few seconds, and several went through the bamboo brush behind which I was hiding so I changed my position and began shooting again at the Spaniard. He soon disappeared and about this time Lt. Thornton, leading two men, crossed the burning bridge on our left. The floor of the bridge was so badly charred that Thomas, (Corporal*

William F. Thomas a Scout from Company K, Dickinson, ND) choked by smoke, fell through but crawled out of the creek on the opposite side and joined in the fight.* After crossing these three (including Thomas) had a flank fire down the insurgents' trenches, and the insurgents began to leave the trenches like a flock of sheep.

"We sat and shot at them at point blank range for several minutes. We were so few that they could not locate us, and we were so close they could not tell how much of the firing we were doing. Those on the left of the bridge crossed over first and those of us on the right soon after and followed the insurgents for a half mile across an open field where they gained a line of trees."[130]

The Battle of the Burning Bridge, as it became known, was at a place called Tarbon, where there was a small church, about a half mile from San Isidro. The church was torn down in order to repair the bridge, without which there would have been several days' delay in getting the artillery, the 13th Minnesota and the 2nd Oregon across to take the town of San Isidro. The Americans were surprised to learn they had been up against a force of about 600 Filipinos, as confirmed by wounded prisoners. Previous estimates were in the 400 – 500 range. One of the prisoners was cooperative and informed the Scouts and General Lawton that there were at least 600 insurgents, one rapid fire Gatling type gun, and two canons along with several Spanish and some American prisoners in San Isidro.

---

* Later when asked by investigating officers if he was the first one over the bridge, Thomas replied "No, I fell in the river" Had he told the entire story Thomas would undoubtedly have been awarded the Medal as well. He was recommended for it, but it was not awarded.

130 Kinne, Diary 1898-1899 CO B First North Dakota Infantry, 55-60.

Titled by the artist "Soldiers in the Sun," a National Guard Painting.

The Battle of the Burning Bridge San Isidro, May 16, 1899, artist Donna Neary[131]

General Lawton had appeared with some mounted cavalry shortly after the Scout's battle and also accompanied by the 2nd Oregon, who were the ones repairing the bridge. His troops were also the bearers of some bad news. One of the Scouts, a good friend of Corporal Anders, and also a new friend of Kinne's was killed in the assault on the bridge. General Lawton, who had a lot of respect for the Scouts and had defended them against possible charges from Captain Birkhimer, had ordered Pvt. James Harrington's body covered with a flag. Even worse news reached them when they found out that William H. Young had died as well. In an article in the *New York Herald* dated Sunday August 20, 1899, Jim Harrington was immortalized

---

131 Kolb, "Blaze in the Boondocks, 2002. Fighting on America's Imperial Frontier in the Philippines, 1899-1913."

with this headline: "The Advance on San Isidro How Harrington, the Fearless Scout Lost His Life"

There was also a photograph of Harrington's body where he fell, probably taken before Lawton had the flag placed over it. Of the twenty-three Scouts who charged over the bridge that day and routed 600 of the enemy, Harrington was the only one killed in action. Many of the surviving Scouts were recommended for the Medal of Honor, seven were awarded, five of them from North Dakota. The recipients:

Otto Boehler, Wahpeton, North Dakota
Charles Davis, Valley City, North Dakota
John Kinne, Fargo, North Dakota
Richard Longfellow, Mandan, North Dakota
Frank C. High, Picard, California (2nd Oregon Volunteers)
Marcus Robertson, Hood River, Oregon
Frank Ross, Langdon, North Dakota

Their citations read as follows:

"With 21 other Scouts charged across a burning bridge, under heavy fire, and completely routed 600 of the enemy who were entrenched in a strongly fortified position."

Mandan North Dakota's Historical Society gives a bit more description of the event in memorializing Richard Moses Longfellow, Jr. (1867 – 1951): *"On May 13. 1899, eleven of (Young's Scouts) earned Medals of Honor in a frontal attack on 300 enemy (referring to the attack on San Miguel). Three days later, the Scouts encountered a large enemy force at San Isidro who had set fire to a strategic bridge. Three scouts sprinted across the bridge, firing at the enemy from point blank range, while the remaining scouts took cover and returned fire on enemy trenches on the opposite bank, only fifty yards distant. Private Longfellow was one of twenty two Scouts that braved the hail of fire to rush the burning, wooden bridge and extinguish the flames, though constantly under fire. They then attacked and routed the enemy forces numbering 600 men.*

"Richard Longfellow was the only individual nominated for the Medal of Honor for both engagements"[132][133]*

Longfellow   **Kinne**   **Robertson**

Photos of Medal of Honor Recipients Ross, Davis, High[134] and Boehler are not immediately available.**

132* (Sic. Not true. Several of the Scouts were recommended for both.)

133 Mandan Historical Society, www.mandanhistory.org/biographieslz/richard-longfellow.html.

134 Wikipedia, the free encyclopedia.

**Frank Charles High (June 7, 1875 – December 13, 1966) was a United States Army soldier awarded the Medal of Honor for his actions during the Philippine-American War. High was one of thirteen members of Young's Scouts awarded the Medal of Honor for actions between May 13 and May 16, 1899. High was born in Yolo County, California, where his family owned a ranch. He enlisted in the Army from Picard, California, and later arrived in Jacksonville, Oregon, from where he joined the 2nd Oregon Volunteers. During the Philippine-American War, he was a member of Young's Scouts. On May 16, 1899, Filipino fighters set fire to an important bridge near San Isidro. The river could not be forded, so High and other scouts rushed across the burning bridge, despite intense enemy fire, and engaged the entrenched Filipino forces. For these actions, High was awarded the Medal of Honor. After returning home, High settled in Ashland, Oregon, where he lived until his death at age ninety-one. He is buried at Memory Gardens Cemetery and Memorial Park in nearby Medford. High Street in Ashland is named in his honor.

American Military Cemetery Manila Decoration* (Memorial) Day 1899[135]

---

* The name was changed to Memorial Day in 1967, and the official day changed from May 30th to the last Monday in May, thus securing a three-day weekend. The first Decoration Day was proclaimed on May 5, 1868, and observed on May 30th of that year. The first Decoration Day in the Philippines was observed on May 30, 1899.

135 Dumindin, "Philippine-American War, 1899-1902."

CHAPTER TEN

May 16 – June 6, 1899

"War is a series of catastrophes that results in a victory." –Georges Clemenceau 1842-1929

John Kinne had an interesting experience some years later while a medical student at Chicago's Rush Medical School. Kinne was also the head waiter at the Men's Commons of the University of Chicago when he became acquainted with a Filipino by the name of Sarabia who was applying for a position as a student waiter. During the pre-employment interview, Kinne discovered that Sarabia was a cousin of General Pilar's orderly during the engagement at San Isidro. Pilar was the opposing insurgent commander. Sarabia had also been there as a soldier in the 1st Manila Regulars, which were Aguinaldo's finest regiment. The defeat of this outfit by the Americans at the Tarbon Bridge was instrumental in Aguinaldo's decision to give up further significant resistance. Sarabia was greatly surprised that there were only twenty-three Scouts in the fight that day.[136]

Kinne continued the tale following the Tarbon Bridge fight: *"The ambulance corps arrived and began taking care of the wounded, which the natives had left on the field. They all belonged to Aguinaldo's crack regiment called the 1st Manila Regulars. They were nearly all armed with Mauser rifles and were under direct command of General Gregorio del Pilar.*

---

136 Kinne, Diary 1898-1899 CO B First North Dakota Infantry, 56.

"The next morning we had breakfast with the Oregon's. Colonel Treumann and Major White came over the river, and while we were waiting to move, General Lawton and staff, followed by Troop I of the 4th Cavalry, (the) 22nd Infantry, and the ND's rode up. With the Scouts in advance the whole line moved out toward San Isidro about two and a half miles before shooting. I shot at a mounted officer but did not succeed in stopping him. Soon the whole line opened fire and the insurgents could be seen running into the woods at the right. They opened with volleys at us from a wall surrounding a cemetery to our left, but soon we dislodged them as the Krag bullets, penetrated the wall."[137]

Following the exchange of bullets, the Americans hurried into the town to the church where they rang the bell telling their comrades they were in possession of the town. After that, they were escorted by Spanish soldiers to the jail where American POWs had been kept. These prisoners were taken by the insurgents into the mountains where the rebels retreated. Kinne copied their names from the jail cell walls.

One old Spaniard civilian had a letter from one of the prisoners to our troops describing the mistreatment and starvation they were going through. The Spaniard also indicated there were sixty-five insurgent casualties both dead and wounded from the fight at the burning bridge.

Harrington was buried in the Spanish cemetery with military honors. William H. Young, who died within the hour that Jim Harrington did, was buried in the American Military Cemetery, Battery Knoll, Manila.[138] [139] See photo page 101.

That evening Mandan's "Mose" Longfellow came back to the Scout's quarters and reported there was a great commotion at Lawton's headquarters.

---

137 Ibid, 58.
138 Durand, The Boys, 1st North Dakota Volunteers in the Philippines, 278.
139 Kinne, Diary 1898-1899 CO B First North Dakota Infantry, 58.

"What's goin' on Mose?" asked Kinne.

"Well," said Mose, "they tell me that there are two of Aguinaldo's Generals over there talking with Lawton."

The Original Young's Scouts (left) William H. Young (right)*

"You suppose they are goin' to surrender?"

"That's the speculation," Longfellow continued, "and I sure hope it's true!"

"You know who the brass are?" Anders chimed in.

"Heard the names Pilar and Looney or something like that," said Mose.

"General Luna, that's who," said Anders, "and he's the head honcho I think."

Indeed! General Anthony Luna, Commander of the Filipino Army and General Gregorio del Pilar y Sempio, known as the 'Boy General' because of his young age of twenty-eight, and who led the initial victory

* *Computer manipulated image from Photo at left which was supplied by The Institute for Regional Studies and Archives, North Dakota State University, Fargo ND. Reprinted with permission.*

over Bell's troops, on April 22nd, were in town to discuss peace terms with the Americans. It was not going to happen for a while, however, and Pilar would not live to see peace, neither would Luna, nor Lawton.

What today is called an episode of collateral damage occurred the day after San Isidro fell. After offering some insurgents, who were in a yard with women and children a peaceful surrender, the Scouts opened up on those who elected to flee. One of the women holding a baby got hit in the chest and died instantly. Kinne stated it was the saddest thing that had happened to them for some time. None of the fleeing insurgents were hit.

General Gregorio del Pilar 1899[140]

Actually after the Pilar and Luna meeting with Lawton, Aguinaldo realized he could not contain the Americans nor win the rebellion at that time, so he arranged for his boy general, de Pilar, to negotiate peace terms along with Captain Lorenzo Zialcita, and two prominent civilians, Alberto Barretto and Gracio Gonzaga. General Luna, whom Aguinaldo feared was too ambitious, was conspicuous by his absence.

The Americans chose Jacob Schurman, Charles Denby, Dean C. Worcester, and John MacArthur, for the peace talks and the group became known as the Schurman Commission. The Commission was actually appointed by President McKinley the previous January to assess conditions in the Philippines and make recommendations for governing the Islands. The leader, Jacob Gould Schurman, was the president of Cornell University. Admiral Dewey was also a member but did not attend the peace negotiations, nor did General Otis, who, as Military Governor, was also a member.

Whatever else that was said about the attitude of the commission, the bottom line was that the commission determined that the Filipinos were not ready for independence, and thus the peace dialogue instituted by Aguinaldo failed and the war continued.

"Ten days later, on June 2, Pedro Paterno, the head of Aguinaldo's cabinet, issued a manifesto recognizing the futility of the peace efforts with the Americans and exhorted all Filipinos to continue the struggle: 'To war, then, beloved brothers, to war.'"[141]

140[Dumindin] *"On December 2, 1899, del Pilar led 60 Filipino soldiers of Aguinaldo's rear guard in the Battle of Tirad Pass against the "Texas Regiment", the 33rd Infantry Regiment of the United States led by Peyton C. March. (The Astor Battery Commander) A delaying action to cover Aguinaldo's retreat, the five-hour standoff resulted in Del Pilar's death due to a shot to the neck (at the height or end of the fighting, depending on eyewitness accounts). Del Pilar's body was later despoiled and looted by the victorious American soldiers. Del Pilar's body lay unburied for days, exposed to the elements. While retracing the trail, an American officer, Lt. Dennis P Quinlan, gave the body a traditional U.S. military burial. Upon del Pilar's tombstone, Quinlan inscribed, "An Officer and a Gentleman."*

141 Ibid.

Jacob Gould Schurman Leader of the First Philippine Commission[142]

After leaving San Isidro,[*] Lawton's Division continued to experience sniping and small firefights as they followed the Rio Grande de Pampanga, now flowing in a south westerly direction. The Scouts crossed the river at a shallow ford in about four feet of water and in a dense fog, which protected them from being seen by the insurgents, and took the small hamlet of San Antonio after being surprised by an insurgent ambush as they watched some of the 2nd Oregon troops wade across the river between them and some other rebels.

The Scouts killed seven of the enemy without a casualty of their own during the fight that ensued during the ambush. There were also some tense moments during the street fight in San Antonio and Kinne documented accurate shooting by Private Ed Lyon of the 2nd Oregon who was also to be a MOH recipient, who killed a Filipino that Kinne had been shooting at but missed. Reaching a small village called Cabiao, the Scouts were pleased to find two Spanish soldiers who had escaped from the insurgents after nine months of imprisonment.

---

142 Dumindin, "Philippine-American War, 1899-1902."
* Because the Americans did not occupy San Isidro, Lawton would have to return and take the town a second time in October of 1899.

The next few days saw the Scouts traveling by foot including river crossings that were time consuming. Approaching Mount Arayat (which the soldiers had christened "Split Rock") and the town of the same name, they found that others from MacArthur's 2nd Division, the 17th Infantry and the 9th US Regulars had entered the town from the south, just as the Scouts and an advanced guard from the 1st Division's 22nd Infantry Regiment came in from the north. The meeting of the two divisions signaled the near completion of the San Isidro campaign and the next day the Scouts were assigned as rear guards as the divisions headed back to Manila. The Scouts stayed in Arayat that evening and enjoyed a fine meal the portions of which Murphy, the surviving civilian Scout, had paid for by pesos stolen from a Chinaman.

They camped at a town called Candaba the next day having caught up with the troop columns and found out that the 2nd Oregon had received orders to proceed to Manila. The Scouts from Oregon which included Lyon, Huntley, Heye, O'Neil, and Lt. Thornton then left to rejoin their regiment. The Scouts who came from the 4th US Cavalry were assigned to eat with Jamestown's Company H.

The war was far from over yet, however, and the remaining Scouts could hear gunfire south of Candaba. Kinne recalled the events in his diary: *"General Lawton sent ten of us across the river to the church tower to see what it (the gunfire) was and from there we could see San Alfonso ablaze. The 3rd Infantry, (and) three troops of cavalry with some artillery were on the road going north and must have met the enemy there. We later heard that there were two Americans killed, 1 wounded and 22 n—ers killed."*[143]

No major action occurred; however, and it wasn't long before Lt. Colonel Treumann gave them permission to join the 2nd Oregon on the train ride from Calumpit back to Manila. The Scouts floated down the Rio Grande de Pampanga with the rest of their brigade on launches, accompanied by the gunboat Laguna de Bay, which was carrying sick and wounded to the hospital. The next morning they hiked three miles from Apalit to Calumpit where they rode on top of a boxcar for the forty-five mile trek to Manila.

---

143 Kinne, *Diary 1898-1899 CO B First North Dakota Infantry*, 60.

Kinne states in his diary that *"Reaching Manila about 3:00pm, the scouts went directly to a picture gallery and had a group picture taken just as we were."*[144] The picture, apparently taken at San Pedro Macati, a suburb southeast of Manila, where they had previously been quartered, is the photo on page 71.

A photographer from *Harper's Weekly* was there on Sunday, the 28th, to record images of the Scouts and the preparations they made for the decoration of William H. Young's grave on Battery Knoll for Decoration (Memorial) Day.

On or shortly after the Decoration Day ceremonies two sailors from the Monadnock (see photo page 19) were captured by insurgents after their small boat was driven ashore by high winds. Subsequent shelling of the insurgent positions by the monitor failed to produce any positive early results. Kinne's diary gave no information about the fate of the sailors, and the Monadnock's captain, Henry Nichols, died of heat exhaustion or heat stroke shortly thereafter, as reported in the *New York Times* of June 13, 1899, and shortly before, the insurgents were driven out of the area, primarily due to shelling by the monitor. The sailors, if they were still alive, most likely were forced to accompany the fleeing rebels.

On June 3rd, following an evening of torrential rains because of a close-by typhoon, the 2nd Oregon was ordered to the Manila waterworks near Marikina and the 1st North Dakota began to move as well. It was General Otis's intention to force the insurgents under Filipino General Pilar, whom Otis had heard was entrenched in the town of Antipolo at the base of the Morong Peninsula to move south. The peninsula, located just a few kilometers southeast of Manila, and which projected into the Philippines' largest lake, Laguna de Bay, also southeast of Manila, would be a place where rebels could be trapped.[145]

---

144 Kinne, Diary 1898-1899 CO B First North Dakota Infantry, 61.
145 Paul Hook, Map Design, Mill City, Oregon.

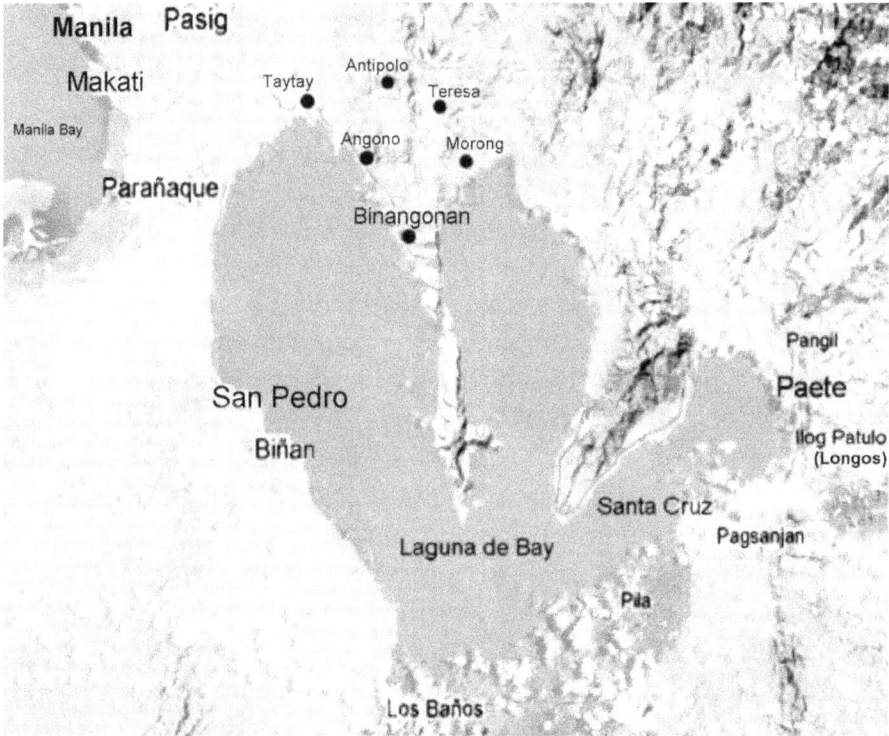

Aerial view[146] of modern day Morong Peninsula extending into Lake Laguna de Bay. Note position of critical towns in General Otis's plan to trap the elusive boy General de Pilar.

Although General Lawton, who was not exactly friendly with Otis, was skeptical of the plan, he was a good soldier who followed orders. There had also been some command changes since completion of the San Isidro campaign. Admiral Dewey was informed on May 8th that his relief, Rear Admiral John C. Watson, had been ordered to Manila. General Frederick Funston was now in charge of all volunteers and served as the 1st Brigade Commander of the 2nd division, under MacArthur. General Robert H. Hall was filling in as 1st Brigade Commander of the 1st Division, replacing General Charles King, who had taken ill at the Battle of Santa Cruz. (King would return later to fight in the end stage battles of the Philippine War.)

---

146 Ibid.

On 3 June 899, the 1st North Dakota led by the Scouts marched to San Pedro where they camped for the night. In the meantime the rest of Hall's brigade was on the march from the Manila waterworks near Marikina, to Antipolo. Hall and his superiors did not, however, anticipate the dreadful heat and humidity. As a result, the troops, some 2500 strong, were quickly exhausted. To compound the problem, Hall's troops were under constant harassing fire, and together with the harsh terrain the results proved too much for them to reach their goal of Antipolo before dark. They wound up spending the night in the rice fields about two or three mile west of the town, having suffered three KIA and ten WIA.

On the 4th, the 1st North Dakota got an early start for Pasig, and after crossing the Pasig River by boats, Colonel Treumann ordered his regiment to form a skirmish line and attack the small village of Cainta along with a regiment of Washington Volunteers. Kinne, along with Anders, Mose Longfellow, and the other Scouts were in the middle of the skirmish line.

"What's the situation, John?" asked Mose. "I heard you talking with Major White."

"White said the 9th Infantry, the 20th Kansas, the Wyomings and the Oregons were going to hit the town from the north east and we are hitting them from the west," replied Kinne.

"Ain't gonna work," said Anders, "I saw a few of those N—ers running north and east of those Washington's on our left."

"You're probably right, Frank," Mose said, "I sure as hell wouldn't chase them in this heat!"

The Scouts were right. Although the Washington regiment under Colonel John Wholley had met some resistance on the left flank, Col. Treumann's troops and the remaining Scouts entered the town of Cainta with little resistance. After spending the night in Cainta, virtually unopposed, the Scouts were directed to find General Hall and deliver a message from Treumann. On the way, Kinne noted replacement troops of the 12th Infantry *"hugging the ground behind the rice paddies (with) not a n—er in site, and not a bullet flying."*[147]

---

147 Kinne, Diary 1898-1899 CO B First North Dakota Infantry, 68.

In reference to the above quote from Kinne, author John Durand[148] remarked on the battlefield maturity Kinne demonstrated compared to his first experience (see page 32). Also according to Durand, the message from Treumann was to inform General Hall that Wholley was on his way to Morong via cascos (small boats) which they would board at the Pasig River. When Hall got the message he sent the Scouts back with orders for Treumann to hold his position at Taytay until he could join him. In the meantime, Hall continued the two miles or so into Antipolo, on the morning of the 4th. There, he found the town deserted. The insurgents under the boy General Pilar had thrown thousands of Mauser and Remington cartridges into a well in the church and left town. The church itself was a well-known shrine where tourists and travelers had worshiped for centuries. Historian Dumindin described it this way: *"The shrine of Mary as 'Lady of Peace and Good Voyage' in the church has for centuries attracted pilgrims from all over the country, particularly those intending to travel, work overseas and, beginning in the 20th century those who have bought new motor vehicles. This belief in the good luck bestowed by the Nuestra Señora De la Paz Y Buen Viaje has its roots in the Manila-Acapulco (Mexico) Galleon Trade of 1565-1815 when the Marian statue accompanied and supposedly protected ships from bad weather, pirates and the Dutch and British blockades."[149]*

148 Durand, The Boys, 1st North Dakota Volunteers in the Philippines, 299.
149 Dumindin, "Philippine-American War, 1899-1902."

Lady of Peace and Good Voyage Church in Antipolo. Photo 1898[150]

The Scouts were now under the leadership of John Killian, who, although only a private, had been with Young's Scouts from the beginning. Killian was from Jamestown's Company H but had joined the outfit from an enlistment in San Francisco. Lt Col. Treumann, recognized the older volunteer, whom the other Scouts called "Dad," as a natural leader as did Major White. Young's Scouts had been disbanded by General Lawton following the San Isidro Campaign and the death of its leader, but Treumann recognized their value as had Generals King and Hall and had continued to use the North Dakota Scouts in special operations as before. Despite Killian's rank, the Scouts responded to his appointment as Scout leader without complaint.

After the Scouts had found General Hall on the way to Antipolo, they did an about face and headed for Taytay, as ordered by the senior officer.

"Geez, Dad, it's hot," complained Corporal Anders.

---

150 Ibid.

"We'll take a break," said Killian, "and take our time getting back."

"What about our orders?" asked Anders.

"Listen to your old Dad, Corporal, sir," Killian replied with the irony appropriate to addressing a superior noncommissioned officer, but knowing he was in charge. "Treumann is not going anywhere. The troops are exhausted and I heard him talking to White that he was going to have to send quite a few to the hospital in Manila. He'll still be in Taytay, if he got that far, when we get there. We'll take our time, and do a little foraging on the way."

"Sounds like a plan to me," chimed in Mose Longfellow.

Kinne's diary confirmed the actions taken by Chief Scout Killian. *"After delivering our message we started back, taking our time, and foraging by the way. We had nine eggs and a big fat Peking duck and after getting to Taytay where the troops had gone we had duck and boiled eggs."*[151]

Actually, Treumann did not get all the way from Cainta into Taytay, but had bogged down in some rice fields just outside of the town. As Killian had predicted the troops were exhausted and author John Durand quoting Major Fraine's *Historical Sketch* noted that *"only 60 officers and men from the four North Dakota Companies were on their feet. The others were lying in all stages of exhaustion from the over-heat along the road."*[152] Exacerbating the conditions was the severe jungle growth, lack of decent roads and the start of mountainous elevations of terrain.

When Hall found the town of Antipolo relatively deserted, he decided to send one regiment south to Teresa before reversing his course to Taytay.

While the Scouts were still foraging and before Treumann ordered them south, General Lawton had appeared on horseback at Treumann's command post in the rice fields. He was accompanied by a touring United States Congressman, Senator Beverage, and ordered Treumann to advance into Taytay which he did and found the town virtually empty. Lawton then ordered Treumann to meet Hall along the road to Antipolo and give him instructions to advance to Morong

151 Kinne, Diary 1898-1899 CO B First North Dakota Infantry.
152 Durand, The Boys, 1st North Dakota Volunteers in the Philippines.

and then go back to Taytay and proceed south along the west side of the lake.

By the time Treumann reached Taytay for the second time, the Scouts were already there enjoying their Peking duck. After they ate, the Scouts were ordered by Treumann to reconnoiter the road to Angona, the next town south along the west lake shore of the Morong Peninsula. Although the Scouts entered the town without significant resistance, Kinne noted that someone had *"carelessly let a flock of turkeys loose in this town and we had 'Thanksgiving' dinner the next forenoon."*[153]

Now, Treumann's depleted regiment was down to a bloated company in strength, divided into two battalions, led by Majors White and Fraine and supported only by Scott's Battery of artillery headed south along the mountainous west shore of Lake Laguna de Bay. In addition, Hall's column has turned around for the second time trying to catch up with the regiment he had sent ahead to Teresa, and General Lawton, who knew the whole scenario was a useless effort since there were so many escape routes for de Pilar, playing out the charade in front of the visiting Senator. Neither Hall nor Lawton knew that Wholley's Washington regiment had successfully traveled by water and already occupied Morong.

As usual the foot soldiers were the ones who suffered from the senior commanders' decisions. Killian and the Scouts welcomed Treumann's column into Angona shortly after finishing their noon "Thanksgiving" dinner, then proceeded further south in front of the column. As they exited the southern limits of Angona, Major Fraine leading the column on horseback, along with Treumann, spotted one of the Scouts, Archie Galt, trotting back along the road in front of the column.

Galt drew up in front of the Colonel, saluted, and came to attention.

"What is it, son?" asked Treumann.

"Sir, there's a whole lot of n—ers hiding in the rocks on both sides of the road about a half mile ahead."

"Where are the Scouts?" asked Treumann.

"Killian has them spread out on the shore side of the road and under cover."

---

153 *Kinne's diary, 68.*

"Son, you go further back in the column until you see the artillery, find Lt. Scott and tell him to get one of his pieces up here pronto!"

"Yes, sir," Galt saluted again, turned and started trotting along the column. As he ran the soldiers who had witnessed the exchange but could not hear what was said started throwing questions at him. Galt ignored them, intent on his mission. Treumann, meanwhile called a halt to the march, turned to Major Fraine and said, "Major, get your battalion in a skirmish line and get ready to deploy as ordered as soon as I get some artillery up here."

"Sir!" Fraine saluted and turned his mount to comply.

CHAPTER ELEVEN

June 6 – 8, 1899

"I hate war as only a soldier who has lived it can, only as one who has seen its brutality, its stupidity." –Dwight David Eisenhower

Major Fraine had his battalion in skirmish formation and ready to go when Lt. Scott arrived with his mule drawn artillery piece.

"Move them out," Treumann ordered Fraine. "As soon as you start to receive fire, take cover and we'll let Scott do his thing."

"Yes, sir," replied Fraine.

When the first shots were fired, at pretty close to the distance of a half mile as Galt had indicated, the troops took cover while Scott set up his artillery and began to fire, targeting both sides of the road.

The insurgents, respecting the artillery advantage of the Americans, fled in numbers too numerous to count, and it wasn't more than a dozen shots before Fraine restarted the skirmish line advancing along both sides of the road as the artillery subsided. Resistance was very light with only a few scattered shots heard from either side with no visible enemy apparent.

The troops continued their march south dreading the climb up each ridge, even though the road was decent along the mountainous shore.

That night they camped just outside of the town of Bunangonan, which was more than twice the size of Angona. Kinne continued the tale: *"The next day the first battalion of N.D 's, led by the Scouts went up over the first ridge of hills to flank a town named Bunangonan on the lake, and the second battalion (of) N.D.'s, 12th Infantry and Scott's Battery took the beach (route). This was some of the worst mountain climbing we had struck, but we saw some beautiful scenery when we reached the top of the bluff.-About noon we entered Bunangonan without resistance."[154]*

While they were in Bunangonan, the Scouts watched the Washingtons, who had already been in Morong, leave from the lake shore on four of the little boats called cascos headed back toward Pasig, shortly after the 12th Infantry and the rest of the North Dakota regiment arrived from the beach approach. The next day, the Scouts passed Hall's column going the way they had just come, from Bunangonan, while the Scouts and the 1st North Dakota were headed for Morong. When they entered Morong, which they cynically spelled "More Wrong," they saw troops of the 2nd Oregon also leaving on cascos on their way back to Manila. The 2nd Oregon was hopeful that they would finally be sent home. Kinne spotted Lt. Thornton on one of the small boats and yelled a greeting.

"Hey, Lieutenant, where're you headed?

"Hey, John, Manila, and we're glad to be going. We lost four KIA and one wounded."

"What happened?"

"Ask those guys from the 4th Cav, they were there. Got to go now. Hope I see you again."

"Good luck, Lieutenant!"

"Ya, you, too."

Talking with the men from the 4th Cavalry, Kinne related the conversation thus: *"We were told that the 2nd Oregon had had hard fighting all the way from the water works to Antipolo and from Antipolo to Morong. They had four killed and one wounded and the 4th cavalry had two killed and six wounded, and the Wyoming had one killed. There were twenty casualties altogether."[155]*

Kinne never said from where the other six casualties came.

The 1st North Dakota was in garrison for a little over a month in Morong. During that time, they experienced a monsoon rainy season, continuing sporadic firefights, mosquitoes, illnesses, including

154 Kinne, Diary 1898-1899 CO B First North Dakota Infantry, 69.
155 Ibid.

malaria, typhoid, cholera, a variety of dysentery, dengue fever, bubonic plague, and a lot of fevers for which there were a variety of names but the etiology of which were unknown. Fortunately, the vaccinations for smallpox protected the Yanks, but the disease was still endemic amongst the natives. The toll was horrendous on the numbers of healthy soldiers, and the numbers of those fit for duty continued to drop.

The casualties from combat also continued to drain Otis's strength, yet he continued to underestimate the numbers needed to win a victory, telling the President and Congress that 30,000 troops would do the job, when his generals in the field estimated the need for thousands more, up to five times that number. The disdain Otis demonstrated for some of his troops is demonstrated by this quotation by a returned POW: *"Leland Smith (who) was to be starved, shot at, set up in front of a firing squad and generally almost walked to death in his three months as a POW."*[156] After suffering months of starvation, brutal forced marches, and severe illnesses Smith had this to say about his first meeting with General Otis: *"Shortly after getting back to Manila, Maj. Gen. Elwel S. Otis, commander of the Department of the Pacific, had all us POWs assembled before him,"* said Smith. *"We supposed he was going to make a speech commemorating all our suffering and making note of our devotion to duty. He came out and stood before us, his retinue gathered behind him. He looked us over for a minute, then he said:*

"'Well, you fellows have had a pretty good time. You've had a vacation and haven't suffered any. I think you can go back to your outfits.'

"Then the general turned on his heel and walked out," Smith said, a disgusted look on his face, *"leaving us with our mouths open, speechless."*[157]

Another quote from Kinne himself also reveals Otis's mindset about the troops, particularly the volunteers: *"This town of Morong was a fierce place. Otis had said when he got through with the volunteers he would be able to send them all home on the same boat, (referring to the number of all volunteers that would survive) and if our experiences*

---

156 *"American Prisoner of War in the Philippines: 1899- Military Forum,"* http://search.aol.com/aol/search?s_it=wscreen-aolexperience-.
    157 *Ibid.*

at Morong had been long continued his prediction would have certainly come true."[158]

On the third day in Morong, the Scouts were sent out to reconnoiter the insurgents but were detected by the rebels first. Although the rebels opened fire from a long distance, the Scouts could see their skirmish line and exchanged several shots with them apparently with no injuries on either side. A day or so later, Chief Scout Killian was approached by a man named Stoddard, who stuttered badly.

"Are ya-ya-ya-you Ch-Ch-Chief Sc Sc Scout K-K-K-Killian?"

"Yes I am. Who are you?" Killian replied.

"My n-n-name is Stoddard, and I'd like to g go with y-you today."

Killian noted that Stoddard carried a Krag-Jorgensen repeater. "I guess I could use another man. Are you any good with that?" he asked.

"So, so, I g-g-guess, but I had s-s-some n—ers and th-they got away from m-me."

"You mean POWs?"

"Y-y-yes and the sergeant said I'd b-b-better get em b-b-back!"

Killian said it was okay for Stoddard to join them. When the Scouts, in a skirmish line, experienced the first shots fired at them, Stoddard *"did a double time to the rear saying don't want any n—ers to get me."[159]* The Scouts returned to Morong without doing much shooting.

The next morning, as they were preparing to go canoeing, Kinne and Jim Miller, a bookbinder from Fargo's Company B, were stopped by Killian who told Kinne the Scouts were going out again and to get his weapon, first aid kit, and matches, which he did.

The Scouts returned to the spot where they had been fired on the day before, but no insurgents were present there. As they progressed around a point of land they saw the enemy a short distance away down the road and opened fire. Kinne stated that two of them spied a Gugu (another label for a native insurgent) and dispatched him with rifle fire. They then charged down the road and found themselves in a fierce firefight in an area lined on both sides of the road by bamboo shacks.

Kinne related what happened next: *"Someone called to us to hold our position while they took back a wounded man. We did so and kept up*

---

158 Kinne, *Diary 1898-1899 CO B First North Dakota Infantry*, 69.
159 Ibid, 70.

a constant fire and on the retreat one of the fellows named Glassley (Pvt. Michael Glassley* from Bismarck's Company A, also a Killian Scout) said to me 'give me your gun and help me carry Killian back.'[160]

Killian had apparently been left to die next to the road after being hit in the firefight. Kinne and Glassley struggled to get "Dad" Killian to safety, almost abandoning him when the stretcher collapsed and they were under significant enemy fire. When Killian moved his lips, they knew he was still alive and resumed the evacuation under fire. After a moment, Kinne spotted troops from the regiment coming to their rescue. They set the stretcher down, and Kinne rushed to meet Major White, who was leading the rescue effort.

"What's the trouble, Kinne?" asked Major White.

"We got mixed up and had a man wounded, sir. He needs a hospital corpsman bad!"

White sent two of his people to fetch the stretcher then turned back to Kinne. "Who is it, John?

"Sir, it's Dad Killian," Kinne said with a catch in his voice, "and I don't think he's going to make it!"

Kinne was right; Killian was dead by the time the corpsman got to him. John Kinne in his diary stated that Killian was the third leader of the Scouts to be KIA, but he was only the 2nd. Both Birkhimer, the self-appointed leader that lasted only until his confrontation with Anders and Harrington, and Lt. Thornton of the 2nd Oregon Volunteers were still alive. Kinne may have assumed Jim Harrington was the natural leader of the Scouts, after Young was hit, and both died at nearly the same time a few days later, although the deaths were the result of different actions.

Because Killian's name was not on the original North Dakota Roster, since he enlisted in San Francisco, the North Dakota newspapers assumed it was Kinne who was killed in action because the spelling was similar. It took two days for the error to be corrected

---

* *Glassley was one of several former Young's Scouts including Gotfred Jensen, Sterling Galt, Pat Hussey, John Smith, Frank Summerfield, and Jim McIntyre to reenlist and be assigned to the 36th volunteer Infantry, which continued the fight in the Philippines after the North Dakota regiment went home.*

160. Ibid, 70.

in the Fargo papers. Lord only knows the anguish that caused for Kinne's family.

There were other incidents that punctuated the difficulties of their time in Morong. After Killian was killed and the Scouts were rescued by Major White's intervention, they could see insurgents carrying their dead and wounded from the field of battle. That evening a sentry fired a shot that startled the Scouts.

"Who the hell is shooting now?" Otto Boehler yelled. Charley Davis set his coffee cup down and said "I'll go see." He returned a few minutes later and told the others who were finishing chow, "The sentry just killed a bolo man who was crawling toward him with a net!"

"Those bastards won't quit, will they?" Boehler said.

Boehler was referring to the reputation these fierce warriors had. Bolo men, as they were called, are probably described best by Robert Fulton:[161] "–.the fact is the Filipinos were as motivated, tough, and potentially as deadly as the Vietnamese, but unlike the NVA and Viet Cong they did not have the relative luxury of an unlimited stream of modern weapons, abundant ammunition, and foreign trainers, all provided gratis by a friendly superpower (the USSR). Otherwise there might have been a far different outcome. Even then 4,234 Americans killed out of 126,468 'cycled through' gave that war (The Philippine-American) the dubious distinction of having one of the higher 'death rates' for American wars, that is troops committed to troops dying, half-again higher than the decade-long Vietnam War……Like all good guerrilla fighters, the Filipinos were improvisers. They took advantage of the tropical topography with its exceptionally high grasses (well over six feet tall), dense jungles, and winding, constricted trails, to mount ambushes using a tactic called 'the bolo rush.' The Philippine bolo is a fearsome, short (16" to 18"), single-edged, razor-sharp cutting weapon. Every farmer had one and knew how to use it, whether for harvesting crops, hacking trails through jungle, or taking off a limb in a fight. A large force, often 100-200 'bolo men' would lie hidden near a trail. When a smaller American patrol came along in single-file, Filipino snipers would fire, forcing them to drop for cover. At a signal, the bolo men would rush*

---

161 Robert Fulton, MOROLAND 1899-1906: America's First Attempt to Transform an Islamic Society 2007.

the soldiers lying prone on the trail, inevitably losing many in their ranks to rifle fire but occasionally overwhelming the Americans with their sheer numbers and the ferocity of the charge. Commissioned officers and sergeants, armed only with Colt .38 revolvers, were a primary target."[162]

Bolo Knife and Scabbard 1899[163]

Bolo Man 1899

162 Ibid.
163 http://www.jjmilitaryantiques.com/catdet.asp?TargetItem=8614&Category Type=Kniv.

CHAPTER TWELVE

June 4 – July 31, 1899

"An ideal form of government is democracy tempered with assassination." –Voltaire

General Anthony Luna, the fiery and volatile Commander of the Philippine Army and a Spanish immigrant, was appointed to the post by Aguinaldo in January 1899. Before that he was Chief of War Operations and had also established the Philippines Military Academy at Malolos. Luna had fought well and bravely in Caloocan, Manila, Bulacan, Pampanga, and Nueva Ecija against the US.

He was an advocate of guerrilla warfare early on, but President Aguinaldo wanted to fight as a recognizable nation. After the meeting of the Schurman Commission on May 5, 1899, members of the Malolos Congress wanted to accept the autonomy and peace offered by the US, but as noted previously the peace talks failed under the newly appointed cabinet headed by Pedro Paterno.

Also, as previously noted, Luna was conspicuously absent at the talks, but that did not prevent him from voicing his strong objections to any deal with the Americans. Luna had a compatriot in this attitude in the Philippine chairman of the commission, Felipe Buencamino, who was also Aguinaldo's Secretary of Foreign Affairs. Buencamino's was a lone voice, however, and when Luna found out the commission had approved a deal with the Americans he confronted the cabinet members, slapped Buencamino, and called him a traitor and his son a coward. He then arrested the entire cabinet and turned them over to

Aguinaldo, but the president, fearful of a Luna *coup d'état,* promptly turned them loose.

On June 4th, Luna received a summons from Aguinaldo to attend a conference in Cabanatuan, some seventy-five miles away from his headquarters. He traveled with a bodyguard of twenty-five cavalrymen and some of his staff. When a broken down bridge delayed the travelers, Luna left his escort and arrived at his destination accompanied by only two officers, Colonel Francisco Roman and Captain Eduardo Rusca.

The first officer Luna saw on arrival at the president's headquarters was a man Luna had previously disarmed for cowardice. His volatile temper was then provoked further by a sentry who failed to salute him, and on top of that, when he climbed the stairs of the building, he saw Felipe Buencamino with whom he exchanged *"heated words."*[164] Hearing a gunshot, Luna ran back downstairs and *"and there, waiting for him, were Capt. Pedro Janolino and members of the Kawit Battalion of Cavite Provence. These were the same soldiers who had refused to take orders from Luna during the battle at Caloocan on Feb. 10, 1899; as punishment, Luna had disarmed and relieved them of their duties."*[165]

What followed was a mob assassination reminiscent of Julius Caesar's. Aguinaldo's mother, Trinidad Famy y Aguinaldo, apparently witnessed the assassination and asked the soldiers if Luna was still alive. One of the killers nudged Luna's body with the toe of his boot. There was no response. Also killed was Colonel Roman who tried to defend Luna. Wounded by a shot in the leg was Captain Rusca, who also tried to help. He managed to flee and take refuge in a nearby church.

Aguinaldo had left town and was nowhere to be seen.

On June 10th, General Lawton led a force some 4500 strong south of Manila along the west side of Lake Laguna de Bay and attacked the coastal towns of Parañaque and Las Piñas. The actual infantry combat was preceded by two days of artillery bombardment which Kinne and the Scouts could hear some distance away at the heights of their quarters in Morong across the lake.

---

164 Dumindin, *"Philippine-American War, 1899-1902."*
165 Ibid.

Historian Dumindin described the infantry battle like this: *"Near Las Piñas, at the base of Telegraph Hill, the Filipinos launched a determined attack, but were beaten back by the Americans defending (their artillery on) the hill. The heat during the battle proved overpowering to the Americans. Most threw away their ponchos, blankets and haversacks, everything but rifles, ammunition, and canteens. It was estimated that forty percent of the troops had heat exhaustion."*[166]

It was a day later that Captain Henry Nichols of the Monadnock, which was involved in the artillery barrage, died of heat stroke.[*]

According to Dumindin, *"The Americans suffered 2 men killed in action and 21 wounded. The Filipinos lost 50 men killed and 20 captured."*[167]

Kinne reported the results a little differently: *"On the 11th it was reported that there were 12 wounded in the 1st Colorado and 2 killed in the 14th Infantry. The 14th had been obliged to charge 3 times before being able to dislodge the insurgents at Las Pinas. They found the entrenchment filled with men and the insurgents had to throw out the dead so as to make room for more soldiers. During the fight there were 65 wounded and 10 killed in 2 companies of the 22nd Infantry. There were 500 insurgents killed and 150 buried in back of our quarters at Manila.—The 14th Infantry brought in 600 (POW's) in one bunch."*[168]

---

166 *Ibid.*

* *The difference between heat stroke and heat exhaustion is that heat exhaustion, although serious if not treated by replenishing fluids, is usually not fatal. Heat stroke results when the victim stops sweating, and body temperature spikes upwards of 106 degrees. It is a medical emergency requiring rapid cooling to avoid death.*

167 *Ibid.*

168 Kinne, *Diary 1898-1899 CO B First North Dakota Infantry,* 71.

***Filipino soldiers – prisoners of war at Las Piñas*[169]**

Also on 11 June, a rumor reached the 1st North Dakotans that Otis was going to send the volunteers home as soon as transports could be provided. For once the rumors proved to be accurate and the 2nd Oregon actually embarked for home the next day, and the volunteers from Nebraska had orders to board their transport on the 17th. Kinne stated that *"the 13th was the 60 day limit after signing of the treaty by the President, entitling us to our discharge."*[170]

169 Dumindin, "Philippine-American War, 1899-1902."
170 Kinne, Diary 1898-1899 CO B First North Dakota Infantry, 71.

While they were waiting for the word to go home, the Scouts were re organized once again, this time with Lieutenant Harrison Gruschus of Dickinson, ND, in command. Gruschus was transferred in January from Dickinson's Company K to Jamestown's Company H. He had not served with the Scouts before. Although there were still a few episodes of shooting and an occasional firefight, the intensity of war for these now battle hardened veterans was considerably diminished. They were anxious to leave "More Wrong," but it would be another six weeks before they finally did.

In the meantime, recently promoted from Captain to Major, James Franklin Bell, the same officer that General de Pilar forced into a defensive position on the way to Norzagaray at the start of Lawton's San Isidro campaign, and the same guy that most likely knew Frank Ander's dad while serving in the 7th Cavalry at Fort Lincoln, Dakota Territory, was snooping around trying to get recruits for his newly formed 36th Volunteer Infantry.

On the 21st of the month, Jim McIntyre* of Fargo's Company B, one of Young's Scouts who had been recommended for the Medal of Honor twice, once at San Miguel and also at the Burning Bridge, signed up for Bell's new regiment. Later, so did Scouts Gotfred Jensen from Devil's Lake, Archie Galt from Valley City, Pat Hussey, John Smith, and Frank Summerfield all from Dickinson's Company K, and Mike Glassley from Bismarck, who helped Kinne carry the mortally wounded "Dad" Killian out of the battlefield at Morong. The word was that all of the Scouts who transferred to Bell's new regiment would be given sergeant's stripes and a $500 bonus.[171]

Sporadic firefights and a cholera scare took up most of the rest of the month. The cholera scare involved one of the North Dakota's Chinese cooks who died during the night of the 22nd after a fierce firefight involving the Scouts, none of whom suffered any hits. The cook's body was subsequently burned along with all his possessions and the shack where he lived. On the 30th, the Grant, the ship from

* There were two McIntyres that signed with Bell. The 2nd was Grafton's Donald, from the Hospital Corp.

171 http://www.iowahistory.org/museum/exhibits/medal-of-honor/huntsman_john_paw/bio.htm.

which civilian Scout Murphy came, arrived back in Manila from San Francisco. This was the vessel that would carry the survivors of the 1st North Dakota home. The regimental loss to that time was fifteen dead (of which eight were KIA), twelve WIA, and thirty-two sent home with illness, injury, or disability.

John Kinne managed to get a pass to Manila good until 7 July and left on a ferry boat, the Oesta, on 3 July. He would not return to "More Wrong."

Talk among the Scouts left behind centered on the choices they had to make about staying in the service, going home, or staying in the Philippines or maybe California.

"Me, I'm going with Major Bell," said Archie Galt.

"Why?" asked Tom Sletteland. "I thought you liked Valley City."

"I do, but there is nothing there for me now. My dad can't work and my folks are going move to Kansas City. I need to make a little more money to help them out and the Sergeant's stripes will do that," replied Galt.

"That's a good enough reason," said Sletteland, "but I'm going home. What about you Frank?" continued Tom Sletteland.

"I've had enough of this crud," said Anders.

"How about you guys from Dickeyville?" Sletteland barbed to Patrick Hussey.

"We're stickin' together," replied Hussey with a wave of his hand to include his Dickinson team mates Smith and Summerfield, "and goin' with Bell. We can use the money, too, and who wants to spend another winter in North Dakota?"

"Might be better than this heat!" chimed in Fred Jensen. "But you have a point. It's going to cool down here in a couple of weeks. I think I'll go with Bell, too, especially if that $500 bonus is true."

"Where's Kinne?" Mike Glassley asked, "I was kind of waiting to talk to him before I made up my mind on this."

"John got a seven day pass to Manila," replied Anders, "but he wants to go to medical school, so I don't think he'll re-up."

"Oh," said Glassley. "Well, I've been leaning on sticking around. Maybe I will."

Glassley did, along with the others so committed.

While Kinne was celebrating the 4th of July in Manila, Anders, Slette-land and the other veterans were gearing up to evacuate Morong. On the 5th, Kinne witnessed two battalions of the 21st Infantry leave Manila to relieve the 1st North Dakota. When John found the weather too rough to return to Morong on the 6th, he had a good excuse to await his outfit's arrival back to Manila, knowing his pass expired on the 7th, and they arrived as expected on the eve of that day.

After days and weeks of turning in equipment, changing uniforms, and doing countless paperwork the only thing preventing an earlier departure from Manila on the Grant, was a typhoon lurking in the area. On the 31st, the Grant weighed anchor and left Manila Harbor. The regiment was on the way home and the reenlisted Scouts were now with the U.S. 36th Volunteer Infantry.

There were many others, including other Scouts who reenlisted from the 1st North Dakota. Not all of them went to the 36th Volunteer Infantry, although the majority did. Some went to the 17th Vol. Infantry, the 34th Vol. Infantry, the Signal Corps, and the 14th Vol. Infantry. Others had extended service because of wounds and were transferred to a regimental hospital. For a complete list, see John Durand's roster of the 1st North Dakota in his book, *The Boys*.

CHAPTER THIRTEEN

September 3 – 18, 1899

"Anyone, who truly wants to go to war, has never truly been there before!"
–Larry Reeves

On September 3, 1899, General Otis announced completion of a railroad line from Manila to Angeles in Pampanga Province. The Americans, under Lt. Col. Jacob H. Smith leading the 12th U.S. Infantry, took the town on August 16th in hopes of catching Aguinaldo there. They were only about a month too late since the rebel leader had left the area twenty-five days earlier, a fact which reflects the status of communications and strategic intelligence in that era of the late 19th century.

The battle for Angeles lasted just about an hour primarily due to the accuracy of the 12th Infantry's volley firing and the overwhelming artillery support by 1st Lt. William L. Kenly's two guns of Light Battery E, 1st Artillery. Historian Dumindin said of the short battle: *"The Filipinos finally withdrew at 11:30 a.m. They took up positions on the northern banks of the Abacan River, at Mabalacat town, Pampanga Province. The Americans lost 2 men killed and 12 wounded. They reported that Filipino casualties aggregated over 200. In addition, they captured 3 locomotives, 25 cars, and a large quantity of unhulled rice."*[172]

Also on September 3rd, while Otis was announcing the completion of the rail line from Manila to Angeles, the Scouts of the 36th U.S. Volunteers under Colonel James Franklin Bell, were engaged in their first

---

172 Dumindin, *"Philippine-American War, 1899-1902."*

significant battle since the regiments' inception. The insurgents had established a defensive line in Pampanga Province extending from Porac to Magalang. The line crossed just north of the recently captured city of Angeles, and the division defending was led by General Venancio Concepcion. Angeles is about thirty-six miles NW of Manila.

Guerilla Line of Defense

After the capture and garrison of Angeles, for the next several weeks, while the Americans were waiting out the monsoon season and building up their numbers, the engineers building the railroad were under constant harassment by the insurgents. The 36th Infantry had been called upon to suppress the harassment, which was why they were engaged in battle on 3 September 1899.[173]

---

173 Paul Hook, Map Design, Mill City, Oregon.

Original caption: "Third Artillery shelling insurgents to protect engineers working to recover wrecked engines at Angeles, August 18, 1899."[174] (Part of the early harassment following the victory on August 16, 1899.) Photo credit[175]

The North Dakota Scouts who had reenlisted with Bell, had made some new good friends, including two "Johns"—Sergeants John Hampton and John Huntsman—who would two months later show considerable courage, resolve, and heroism. Another couple of soldiers included in the close knit group were Pvt. Cornelius ("Irish") J. Leahy and Lt. ("El Tee") Arthur M. Ferguson, who was one of the Scouts assigned by Bell to lead. As before, when they were with Young, the Scouts were relieved of Company responsibilities, in order to do their job, and were an elite force within the 36th.

Leahy was an Irish emigrant born June 1, 1872. He had enlisted in San Francisco and reenlisted with the 36th Volunteers. Ferguson was the son of a Union Soldier, born in 1877, and had enlisted with the

---

174 Dumindin, "Philippine-American War, 1899-1902."
175 Ibid.

20th Kansas Volunteers before being assigned to the 36th. He had previously been cited for gallantry as a corporal in the 20th Kansas and had been commissioned as a result. Another Scout, James R. ("Jim") Gillenwater born in Rye Cove, Virginia, a Corporal in Company A, would also play an important part in the day's battle.

At the direction of Colonel Bell, Ferguson took his group of Scouts the morning of the 3rd of September and headed for the southwest corner of the insurgents' line of defense near Porac, Pampanga Province. Their mission was to reconnoiter the insurgent defensive line in order for Colonel Bell to come up with a reasonable plan to suppress the harassment of the newly completed Manila to Angeles railroad and telegraph line.

Included in the group of Scouts were the three from Dickinson: John Smith, Pat Hussey, and Frank Summerfield. Also tasked for the mission were Fred Jensen, Mike Glassley, Jim McIntyre, and Archie Galt, from the North Dakota contingent and Irish Leahy and Jim Gillenwater mentioned above and their friend Wilton O. Allen from Long Island. On another "Oh Dark Thirty" (e.g., time of 0430) mission, Ferguson had his Scouts in position before dawn on September 3rd.

"What's the plan, El Tee?" asked John Smith.

"Since you asked, Smitty," replied the Lieutenant, "you can take the point, and you," pointing to Gillenwater, Leahy, and Allen, "flank him on either side, and stay a couple of steps behind. I'll take the far left flank and change places with Smith every 200 yards or so. Frank you take the same position I have on the other far flank. Smith will stay on the road, until I replace him. The walking will be easier on the road so take it easy and don't get too far ahead of us guys in the boondocks!"

"What about us, Lieutenant?" asked Archie.

"The rest of you double up the same formation we have, except you'll have only two close-in flankers and stay behind," said Ferguson. "We'll switch groups every half mile or so. If we draw fire, hit the dirt, until I can sort things out. You've been here before, guys. You know what to do!"

"How far out are you goin' to flank the close-in flankers, El Tee?" asked Summerfield.

"No more than 100 yards," replied Ferguson. "And as for the group behind, Archie, stay about fifty yards back. Any other questions?"

The Scouts looked at one another and when no one said anything, Ferguson had one more instruction.

"Keep an eye on me. I'll wave my Krag like this," Ferguson continued, demonstrating the signal, "when it's time to rotate our positions within each group. The same signal after that will tell you to rotate the groups, but I'll stay either as the out flanker or point in the lead group. Archie you are my counterpart in the second group, so stay back, even when the groups change places."

"Yes, Sir."

As dawn was breaking, the eleven Scouts started out with more than a little trepidation. Lt. Ferguson gave the first wave of his Krag when Smith was at about a city block up the road, starting to head for Smith's position on point and waving toward himself at the same time. Everyone caught the signal, and the first exchange of positions went well without any hitches, the group behind coming up to and then passing the group in front.

Things were about to change, though and it wasn't going to be good. After the second change, Ferguson was still on point, but now with Jensen and Glassley as close-in flankers and McIntyre and Hussey out wide. Unbeknownst to the Scouts, their presence had been detected by Concepcion's night sentinels who were guarding their sleeping comrades. As they approached a small village, which was just a collection of shacks southwest of Angeles, Ferguson gave the signal to halt and take cover. While he pulled out a telescope to view what was in front of him, all hell broke loose.

The insurgents had allowed the first group of Scouts to pass their first positions without challenge and now had the Scouts virtually surrounded. Thus, the first to get hit was the far left flanker of the second group, who now was Dickinson's Sgt. John Smith, who had rotated to the far flank when Ferguson came in to the point. Smith took a round through the heart and was dead before he could respond to Ferguson's signal to take cover.

Before Smith fell to the ground, the second Scout hit was one of the close-in flankers of the second group as well, ex Long Island,

New York police detective Wilton O. Allen. When the Scouts realized they had been ambushed, they opened devastating return fire into the insurgents.

Both Gillenwater and Leahy saw Allen go down, realized he was still alive, and, using the repeater capability of their Krags, returned .30 caliber rounds into the bushes from where smoke was rising as they dashed to Allen's aid. Bullets snapped twigs off of nearby bushes as the men, approaching the wounded Scout from different directions, traversed the deadly enemy fire. Gillenwater got to him first, saw that his wound was a penetrating belly wound and waved Leahy in to grab Allen's feet.

"I've got his shoulders, Irish; head for those rocks," he said, pointing to some nearby cover. Both rescuers then threw their rifles over their shoulders with the straps, picked up their wounded comrade, and made a run for it to the rocks, with bullets tracking them all the way.

One of the insurgents, seeing an opportunity, made a dash to recover Allen's rifle. Archie Galt saw the opportunist, said to himself, "Oh no you don't, you SOB!" and quickly dropped him with an accurate shot to the chest. The firefight then picked up intensity.

Since the Scouts under cover were spread out fairly well, it was hard for the ambushers to concentrate their fire. Before long the accuracy of the Americans with their Krags began to tell. Lt. Ferguson, far in front was in the ditch by the road with his two far flankers seventy-five to one hundred yards on either side, and his close-in flankers about twenty to thirty yards from the road and a few paces in back of the Lieutenant. The closest one to Gillenwater, Leahy, and the wounded Allen was Fred Jensen. He hollered to the huddled group, "How bad's he hit?"

"Belly wound, Fred. Can you cover him? Smitty was hit with the first volley, too, and we've got to go get him," Irish yelled back.

"Got it covered. Go for it!"

With that the other Scouts, who had heard the exchange, opened up a deadly covering fire as the two rescuers started running to the far left flank where Smith had gone down. Firing as they ran, their surprising charge directly into the enemies' face elicited a flight response from the insurgents who high tailed it in numbers out of the area as fast as their legs could carry them.

Seeing their comrades flee elicited the same response from those ambushers not directly in the line of American fire, so that before long there was no further enemy resistance except for a few shots at Gillenwater and Leahy as they returned with Smith's body. Once they were under cover of the rocks all firing ceased.

Ferguson cautiously stood up and when he did not draw any fire, he yelled at the group in the rocks. "Cover me. I'm coming in!"

He did so without incident, and when he got there, shouted for the others to come in as well.

American Scouting Party 1899 (location not specified)[176]

---

176 Dumindin, "Philippine-American War, 1899-1902."

Scouting Party Dashing for Cover 1899 (location not specified.)[177]

Once the Lieutenant had assessed the situation he dispatched the fastest distance runner, who was Fargo's Jim McIntyre, to get an ambulance for Wilt Allen. Since it was still monsoon season, the Scouts were all carrying their ponchos.

"You fellows," he said, pointing to Glassley and Jensen, "rig a stretcher with your ponchos. We'll trade off carrying Wilt until we meet the ambulance." He then knelt down close to the wounded man and asked softly, "How'er ya doin', Wilt?"

"Hurts pretty bad, El Tee."

"Hang in there, Wilt."

Wilt's eyes filled with tears. He just nodded. The aftermath was illustrated by this article published in the *New York Times* on September 4, 1899,* made possible by General Otis's daily telegraph report.

---

* 6pm in NYC on Sept 4th would already be 6am on Sept 5th in Manila. The action was on Sept. 3rd.

177 Ibid.

WILTON O. ALLEN'S DEATH.

Gen. Otis's Report Clears a Mystery in Elmhurst Home.

The death reports of Gen. Otis from the Philippines have solved a mystery that has troubled a little home in Grand Street, Elmhurst, L. I., for some time. In the last report of Gen. Otis appeared the name of Wilton O. Allen in the death list.

Allen was a member of the police force of the City of New York. He had been a soldier at West Point, and while attending the military tournament at Madison Square Garden in 1897 was attracted by the request of Police Commissioner Theodore Roosevelt for the services of stalwart men and joined the force. He was then assigned to Capt. Chapman's district. He had hardly served his probation when Capt. Chapman made him a precinct detective.

From Capt. Chapman's precinct Allen was sent to Newtown just after consolidation, where Capt. Dimond was in command. Allen proved himself a valuable man. He made a map of the Newtown District which was accepted by the Board of Elections. As Capt. Dimond's wardman, Allen waged a fierce war against violators of the excise law. While at Newtown he married a well-known young woman of the place.

After Capt. Dimond was transferred Allen was ordered to the Fifty-first Precinct. He never reported there for duty, and neither his wife nor any of his friends knew of his whereabouts. It now appears that Allen joined one of the regiments sent to the Philippines. He was dangerously wounded while in the front ranks during an attack on a Filipino village.

Allen applied to Col. Roosevelt to be made a member of his Rough Rider troop. The Colonel, who knew Allen's ability, advised him to remain in the police force.

The New York Times
Published: September 4, 1899
Copyright © The New York Times

Kinne, who was being mustered out in San Francisco, received word on September 18th that *"Smith of K Company, one of Young's Scouts, who had been discharged in Manila and joined Bell's Regiment, had been killed at San Fernando."*[178]

---

[178] Kinne, Diary 1898-1899 CO B First North Dakota Infantry, 85.

The town of Angeles was once a part of the town of San Fernando as indicated by this excerpt from Wikipedia: *"In 1796, after serving as gobernadorcillo the previous year, Don Ángel Pantaleon de Miranda retired to Barrio Saguin, from where he started setting up his hacienda in Barrio Culiat. The barrio was separated from San Fernando on the December 8, 1829 as the new town of Angeles, with the Los Santos Ángeles Custodios as titular patrons."*[179]

Today, the San Fernando of 1899 has been absorbed into the metroplex. In addition to the slight discrepancy of the apparent site of Smith's death, John Durand also states in *The Boys* that *"Smith's name does not appear on lists of casualties in Official Correspondence, Vol. 2."*[180] To our knowledge his remains were never returned to the USA. However, the date of action and MOH citations of record for Leahy and Gillenwater fit the story and Smith was the likely first victim of the firefight of September 3, 1899.

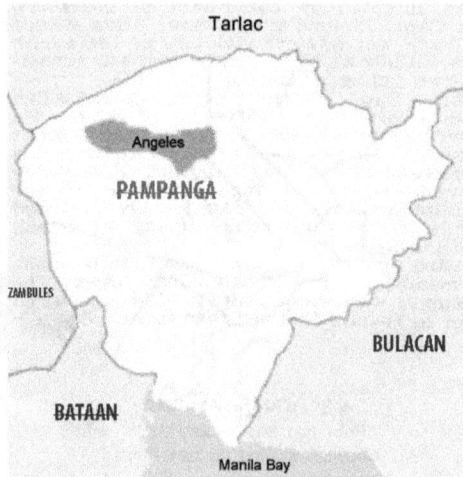

2010 relative position of the 250k+ population town of Angeles.

---

179 http://en.wikipedia.org/wiki/City_of_San_Fernando,_Pampanga.
180 Durand, *The Boys, 1ˢᵗ North Dakota Volunteers in the Philippines.*

Tarlac

San Fernando

PAMPANGA

Zambales

Bulacan

Bataan

Manila Bay   181

***2010 relative position of the 250k+ population town of
San Fernando.***

Pvt. Cornelius J. Leahy, "Irish" to his comrades, was born in Limerick, Ireland on June 1, 1862. He was killed in action at Pilar, Luzon Philippine Islands on December 1, 1899, three months after the action of September 3rd. He was awarded the Medal of Honor posthumously on May 9, 1902 (the medal received by his mother), for actions near Porac, Pampanga Province, Luzon, Philippine Islands on September 3, 1899. His citation reads as follows: *"For most distinguished gallantry in action for defending and driving off a superior force of insurgents and with the assistance of one comrade bringing from the field of action the bodies of two comrades- one killed and one severely wounded. This while on a scout near Porac, Luzon, PI September 3 1899."[182]*

Leahy is buried at the San Francisco National Military Cemetery, Presidio, San Francisco, California. The posthumous award is really unusual for a Philippine War veteran, since it was General Arthur MacArthur's policy and apparently the Army's at the time not to award posthumous medals of valor. We can only surmise that the award was approved before Leahy's death.

181 Map designed by Paul Hook, Mill City, Oregon.
182 http://www.archives.gov/publications/prologue/2000/summer/philippine-insurrection.html.

Corporal James Robert Lee Gillenwater's citation is identical to Leahy's but issued March 1, 1902. Gillenwater was born and entered service in Rye Cove, Virginia, and transferred to the 36th Volunteer Infantry after having been recruited by Bell. He survived the war and died January 19, 1946, and is buried in Highland Cemetery, Rogersville, TN.[183]

Photo credits findagrave.com

183 Wikipedia, the free encyclopedia, http://en.wikipedia.org/wiki/James_R_Gillenwater.

CHAPTER FOURTEEN

September 28, 1899

"In case of doubt. Attack!" –General George S. Patton

Arthur Medworth Ferguson, called L-T (El Tee), for Lieutenant, by his Scouts, was born in Coffey County, Kansas, on December 11, 1877. He had been cited for gallantry as a Corporal with Company E of the 20th Kansas Volunteers. Ferguson's action to earn that citation on April 26, 1899, is a remarkable story in itself. Quoting from the Arlington National Cemetery Website, which in turn quotes from the Burlington (Kansas) Daily Republican of February 21, 1923, is the following:

"The insurgents were entrenched strongly at the Rio Grande and General Wheaton and his brigade, including the 20th Kansas, was bent on taking the position, by long odds the most formidable yet encountered. The ties and girders had been removed from the bridge and a small fortification at the end of the bridge commanded the approach so effectively that any attempt to carry it would be suicide. Colonel Funston was anxious to make the effort, however, and Ferguson volunteered to cross the bridge in darkness and determine the feasibility of an attack. Stripping off his clothes he made his way along the slippery and dangerous footing, where a misstep meant death in the river beneath, and the slightest noise meant death from an insurgent bullet. Ferguson got up to within 20 feet of the insurgent fortification and then returned. He reported that any assault was impracticable and the project was abandoned. The next day Privates Trembley and White swam the river, and with 14 men, Colonel Funston put to route 3,000 insurgents and captured the position, thereby winning the star of a Brigadier General."[184].

---

184 http://www.arlingtoncemetery.net/afergus.htm.

Ferguson was later awarded the Distinguished Service Cross for the same actions in the Philippines, but the DSC was not authorized until WWI was in progress in 1918. His citation is shorter but more graphic than the description of his gallantry by the Burlington newspaper:

"At the imminent risk of his life, Corporal (later Captain and eventually Lt. Col.) Ferguson voluntarily crawled through a network of iron beams underneath a bridge and inch by inch, worked his way hand over hand across the bridge until he was underneath an insurgent outpost, obtaining a complete description of the condition of the bridge."[185]

The DSC is the Army's 2nd highest award for valor exceeded only by the Medal of Honor. It is equivalent to the Navy Cross.

Lieutenant Arthur M. Ferguson[186] Army Distinguished Service Cross

185 *Ibid.*
186 *http://www.arlingtoncemetery.net/afergus.htm.*

On September 28th, just twenty-five days after the Ferguson-led Scouts were bloodied by an ambush in which they gave back more than they got, they found themselves in a similar situation in almost the same location near Porac at the southwest end of the insurgent line of defense.

Because he was a "*Mustang*," a term used more by the Navy than the Army and meaning a commissioned officer who came up through the enlisted ranks, Ferguson understood his men more than most young officers of his age. He also had a rapport with them that was otherwise difficult to appreciate by anyone who had not served as an enlisted rank.

Regardless of his Scouts using the familiar term L-T, they had a great deal of respect for him in spite of his young age of twenty-one. They would never call him names behind his back as some senior officers might. That was a good thing too, since the young officer eventually would rise to the rank of Lieutenant Colonel, which, with an occasional exception, was about as high as a "*Mustang*" could get.

The Scouts' mission on this particular day was once again to reconnoiter the enemy positions and suppress any potential harassment by the Filipinos of the railroad workers and trains. It wasn't that they had been idle from combat the last three weeks, they hadn't. But Generals Lawton and MacArthur in trying to carry out General Otis's policies were hampered by lack of intelligence. So in addition to the usual Scouting mission Colonel Bell had called in Ferguson for a private chat prior to the Scouts' departure.

"Well, Arthur," Bell addressed the young Lieutenant by his first name, "how's it going with your group of Scouts? I know it was hard on them to lose Smith and Allen."

"Yes, sir, it was, particularly Summerfield and Hussey. They grew up together with Smith in Dickinson, you know."

"I knew that," said Bell. "I was stationed at Fort Lincoln with the seventh Cav south of Mandan in the late seventies. It's about a hundred miles from Dickinson."

"Yes, Sir."

"Anyway, today when you are out there, if you get a chance get me a prisoner or two, an officer if possible. I need some decent intelligence on these insurgents. Those three I caught a couple weeks ago were a big help for a while but the information is old now," Bell said. He was referring to his own actions on September 9th when he captured along with Lt. Colonel William Grove an officer and two enlisted men of the insurgent army. Bell and Grove were later awarded Medals of Honor for the action.

"I'm going to trail your outfit with one battalion, so if I hear firing we'll be close by to help, just send someone back with the information," the Colonel continued.

"Yes, sir, we'll do that," replied Ferguson.

The Scouts going with Ferguson this time were the same ones from September 3rd, minus of course Allen and Smith. Filling in were other experienced soldiers from the original North Dakota Volunteers. One of these was another Dickinson native from Company K who re-enlisted in the 36th, Dennis Mahoney a stone cutter in civilian life. Another was Frank Lee originally from Fargo's Company B.

Mahoney, a very capable marksman, asked to go along with the Scouts when he heard about Smith's death. All of the 36th volunteers were equipped with Krags. Lee was recruited to the Scouts by Ferguson after he had consulted with Jim McIntyre on who would be another good replacement for Smith or Allen.

The tactical situation was about the same as it was on September 3rd; the only difference being it was full daylight by the time the Scouts got to their original departure point of September 3rd near Porac. Ferguson, having learned a bitter lesson, kept his flankers in closer than they were before. Now they were in more of a skirmish line on both sides of the road, which they had approached in a wide half circle swinging south from their quarters in Angeles. Bell and his 1st Battalion were about fifteen minutes behind.

The insurgent's line of defense extending from Porac to Magalang and passing just north of Angeles was really part of what would eventually be called the Paruao Defense Line (from the name of the river). It extended along the Pampanga-Tarmac border and included Bamban and its mountains extending from southwest to east of Mt. Arayat. It was here that the Americans coined the term "Boondocks," which was a derivative of the Tagalog word bundok meaning mountain. It eventually came to mean any rough terrain, which is remote in mountains, backwoods, rural areas, or hinterland.

The Scouts had walked their skirmish line about a mile and a half with Ferguson on point when he spotted a white clad figure dart off the road in front of him about a quarter mile ahead. Without hesitation the Lieutenant, turned to his left, tossed his Krag to the closest flanker who happened to be the new Scout, Mahoney, drew his pistol and sprinted after the white clad insurgent startling the Scouts on either side.

Archie Galt, who was the close-in flanker on the other side, reacted quickly. He turned to Mahoney and the rest of the Scouts and yelled, "Come on, let's go!" and started running after L-T. Ferguson had briefed the Scouts on Colonel Bell's request for a prisoner, so Archie and the others knew immediately what he was up to doing.

Ferguson had not gone more than a hundred yards when the trailing Scouts saw dust kicking up on both sides of him before they heard the gunshots. The firing then broke out with intensity. When they saw Ferguson dive for cover the Scouts did too. As they looked out from positions of relative safety and got set to return the enemy fire, the Scouts were further startled to observe their leader jump up and charge the enemy positions all by himself, firing his pistol as he went.

"Geez, Arch, is he crazy?" asked Mahoney, who was holding the Lieutenant's Krag.

"I don't think so," replied Galt. "Watch!"

Ferguson ran right up to three insurgents, one of whom was an enemy officer, leveled his pistol at the group and had them all on the ground, himself included, in a matter of seconds. The Scouts watched in amazement as a hoard of white clad figures suddenly appeared from the bushes and started fleeing to the northeast, some of them running openly down the road they were just on. When the firing ceased, most of it from the Americans, Ferguson started to march the three prisoners back at pistol point, when the two enlisted insurgents bolted for cover.

Ferguson quickly shot at them with his pistol, but they kept running. Both were dropped by rifle fire from the Scouts. The Lieutenant then coolly marched the officer back to the Scouts and had him sit in the middle of the road.

"I'll take my Krag back now, Dennis."

"Yes, sir," said Mahoney, handing over the rifle.

"Archie, you and McIntyre keep an eye on the Gugu. The rest of you, except Irish and Gillenwater, take defensive positions in front and on the flanks. Pat, you and Jim head back down the road and report to Bell that we have his prisoner. He shouldn't be too far if he heard the firing."

The aftermath of the engagement is related in Ferguson's MOH citation awarded February 7th, but actually issued on March 8, 1902.

"For most conspicuous gallantry in action near Porac, Luzon, Philippine Islands, on 28 September, 1899, when as a First Lieutenant, 36th Volunteer Infantry, he charged the enemy alone and captured a captain."[187]

Neither the citation nor the NY Times article of 14 February 1900, mentions the two enlisted men also captured by the Lieutenant. Ferguson went on to re-enlist in the regular Army 14th Regiment in February 1901 as a 2nd Lieutenant, but continued to serve as a volunteer 1st Lieutenant until mustered out of the Volunteer service in June 1901. He was promoted again to 1st Lieutenant in February 1902 and eventually to Lt. Colonel after having served in the Mexican Campaigns and in World War I, as a regular career Army officer. Ferguson served with distinction for many years. He received praise from General Pershing and from Army Secretary Baker. Ferguson married twice, his first wife having died in 1913. He died unexpectedly after hernia surgery in 1923 and is buried in Arlington National Cemetery with both wives at his side.

"1896 Army Medal of Honor" and "2011 Army Medal of Honor"

187 http://en.wikipedia.org/wiki/City_of_San_Fernando,_Pampanga.

CHAPTER FIFTEEN

Review events of February 1899. Porac, Luzon, Oct., Nov., & Dec. 1899

"Weather ain't neutral." –Murphy's *Law of Combat*

In order to understand what the beginning and sustaining of the insurgents' change to guerrilla tactics and what the Americans' response with counterinsurgency warfare is all about, one must explore the commanders'-in-the-field thinking on both sides of the conflict. Sources for that include regimental histories and after action reports, some of which are the 22nd Infantry's.[188]

According to those records, the Americans were concerned that the insurrection led by Aguinaldo reflected his specific intentions. They considered him a *"wily and unscrupulous enemy,"*[189] which was reflected in his actions after Dewey's destruction of the Spanish fleet in Manila, when Aguinaldo proceeded from Hong Kong to Manila with the intention of *"securing as much aid as possible from the United States and then, when sufficiently strong, of driving out the Americans."*[190]

The American soldier-historians apparently did not know or perhaps ignored the fact that Admiral Dewey himself had sent for the rebel leader and even dispatched a United States vessel to fetch him and his exiled junta from the Asian metropolis.

---

188 http://1-22infantry.org/history3/pasig.htm.
189 Ibid.
190 Ibid.

The 22nd Infantry historians' attitude, however, reflects that of new troops and commanders arriving after the shooting had already started. The 22nd Infantry did not arrive in the Philippines until March 5, 1899, and their first combat was in the Pasig River Campaign. There is, however, some justification for labeling Aguinaldo as wily and perhaps even unscrupulous. Historians of the 22nd Infantry noted that Aguinaldo had:

- Declared independence in June 1898.
- Had subsequently captured several weakly garrisoned (Spanish) posts and thus the gained a supply of arms and ammunition.
- Concentrated his troops and fortifications around Manila.
- Had public demonstrations at Malolos (the first Rebel headquarters city), celebrating victory before hostilities had even begun.
- Had sent communications to General Otis on his efforts to maintain peace, which included representatives to the peace (Schurman) commission.
- Showed duplicity, the most damaging of which was the duplicity demonstrated on January 9, 1899, the same day he appointed members of the peace commission. On that date Aguinaldo issued a proclamation to his troops with detailed instructions for *"waging of treachery and death upon the Americans."*[191] These included having his troops dress as women, and using rudimentary napalm-like firebombs made of oil soaked rags and molasses, the components to be made ready long before hostilities broke out.

Not mentioned by the 22nd Infantry historians were the events (in detail) of Pvt. Grayson's first encounter that started the shooting war. Another clue to Aguinaldo's (or perhaps General Luna's or others') intentions was the immediate return of fire up and down the line by all of the insurgents after the first American shots were fired. In other words, they were apparently ready when the first shots were fired, and as noted previously the Insurgent leaders were conspicuously absent from the front lines.

Aguinaldo immediately issued his declaration of war against the Americans although officially war on the USA was not declared by the Filipinos until the Malolos Congress declared war on the United States (June 2, 1899). He did it by issuing a general order to his troops:

---

191 *Ibid.*

"Nine, o'clock, p.m., this date, (February 4, 1899) I received from Caloocan station a message communicated to me that the American forces, without prior notification or any just motive, attacked our camp at San Juan del Monte and our forces garrisoning the blockhouse around the outskirts of Manila, causing losses among our soldiers, who in view of this unexpected aggression and of the decided attack of the aggressors, were obliged to defend themselves until the firing became general all along the line.

No one can deplore more than I this rupture of hostilities. I have a clear conscience that I have endeavored to avoid it at all costs, using all my efforts to preserve friendship with the army of occupation at the cost of not a few humiliations and many sacrificed rights. But it is my unavoidable duty to maintain the integrity of the national honor and that of the army so unjustly attacked by those who, posing as our friends and liberators, attempt to dominate us in place of Spaniards, as is shown by the grievances enumerated in my manifest of January 8, last; such as the continued outrages and violent exactions committed against the people of Manila, the useless conferences, and all my frustrated efforts in favor of peace and concord.

Summoned by this unexpected provocation, urged by the duties imposed upon me by honor and patriotism and for the defense of the nation entrusted to me, calling on God as a witness of my good faith and uprightness of my intention.

I order and command:

1.—Peace and friendly relations between the Philippine forces and the American forces of occupation are broken, and the latter will be treated as enemies, with the limits prescribed by the laws of war.

2.—American soldiers who may be captured by the Philippine forces will be treated as prisoners of war.

3.—This proclamation shall be communicated to the accredited consuls of Manila, and to congress, in order that it may accord the suspension of the constitutional guarantees and the resulting declaration of war."

"Given at Malolos, February 4, 1899.
(Signed) EMILIO AGUINALDO,
General-in-Chief."[192]

192 *Ibid.*

It is interesting to note that Pvt. Grayson's narrative of the events is dated "around 8:00pm" on February 4th and Aguinaldo's general order above is dated 9:00pm the same date. Malolos is about thirty-two km north of Caloocan. Even with the telegraph line along the railroad from the Caloocan station, the message would have to be typed and delivered, so it seems unusual to have a well drafted general order released within the hour of the events. You draw the conclusion!

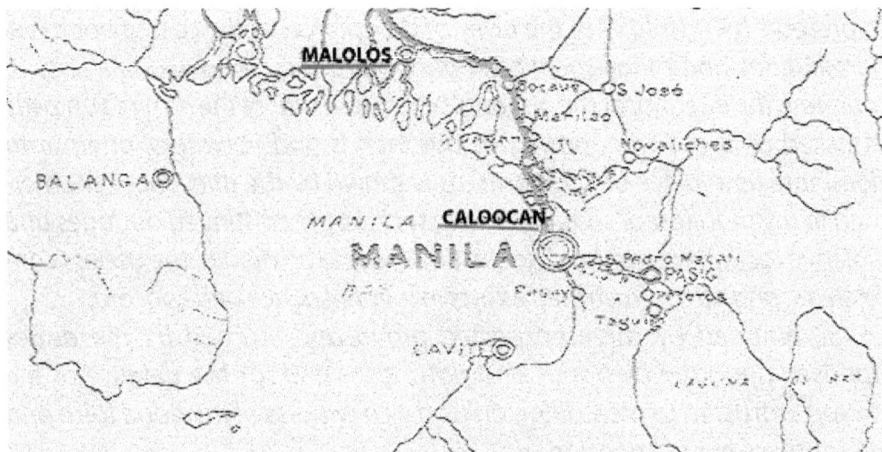

Malolos was close to twenty miles northwest of the Caloocan telegraph station.

Another clue to Aguinaldo's state of mind was a proclamation with instructions to massacre all Americans including children for the sake of Independence. English, French, and Germans, lives and property, were to be spared, for policy's sake, and all Chinamen were to be put to the sword.[193]

There is no way to conclusively judge who was right or wrong but the proclamations and general order by Aguinaldo seem to explain why the fighting became so atrocious on both sides. All of this information may help to explain the persistent actions around Porac

___
193 *Ibid.*

and Angeles in the fall of 1899. It was here that the 36th Volunteer Infantry Regiment earned their reputation as the "Suicide Club"[194] as they searched out and sometimes destroyed elements of Aguinaldo's elusive guerrillas.

Six of the eight Medals of Honor awarded to members of the 36th were earned in the Porac *kill zone*, including the ones presented to Colonel Bell and his companion Lt. Colonel William Grove, in the charge which captured three insurgents. The other four in the Porac area were Ferguson's, Leahy's, Gillenwater's, and another to a second soldier named Bell, but this time to a Captain with the first name of Harry.

According to Rhonie Dela Cruz,[195] the purpose of the Paruao Defense Line was to delay the Americans advancing further into Tarlac and give the army time to prepare for guerilla warfare. It would also allow the Filipinos to move their artillery from Bamban to more strategic locations. Aguinaldo had recognized the superiority of the American firepower and for that reason he elected to switch from frontal defense and confrontation to guerrilla tactics. Thus there appeared the tactical delaying guerrilla assaults and firefights in the Porac "kill zone" in which the 36th Volunteer Infantry found itself embroiled.

The assassinated General Luna had initially been in charge of building the Paruao Line of Defense and the American high command, recognizing the potential cost of destroying it to get to Aguinaldo, was intent on his capture before the insurgents could complete the task and the extension of defense infrastructure (artillery, escape and supply routes and quarters) into the critical heights of the Bamban mountains. Gen. Otis conceived a plan of frontal attack against the Filipino forces on the railroad, with one brigade on each side of the tracks.

The 36th Infantry under Bell was representing 1st Division commander General Lawton and was assigned the left flank of a three

194 Kolb, "Blaze in the Boondocks, 2002. Fighting on America's Imperial Frontier in the Philippines, 1899-1913," 28.

195 Rhonie Dela Cruz, THE PARUAO DEFENSE LINE 1899: THE LAST BATTLE OF THE REPUBLIC, Bamban Historical Society, BHS Journal No. 5, August 14, 2004.

pronged attack. Their position was west and southwest of Bamban (see map on next page). The 32nd Infantry, which had also seen considerable action around Porac, was delegated to secure the supply lines north of Angeles, where most of the Americans were quartered. The center of the attack was a brigade commanded by Brigadier General "Fighting Joe" Wheeler, who earned the nickname actually fighting for the Confederacy during the Civil War because of his aggressiveness and tendency to exceed beyond the military objectives. He had at his command the 9th and 12th regiments, a battery and a half of field artillery and a company of engineers, all representing 2nd Division commander Major General Arthur MacArthur. The 12th US Volunteers were the regiment of Infantry under Lt. Col. Jacob Smith that had captured the city of Angeles on August 16th. The 3rd prong of the attack was now assigned to this same Col. Smith now commanding the 17th Infantry regiment on the right flank.[196] Smith's responsibility included the towns of Magaland and Concepcion.

The time span from November 5 – 20, 1899 has been designated by military historians as the *Tarlac Campaign*, but was in fact a series of battles fought along the Paruao River and its downstream extension called the Bamban River. The battles were fought from Angeles north to points along the river and culminated in the collapse of Aguinaldo's forces in Bamban and allowed the capture of Tarlac on November 12, 1899. On November 9, 1899, elements of the 36th were involved in their mission as part of the left flank probe south west of Bamban.

---

196 Ibid.

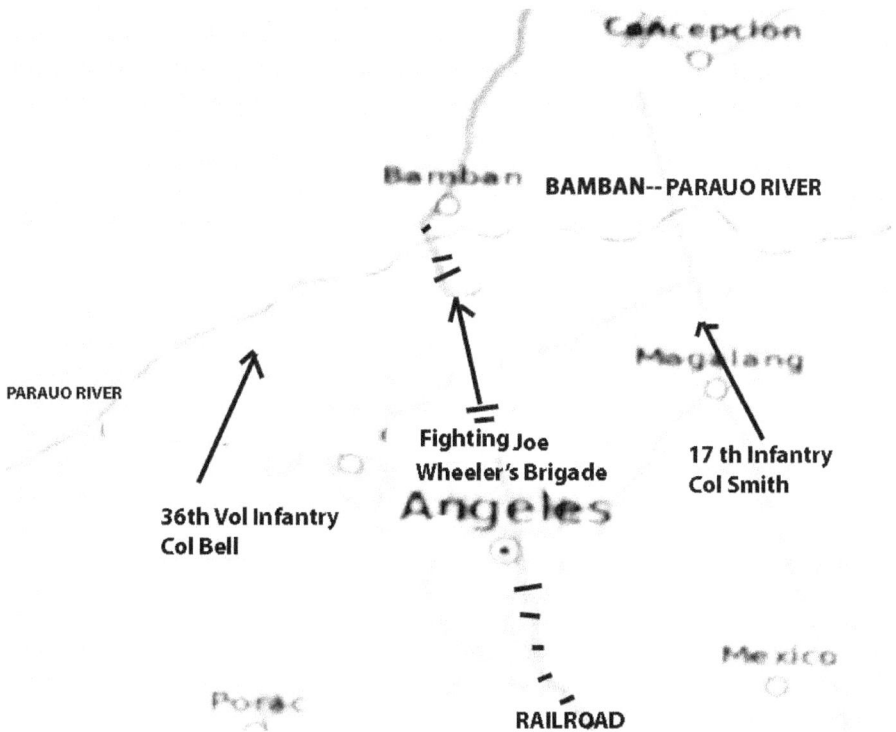

Concepcion

Bamban   BAMBAN--PARAUO RIVER

PARAUO RIVER

Magalang

Fighting Joe
Wheeler's Brigade

17 th Infantry
Col Smith

Angeles

36th Vol Infantry
Col Bell

Mexico

Porac

RAILROAD

Infantry Positions at the Start of the Tarlac Campaign[197]

The new sergeants of the 36th couldn't yet wear their new stripes until the promotions were official, but they were in for a real education serving under Major Bell, quoted by some as *"probably the finest Army commander in the Philippine War."*[198]

He was born in Kentucky in 1856, graduated from West point in 1878, and, posted to the 7th Cavalry in Fort Lincoln, just south of Mandan, North Dakota following Custer's disastrous battle at the Little Big Horn. There, he most likely knew Frank Ander's father, and was later impressed by the 1st ND Volunteers after having observed them in action in the Philippines. Although he first entered combat as a volunteer captain (regular Army 1st lieutenant) in the Philippines, he

---

197 Hook, Map Design.

198 Robert D. Ramsey III, *A Masterpiece of Counter guerilla Warfare: BG J Franklin Bell in the Philippines, 1901-1902, Combat Studies Institute Press.*

was a major of volunteers when recruiting for the 36th Infantry and would quickly be promoted through volunteer colonel to regular army flag rank as previously noted. Bell had also earned a law degree and passed the bar while serving as a professor of Military Science and Tactics at Southern Illinois University in the 1880's.

One of the first American officers to arrive in the Philippines, Bell worked with Aguinaldo's rebel's scouting out weaknesses in the Spanish fortifications, prior to the "mock battle of Manila" and quickly earned a reputation for competence. During Lawton's and MacArthur's San Isidro Campaign, Bell *"aggressively led numerous reconnaissance operations during the spring campaign north of Manila. Time after time Bell found weaknesses in the insurrecto defensive positions and exploited them to the benefit of the American forces."*[199]

Bell raised, and trained the 36th Volunteer Infantry regiment, recruited from discharged state volunteers like those who signed up from the 1st North Dakota. One subordinate who later retired as a major general himself had this to say about Bell: *"In all my service since (the Philippine war), I have never known an officer who was held in such high regard by the officers and men of his command as was Colonel Bell. (He had) an uncanny ability…to value correctly the powers and limitations of the enemy, …and to take advantage of his weaknesses. The Colonel organized, equipped and trained the 36th Infantry for the character of service it was to be called on to perform. But behind it all was the Colonel's exceptionally able leadership of men in war. The officers and men loved him personally. They had almost divine confidence in his military judgment and decisions."*[200]

After a month of additional training in guerrilla and counterinsurgency tactics, Bell led the 36th Volunteer Infantry in a battle near the town of Porac, Luzon, for which he was later awarded the Medal of Honor, thus further enhancing his reputation as a warrior and leader of men.

His citation reads in part: *"while in advance of his regiment [Bell] charged 7 insurgents with his pistol and compelled the surrender of the*

---

199 Ibid.
200 Ibid.

captain and 2 privates under a close fire from the remaining insurgents concealed in a bamboo thicket."[201]

The action occurred on September 9, 1899.

I WOULD RATHER DIE AT THE FRONT -artist RICK REEVES

Colonel James Franklin Bell leading the 36th Volunteer Infantry Titled by artist Rick Reeves. Reprinted with permission

On November 9, 1899, and after weeks of a combination of garrison duty combined with intermittent search and destroy missions in the provinces north of Manila, Scouts Galt, Glassley, McIntyre, and Jensen were leading a patrol along the banks of the flood swollen Parauo River (the upstream name of the Bamban River), which defines the boundary between the provinces of Pampanga and Tarlac.

The Scouts had been running into nests of guerrilla snipers carefully concealed amongst the bamban plants, volcanic lava rocks, and

201 http://www.arlingtoncemetery.net/jfbell.htm.

riverbank vegetation, with the hazardous conditions compounded by a torrential rain.

"Geez, Archie," said Fred Jensen, "look behind us." Archie peeked out from under his poncho, turned, and saw what Fred had just seen: flood waters starting to overflow the ground they had just covered.

"Holy smokes, Fred, we've got trouble!"

"Keep your head down, Arch; we've got two hundred guys drawing fire from the Gugus on the other bank. We've got to get out of here before the waters cut us off!"

"We've got no place to go, Fred, and a lot of the guys can't swim."

"I'll get the other guys up here," Fred replied. "Maybe we can figure something out. Cover me!"

With that, Fred started a belly crawl over the wet ground as Galt started firing his Krag. The first Scout he ran into was Jim McIntyre.

"Where's Colonel Bell?" Fred asked.

"He's over there on the right flank. What's up?" McIntyre replied.

"Pass the word to the other Scouts to get up here quick. Don't tell them why or we'll have a panic…the water is flooding in behind us. Get to Bell and let him know what's going on. Do it quietly, and tell him he can see for himself from Archie Galt's position over there," he said, pointing to Archie.

"On my way," McIntyre said, and started off in a running crouch with bullets chasing him, as he darted and dashed. Jensen watched him arrive safely at Bell's position, before starting back the way he came. McIntyre explained the situation to Colonel Bell, who promptly acknowledged its seriousness, told McIntyre to bring the Scouts as Galt had suggested and added the order for them to bring along as much rope as they could manage to find in a hurry. Colonel Bell then started his own running crouch to Galt's position.

"I'm told we have trouble," said Bell, somewhat out of breath.

"Yes, sir," Galt replied, pointing to the flood waters easily visible from their position, but not well seen by the rest of the troops. Colonel Bell took a long time looking from the approaching flood to the raging river in front of them.

"Who is the best swimmer of the Scouts?" Bell asked Artificer Galt.

"I'm as good as any, better than most, sir." Archie replied.

"I need a good swimming volunteer to get a guide rope to the other side."

"I'll do it," said Archie.

"It's dangerous, son; you'll be under fire, and that water is treacherous!"

"I'm your man, Colonel," Archie said, not as confident as he sounded. The other Scouts started to arrive. The first to carry a coil of rope was Mike Glassley.

"How far across do you think that river is?" Colonel Bell asked him.

"From that tree near the bank, at least 100 yards, may be more," replied Mike.

"Those are 100 foot coils, are they not?" asked Bell.

"Yes, Sir," replied Mike.

"Do we have enough?"

"Each platoon has three," answered Glassley.

"Good. We have enough. Get half a dozen coils over here and anchor the tether at that tree you pointed out. Feed Artificer Galt additional rope as he needs it, but don't add to the weight he has to pull until the last minute as the rope plays out."

"Yes, sir."

"The rest of you sharpshooters get in a good shooting position and give Galt some cover. You know what to do!" ordered Bell.

"Archie," Bell addressed Galt by his common name, which surprised the young soldier, "when you get to the other side, just find a good tree and tie a good knot. We have the muscle to stretch it taught on this side. You'll be tired, so don't waste your strength. As soon as you catch your breath, give us a signal and then find someplace where you can hide. You won't have a weapon until we can get one to you."

"Yes, Sir," Galt said with some trepidation.

"Atta boy!" said Colonel Bell. "I'm going to send two other volunteer swimmers with you. Who would you recommend?"

"Sir, Sergeant Hampton from Lawrence, Kansas, is damn good, and he's got a friend who is good, too, but I don't know his name."

"I'll find out," said Bell. He did. After Bell secured his two volunteers and after the rest of the rope coils arrived, Galt stripped to his waist, took off his leggings and boots, gave the rest of the Scouts a nod, and when they started an intense covering rifle fire, waded into the swollen river with the rope in one hand. As the swift current reached his waist Archie transferred the rope to his teeth and plunged ahead with a strong free style swimming stroke. His two companion swimmers followed. At first the insurgents didn't see him or were keeping their heads down because of the fierce covering fire the troops were providing. When they did, all hell broke loose, with numerous bullets splashing around his barely perceptible head. He made steady progress without being hit.

His two companion swimmers were not as fortunate. The one who Galt did not know was a soldier named Johnson was shot before he had swam ten yards.

When Johnson was hit and Sgt. Hampton was struggling to keep him afloat another Scout, John A. Huntsman of Company E, who had been with Bell in previous campaigns and had been personally recruited by the Colonel, saw the crisis. He threw down his Krag, stripped off his boots, ran barefoot along the shore, and plunged into the water at a point where he could catch up with Hampton and Johnson. Using strong freestyle swimming strokes, Huntsman caught up with the two, got one of Johnson's arms around his neck and said to Hampton, "Hang on to his other arm, John; we're drifting toward the other shore."

"I've got it. See if we can get to that clump of lava rocks."

"I see it."

The two Scouts paddled with their feet and one arm each, trying to keep Johnson's head above water, not realizing he was already dead, until Huntsman's fingers slipped into a huge hole in the back of Johnson's head.

"Oh shit!" Huntsman said. "He's gone. John. I just put my hand into the back of his head."

"Hang on to him anyway; we're out of range of the shooters, or else they don't care about us."

They managed to finally get to the lava racks with Johnson's body. Galt had aimed his path upstream from his target on the opposite shore, hoping the angle would allow the stream to carry him where he wanted to be without having to swim against the current.

By the time he reached midstream, he realized his angle was insufficient, but he was already too tired to fight the current.

When he reached the three quarter point, still unscathed, he could barely lift his arms, and his clenched jaw around the rope was beginning to spasm. He stopped for a moment, floated on his back, and took the rope from his mouth. One bullet ricocheted off a piece of nearby driftwood. As he turned to look, he realized he was drifting toward the targeted shore, so he let the current carry him. When another bullet came close, he ducked under the water.

When Colonel Bell saw him disappear, he thought for sure he was hit, as did the Scouts from Dickinson, Pat Hussey, and Frank Summerfield, who were in a better position than most to see Galt in the water. When Archie appeared a few seconds later, a cheer went up from those who could see him.

Archie's feet hit solid ground. The bullets, coming closer than ever, increased in number. One nicked his submerged trousers just above his right knee, its momentum slowed by the water, which still covered Archie to his hips. He scrambled ashore hanging tightly to the end of the rope, and dived under a bush next to a large chunk of volcanic lava. Archie finally saw a place where he could tie the rope. It wasn't the original tree, but it would do. When he got it secured he stood on the "safe side" of the tree and waved to his comrades across the river. Another cheer went up. Archie flopped back down under cover.

The danger for Bell's column was far from over. The Colonel now had to get his troops across a raging current during a heavy rain, under fire, using only the slippery rope for a guide. Some of his troops could not swim, and time was short with the rear approaching flood waters threatening to swamp the "island" they were on. Without the rope, death was almost a certainty for some 200 soldiers, who would either drown or be picked off by the insurgents as they tried to swim to safety. The only way out was for Bell to get enough firepower across first to protect the troops as they crossed. Here, Bell's Scouts led by the North Dakota Volunteers led the way.

Mike Glassley was first. Mike had experience swimming in the tough treacherous currents of the Missouri River near his Bismarck ranch home. Mike also agreed to carry Archie's Krag and some ammo since he could hang onto the rope and pull himself along with the rifles and ammo strapped to a quickly put-together-raft and towed behind him and with his boots around his neck. When Colonel Bell saw Glassley's homemade rig he ordered his officers to have the rest of the troops do the same. Laces from their leggings and boots sufficed to hold the homemade floats together. The covering fire from Bell's outfit was sufficient to get all six (including Galt but not Huntsman or Hampton) of the North Dakota Scouts across without serious mishap.

When that was accomplished and the sharpshooters were in action the tide stared to turn in their favor. After Glassley, the next two Scouts over were the two survivors from Dickinson.

"Hey, Arch. Hey, Mike," said Frank Summerfield.

"Hey yourself," said Mike, offering him a hand up. Summerfield then turned to give a hand to Hussey who was right on his heels. When the first three were settled and under cover Galt turned to them and said, "We've got a minute or so until those two get here." Waving at two more in the water about fifty yards out, he asked "Is that McIntyre and Fred?"

"Yup, Colonel Bell wants us to give covering fire for the rest. Where should we set up, Arch?"

"I figured that," said Archie. "There are a couple of high spots with some cover up there, and a couple of more over there," he continued pointing to the locations. "Most of the fire is coming from those rocks over there and those trees," he said pointing to two more locations. "When Fred and Jim get here I'll take them over there," he continued, pointing to a third spot. "You guys split up and take the spots I pointed out."

"We'll do that," said Summerfield. "C'mon guys," he continued, starting his run in a crouch, which triggered more firing from the hidden insurgents. It was just as well since the distraction allowed McIntyre and Jensen to scramble out of the water safely.

Downstream, Huntsman and Hampton left Johnson's body and started scrambling their way back upstream. They saw Archie Galt helping Jensen and McIntyre out of the water. Both were dragging extra Krags and ammo on their makeshift floats. Jensen spotted them before the others and hollered.

"Over here, you two. We've got your weapons! The Colonel thought you might need them; boots, too."

"Geez Fred, couldn't you keep the socks and leggings dry?" bitched Hampton.

"Screw you, Sergeant John. Go barefoot then."

"How's Johnson?" asked Archie.

"Didn't make it," said Huntsman.

Twenty seconds of silence. Then, Archie said, "After you get dressed follow me. I've got spots picked out for the covering fire the Colonel wants."

On the way to their shooting positions, the five of them came under an intense firing barrage. Four of them dived for cover, but Huntsman started cursing at the guerrillas and charged the bushes where the shots were coming from. He ran full speed into the midst of the attackers. With an American rebel-like yell, he fired five quick shots as fast as he could work the bolt action on his Krag.

The four Scouts under cover could not believe what they had just witnessed. They still couldn't see what had happened. But there was no sound except heavy breathing coming from the bushes about twenty five yards away.

Archie raised his head and yelled, "John?"

"Yeah, all clear, here," replied Huntsman.

When the others entered the clump of bushes there were three dead insurgents, sprawled in grotesque positions, and Huntsman was leaning on his rifle breathing heavily.

"Two of 'em got away," he said.

"Geez, John, why'd you do that?" Fred said.

"They pissed me off, Fred. Johnson was a friend."

Nothing more was said and the group started out for their positions. Once all of the Scouts were in position and started their deadly accurate fire, it wasn't long before the return fire from the insurgents dwindled to a few scattered ones, then to nothing. Bell then entered the water himself and led the column to the safety of the other side, just barely ahead of the flood waters. It was still pouring heavy rain as the last of the troops crossed safely.

Two and a half years later, on April 30, 1902, Battalion Sergeant Major Sterling Archibald Galt was presented with his nation's highest award for valor. His citation was brief. Huntsman's citation for the Medal of Honor for the same date is identical.

"For distinguished bravery and conspicuous gallantry in actions against insurgents at Bamban River, Luzon, Philippine Islands on November 9th, 1899."[202]

Information on Huntsman is scant. Part of his childhood in Oskaloosa (Iowa) involved farming. He must have moved to Kansas before he enlisted in the Kansas National Guard. Huntsman initially served with the 20th Kansas Volunteer Infantry that arrived in Manila in November 1898. His unit partook in the initial hostilities between Aguinaldo and the Americans in February 1899. Huntsman indicated in an official government document that he took part in engagements from February 4, 1899, to April 14, 1899. The 20th Kansas made one of the most celebrated river crossings of the war in a battle outside Manila. From April to June, he served with Major J. Franklin Bell's Scouts. Bell, of the 2nd Division, was its engineer but was often its chief Scout.

In Guagua, he heroically staved off a disaster for an American gunboat. As an advance Scout, he and a dozen others entered Guagua ahead of the American units. Huntsman was supposed to signal the gunboat to attack. Before he did so, Huntsman encountered a much larger force of insurgents than expected. Instead of withdrawing to safety, Huntsman and his men surprised the insurgents by attacking them and driving them back, averting a deadly ambush. He also led some aggressive charges in the Mangarterem mountain area, inflicting heavy casualties on the insurgents and seizing a large supply of munitions. Huntsman was greatly respected in his unit for bravery, resourcefulness, and superb fighting instincts. Huntsman's unit was relieved from active duty in June 1899. After that, Huntsman joined the 36th Infantry, U.S. Volunteers. The army offered a $500 bonus to those reenlisting from state regiments. The 36th consisted primarily of those recruited in the Philippines to reenlist. He had become a lieutenant before he mustered out of military service. He died of cholera

---

202 *Wikipedia, WEB Free Encyclopedia , MOH Citation for Stirling A. Galt.*

July 10, 1902, in the Philippines while serving as superintendent of construction of the Benguet Road in the Phillippines.[203]

Sergeant John Huntsman

For Archie Galt, a more appropriate memorial was presented to the world on Memorial Day, 1991, in Harrisonville, Missouri, where Galt is buried. The story of that service and more on Sterling Archibald Galt is told by this invitation written to the members of the Cass County (Missouri) Genealogical Society by Errol F. Durbin, May 18, 1991:

---

203 Wikipedia.

May 18,1991

Cass County Historical Society &
Cass County Genealogical Society

Dear Members,

I am writing this letter to invite you to the Dedication of
the Sterling Archibald Galt, Medal of Honor Memorial, that
has been placed at the foot of his grave commemorating the
fact that he was awarded the Medal of Honor during the
Spanish American War before the turn of the Century. When
the Cass County Genealogical Society had Harold F. "Sonny"
Wells speak at the April meeting, his program on the Medal of
Honor Society was overwhelming. There were over 50 people in
attendance and the Galt Memorial had never been dedicated so
some of us thought Memorial Day would be very fitting for the
occasion. I am sending the press release as it was given to
me by Mr. Wells so I don't know if the County newspaper will
edit it or not but here goes.

                        LEST WE FORGET

        A young, highly decorated soldier takes ill on the train
between Denver and Kansas City in the Summer of 1903.
        A family from Harrisonville traveling on the train
befriends the stricken soldier.
        The friendship continues until the disease, contracted
while on duty in the Philippines, finally overcomes the young
soldier just 5 years later.
        At 11:00 AM on Monday, May 27, Area Veterans will gather
at the Orient Cemetery for a traditional Memorial Day
Service. In the process they will at long last be paying
their respect to this long forgotten young soldier who had
been presented his Country's highest military award, the
Medal of Honor, in 1902, over 89 years ago.
        Sterling Archibald Galt, Battalion Sergeant-Major, 36th
U.S. infantry, awarded the Medal of Honor on the 30th of
April, 1902 for actions at Bamban River, Luzon, Philippines
Islands on November 9th, 1899: so says the book of Americas
Medal of Honor recipients.
        Galt's Medal of Honor citation says: Distinguished
bravery and conspicuous gallantry in action against
Insurgents.
        Neither the book or the Citation make mention of the
fact he swam a rain swollen river with a tethered rope held
in his teeth, tied the rope to a tree on the far shore and
guided the men and officers to safety, (between 165 and 300
men), all the time under a grueling cross fire from the
Insurgents.
        You see had it not been for his actions the encircled
Command might have been wiped out - to a man. Shortly after
the escape the entire Island the column was trapped on was
under water.

The file on Galt in the National Records Center is very thin. He is known to have been born in Taneytown, Maryland in October of 1866, the son of Henry & Analiza (Aumon) Galt. Military records show he joined the First North Dakota Infantry on April 27, 1898. The enlistment paper shows that he was 5'- 8" tall, fair complexion, and had dark brown hair and occupation was listed as a painter.

He was discharged on July 15, 1899 for the purpose of Re-assignment and re-enlisted in the 36th U.S. Volunteers on July 17th. His age was shown as 32 years and 9 months on those papers.

He was discharged for medical reasons, complications from malaria on January 23, 1901.

Little is known of his marriage to Minnie Allison in 1902. No record of the marriage or a possible divorce has been found. In a 1931 pension application Minnie listed her home as Riverside, California. No children were listed on the form. She died in California in 1939.

Galt had moved to Kansas City in the Spring of 1908 and took a job with the Monarch Life Insurance Company. He was living at 1400 College Avenue in East Kansas City when he died on October 21, 1908. The cause of death was listed as Nephritis. Literally unannounced, he was buried on October 22, 1908 in what may have been a donated grave site.

It is believed his mother was with him at his death as an "A. Galt" is listed on the death certificate as provider of data.

Galt's Medal of Honor Memorial Marker was put in place last Summer. The Dickey Funeral Home working with the Medal of Honor Historical Society arranged for the placement.

A Dedication Ceremony was postponed by rain the first time and the Persian Gulf War a second time. The combined efforts of the Cass County Genealogical Society and the Medal of Honor Historical Society have resulted in the planned Memorial Day Ceremony. The Cass County Honor Guard will participate in the Ceremony.

All Area Veterans Groups and Civic Organizations are invited to send Color Guards or Representatives.

We hope to see you at this Memorial Service and thank you for your time.

Errol F. Durbin

Errol F. Durbin
Cass County Genealogical Society
P.O. Box 406, 887-2393
Harrisonville, MO 64701

This article appeared in the Cass County (Missouri) Demo on May 24, 1991:

"Monday Ceremony Will Recognize Medal Winner
By Linda Thomas
Staff Writer
Since its inception in the 1860's, only 3399 persons have been awarded the Medal of Honor, the highest decoration awarded in the armed forces. Seventeen persons have received two of the medals making the total number of medals awarded 3416.

One of those persons is buried in Harrisonville and will be recognized in a memorial service Monday. The service will be at Orient Cemetery at the grave site of Sterling Archibald Galt.

The Medal of Honor was established by an Act of Congress in 1861 for the Navy, and in 1862 for the Army. It is awarded in the name of Congress to any person who has distinguished himself in conflict with the enemy by gallantry and courage, at the risk of his life and above and beyond the call of duty.

On April 30, 1902, Galt received the medal for his gallantry in saving lives during the Spanish American War, a conflict between the United States and Spain. The United States intervened in a war for independence, which Cuban authorities had been waging against Spanish authorities in Cuba.

According to local historian and genealogist "Sonny" Wells, at Luzon in the Philippines Islands, Galt and two other men swam the rain swollen Pampanga River, about thirteen miles north of Manila with a rope held between his teeth. When he reached the far shore, he tied the rope to a tree. Under crossfire from the insurgents, Galt guided his fellow soldiers and officers across the river to safety.

Wells said that if it had not been for his actions, the encircled command consisting of 150 to 300 men could have been "wiped out to the man."

Shortly after the escape, Wells said the island on which the column had been trapped was underwater.

Galt's medal says, "Distinguished Gallantry in Action Against Insurgents," Wells said.

Wells said acting in concert with Galt to save the men were Sgt. John A. Hampton from Lawrence, Kan., and another man, whose name is not known, and who was shot while in the water. Wells said the file on Galt at the National records center is "very thin."

He said Galt was known to have been born in Taneytown, MD, in October 1866, the son of Henry and Analiza Aumon Galt.

Military records show Galt enlisted April 27, 1889, at Valley City, ND, where he was assigned to Company G of the 1st North Dakota Volunteer Infantry, Wells said.

The enlistment papers indicate Galt was 5 feet, 8 inches tall, having a fair complexion, and dark brown hair. His occupation was listed as a painter. Wells said Galt was discharged July 15, 1899, for purposes of reassignment. Wells said Galt reenlisted July 17, 1899, and was assigned to the 36th U.S. Volunteers where he was a battalion sergeant major. His age at the time was thirty-two years and nine months.

Wells said Galt, who had contracted malaria while in the Philippines, was discharged June 23, 1901, for medical reasons listed as complications of malaria.

While little is known of Galt's personal life, Wells said it is believed Galt was married in 1902 at San Francisco, Calif., to Minnie Alison."[204]"

---

[204] *Cass County Demo on May 24, 1991, Newspaper, Harrisonville, MO.*

"America waged war against one of its fiercest foes-the Moros- in the southern Philippines. The fight against these fanatic followers of Islam lasted from 1902 to 1913. In the end, some semblance of peace prevailed, but the Moros were never permanently subdued during U.S. occupation." –Richard K. Kolb. Editor of Blaze in the Boondocks, a VFW, publication, 2002

PART II

FRANKLIN HOOK

SETTING THE STAGE

Ferdinand Magellan, honoring his king, Phillip II, first claimed the archipelago of over 7000 islands, which we now call the Phillipines, in 1521, nearly 500 years ago. Forty-four years after his claim, the Spanish conquistadores attempted the subjugation of the islands' inhabitants, but *"to their consternation and rage, they discovered that many of the people they sought to subjugate were Muslims,"*[205] of the same religion and beliefs as their ancient enemies from the Barbary Coast of present day Morocco. These ancient warriors were called Barbary Moors, from African homelands known as *La Tierra de el Moros*, the Land of the Moros. The Spanish never did control the Southern Philippines with any degree of sovereignty and were forced to abandon their posts to the USA upon losing the Spanish American War.

On May 19, 1899, three days after the Battle of the Burning Bridge in which Young's Scouts played such a significant role, two battalions of the 23rd Infantry landed on the Island of Jolo in the Sulu Archipelago. The small force of just over 750 men was commanded by forty-seven-year-old Captain Edward B. Pratt, who had been sent by Major General Otis to evacuate a small Spanish garrison. It was the first entry of American troops into "Moroland" as labeled by historian Robert A. Fulton.[206]

Departing commander of the Spanish garrison, General Rios, had not expected the Americans and on his own had turned over the Island of Siasi to the Sultan of Sulu, the Islamic ruler who was already on the supposedly new island acquisition consolidating his gain. Other complications had also occurred ninety-five miles to the north in Zamboanga, *"a mixed community of Christians, Moros, and Chinese,"*[207] where *voluntarios*, who were Filipino Christians sympathetic to Aguinaldo, had seized arms and ammunition, and former Spanish gun boats, probably with the collusion of the Spanish commander of the fort, General Monteros.

---

205 *Robert Fulton, http://www.morolandhistory.com/.*
206 *Robert A. Fulton, MOROLAND 1899-1906: (2007-2009), Tumalo Creek Press, Bend.*
207 *Ibid.*

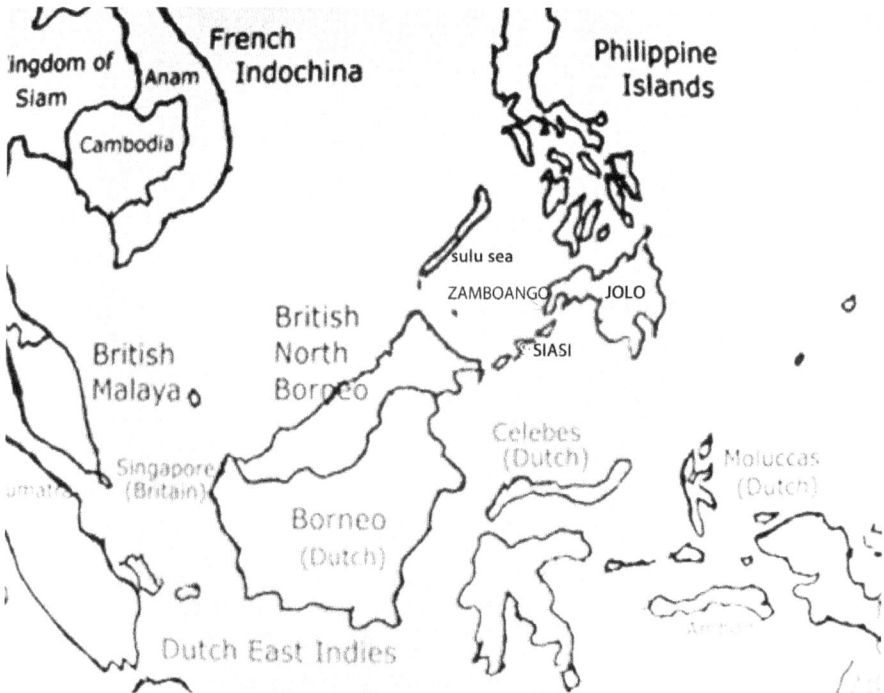

Map courtesy of Robert Fulton-86 modified by author.

All of these problems would land in the lap of Otis's newly arrived Brigadier General John C. Bates, who was charged by Otis with the *"transfer of authority"*[208] from Spain to the United States. Historian Robert A. Fulton described it this way: *"Preparing for their mission, Bates and his staff scoured the Spanish archives in Manila and discovered that Spanish sovereignty had in fact been no more than a myth and a contrived fiction. Of greater significance, it was dubious Spain had ever had the "right" under international law to cede the lands belonging to the Moros as a part of their holdings in the Philippine Islands. This discovery prompted Otis to revise Bates mission to one of gaining acceptance of U.S. sovereignty by the various Moro peoples, and a pledge for them to stay neutral and on the sidelines during the fighting to come, a daunting task.*

"Despite odds against him, Bates succeeded. For the next four and one-half years the relationship between the Moros and the American

---

208 *Ibid.*

government was largely peaceful and governed by a series of power-sharing agreements and understandings between the Muslim leadership and Army commanders. The best known of these agreements, although often mistakenly assumed as being the only one, was The Bates Agreement negotiated with the Sulu Sultanate. Under these arrangements, the Moros recognized the protection of the American flag and permitted the unrestricted occupation of their territories by American troops in return for the retention of local control by their hereditary leadership, non-interference by the Americans with their laws and customs, and especially respect for and non-infringement upon the establishment of Islam. For their part, throughout the Philippine-American War the Moros avoided any alignment with or support to their Christian cousins in the north.

"Following Bates mission, Otis established the Military District of Mindanao and Sulu, headed by a series of four Brigadier Generals, the first being Bates. Bates and those whom followed him in the position were all nearing the end of their military careers and had fought with distinction in the Civil War on the Union side. All did an exceptional job, maintaining the occupation of Moroland with less than 3,000 troops and with minimal friction and bloodshed."[209]

Fast forward from Bates's arrival to nearly a year later to the spring of 1900, where further north and east from "Moroland" on the Island of Samar, a catastrophe for the USA was brewing as the war of Aguinaldo's Philippine Revolutionary Group or PRG as labeled by historian Robert A. Fulton, was about to drastically change.

General Arthur MacArthur's forces had pinned down the insurgent forces of the PRG in central Luzon, while Lawton's division was in position to prevent their escape through the mountains to the East. When General Lloyd Wheaton's landing at Lingayen Gulf cut off their northern retreat, the PRG (also called the Republican Army by military historian Brian McAllister Linn[210]) broke up into small highly mobile units, which gave Otis the illusion that he had for the most part pacified the Philippines.

It was the perfect time for the wily Aguinaldo to switch to guerrilla tactics which he hoped would prolong the war, wear down the

---

209 *Ibid.*
210 Brian McAllister Linn, *The U.S. Army and Counterinsurgency in the Philippine.*

Americans, and if he could, influence the upcoming American presidential election in his favor.

The catastrophe at Catubig is described next, and is also written about by among others author Gregory J.W. Urwin,[211] who indicated that the Filipinos would materialize out of nowhere, kill, run, and then wait for a chance to kill again.

---

211 Gregory J.W. Urwin, The United States Infantry-An Illustrated History 1775-1918, U. of Oklahoma Press, by arrangement with Sterling Pub Co NY, NY, 2000.

CHAPTER SIXTEEN

Catubig, Samar Island, Philippines, April 15 – 18, 1900

"There are no facts, only interpretations." –Friedrich Nietzsche

If anyone attempts to find out what circumstances actually provoked the "Catastrophe at Catubig," as labeled by Richard Kolb[212], the investigator is sure to find conflicting stories as seen through the eyes of those with different upbringing or political exposures. Mona Lisa H. Quizon[213] writing for the National Historical Commission of the Philippines on the 150th anniversary of the birth of guerrilla hero Vicente Lukban, acknowledged that for his enemies he was the terror that couldn't be seen and a relentless terrorist, but, for his people, a warrior of defiance and carrier of hope.

Today, descendants and/or relatives of American soldiers slaughtered during the siege of Catubig might feel Quizon went a little overboard in calling the rare victory over the American troops glorious.[214]

Quintin L. Doroquez[215] describes his version of events that led up to the massacre. Doroquez admits that his story is a recollection of tales he listened to as a youth growing up in Catubig, but some might disagree that that the eye witness accounts related by Doroquez had no ax to grind,[216] particularly with regard to whatever provoked the events.

---

212 Kolb, "Blaze in the Boondocks, 2002. Fighting on America's Imperial Frontier in the Philippines, 1899-1913," 15.

213 MLH Quizon, http://www.nhi.gov.ph/.

214 Ibid.

215 Quintin L. Doroquez, http://www.samarnews.net/gugma/articles/article29. htm.

216 Ibid.

Doroquez indicated, according to the word of mouth tales he recalled, that a number of Americans masquerading as surveyors,[217] began to appear in Kagninipa (later called Catubig*) in February of 1900 and as the days progressed uniformed soldiers arrived (which the surveyors proved to be also) as H Company of the 43rd Volunteer Infantry. The stories went further. As repeated, they tell the resentment the native Filipinos felt of the deception the Americans showed posing as surveyors when their real mission was to deny General Lukban access to the bountiful rice harvest in the Kagninipa Valley as well as a safe haven.

Doroquez's story is not too far from the truth since the 43rd Regiment had been sent to Catubig a few days before the battle[218] but it's highly unlikely that the troops would transport heavy surveying equipment such as transits, levels, and chains just to pose as surveyors, when maps of the area on Samar were scarce not to say relatively useless. It is more likely that Lukban fanned the flames of war by painting the Americans as deceptive and sneaky in order to recruit more rebels to the cause. He was highly successful at just that, while the Yanks were doing as ordered to survey and map the area and see if the rumors of sympathizers helping the insurgents were true, and, if so, try to stop them.

It was the U.S. Army's high command (General Otis in early 1900) failure to recognize the insurgents' switch to guerrilla tactics or even acknowledge that the guerrilla war was a problem, that gave the rebels an advantage. Under General Order #40 of that year, Army officers were instructed to establish municipal governments with a mayor (*el president or alcalde*), a town council (*consejo ayuntamiento*), and a police (*policia*) force. It was recognized, at least by some of the officers, that the natives could only be controlled through their own leaders. Since the Catholic Church was a significant factor in the local leadership in many Filipino communities, Captain H. M. Day, commander of H Company, established his command post in the local priest's rectory by invitation, and since the priest was scheduled to travel through the Samar hinterland

217 Ibid.

* Doroquez tells an interesting anecdote of the origin of the town's name involving the American/English word cat and the Filipino dialect word tubig meaning water of the brook. The tale enforces the initial friendly relations and belies the hostility later implied of the natives toward the American soldiers.

218 Richard Johnson, Reply to a query on the web concerning the Siege of Catubig. Johnson formerly maintained a website on Fort Drum, http://www. concretebattleship.org. No longer active.

for the next several weeks, was allowed to use the rectory, the vacant convent, and the grounds for his company business while he was gone. The church, although vacant, was left open for parishioners to use for daily prayers. The convent became the troop barracks.

The 43rd Regiment had only been in country about four months arriving Dec. 19, before their journey to Samar and although there are many sources repeating the myth that the troops of the 43rd were raw and inexperienced the records of the War Department suggest otherwise.

43rd Infantry Combat Engagements Jan. – April 15, 1900[219].

Place	Date	Company/Det	KIA	WIA
Calbayog	Jan. 26	I, K, L, M	0	0
Catbalogan	Jan. 27	E, F, G, H	1	2
near Catbalogan	Jan. 29	I, K, L, M	0	0
near Najpore	Feb. 3	H	0	1
near Magtuguinao	Mar. 8	H	1	5*
near La Paz	Mar. 8	A	1	0
Paranas	Mar. 11	M	0	3
near Jaro	Mar. 16	B	1	0
La Granja	Mar. 21	E	0	1
near Hiabong	Mar. 24	I, L	0	2
Calobayog	Mar. 26	E, F, G, H	1	3
Gandara	Mar. 27	43rd Inf det	0	0
Malitbloe	Mar. 29	43rd Inf det	0	1
near Baruso	Mar. 30	B	0	1
near Dagami	Mar. 31	Scouts	0	1
near San Jose	Mar. 31	I	0	2
Santa Margarita	Apr. 7	G	0	0
La Vezares	Apr. 10	E	0	0
near Nippero	Apr. 12	E,G	0	1**
Catubig	Apr. 14-19	H, F	18	5

219 *Annual Reports of the War Department Ending Fiscal Year June 30,1900*, *Government Printing Office, Washington, DC, 1900. Available on University of Michigan's Library Website, http://books.google.com/.*

The above table indicates that the 43rd not only gained a considerable amount of experience in their three and one half months in combat, but also suffered a significant number of casualties, including Lt. J.T. Sweeney, who was wounded in the arm just five weeks before his encounter with the rebels at Catubig. Company H personnel had been in four separate fights with three KIA and eleven WIA.

Despite their experience in combat and guerrilla warfare, the soldiers of H Company were naïve in their trust of the apparently friendly natives of Samar who were customarily hospitable to visitors. Had the naturally friendly native attitudes not been affected by ardent revolutionaries like Vicente Lukban y Rilles, perhaps the peaceful attempts encouraged by General Order # 40 (above) would have worked. However, native Filipino opinions were also influenced by others such as local rice producer and wealthy real estate owner Francisco Fincalero, who, according to Quintin Doroquez, informed his tenant farmers to resist any American attempts to commandeer the harvest despite lack of any evidence of such a threat.

Domingo Rebadulla, who would later become mayor of Catubig, was one of the leaders responsible for organizing the local resistance along with Probo Plagata and Juan Alaras, also future mayors according to Doroquez. A series of secret meetings resulted in a recruited militia some 300 strong, albeit poorly trained. Another young insurgent by the name of Homobono Joli-Joli from neighboring Las Navas, came on board with twenty-five volunteers to supplement the new force. Other wealthy locals donated arms such as Mauser rifles and revolvers. Local blacksmiths were recruited to make *palteks*, [220] which were locally handmade firearms, and *baids*[221] designed like Japanese Samurai blades.

Rebadulla, in an astute move, sent his teen age son along with two others, to find General Lukban and the rebel leader promptly responded by sending back one of his senior officers, Colonel Enrique Villareal Dagujob to oversee the upcoming mission. He also sent an expert in the manufacture of gunpowder to use in recycled

---

220 Doroquez, http://www.samarnews.net/gugma/articles/article29.htm
221 Ibid.

cartridges.[222] Lukban also promised 500 reinforcements if fighting broke out. *(Author's note: There is little doubt that a fight was inevitable if Doroquez's tale is true, and events indicate that it is.)*

After inspecting the insurgents' set-up in Catubig, Villareal-Dagujob returned to Lukban's HQ in Blanca Aurora and was immediately sent back with 600 Raiders because according to the story told to Doroquez the General *sensed* immediate hostilities.

Although they were just a day's heavy jungle marching to Catubig when they learned the siege had already began, the Raiders were not too concerned because the local "bamboo telegraph" (the Philippine version of the American "grapevine") indicated the steam vessel To-nyik was said to be on the west coast of Samar and would therefore be at least three days away from rescuing the besieged American troops. Unbeknownst to the rebels, routine reinforcements, headed by 1st Lieutenant J. T. (called Jay-Tee by his men) Sweeney, were already on the way although ignorant of the underway attack.

---

222 *Ibid.*

Rebel leader General Vicente Lukban pictured in Hong Kong in 1897.[223]

The ides of April 1900, Sunday morning of the 15th, was a bright, sunny day in Catubig. Noncommissioned officers Sergeants Dustin (Dusty) L. George and John (Jack) Hall each had a platoon of Company H along with a few soldiers from CO. F going through marching drills in the courtyard outside of their Convent quarters next to the Church of St. Joseph.

223 *Philippine Culture: History-Philippine- American War-Miscellaneous Photos, http://www.yonip.com/archives/history/history-000054.html.*

***Church of St. Joseph, Catubig, Samar Island Philippines. Photo
taken in 2006 modified by the author.[224]***

At the Catubig River docks, longshoremen were stacking bales of
abaca (the source of hemp) to be loaded aboard a ship which was currently unloading cans of kerosene, and while the soldiers were going
through their drills, excited teenage boys in the church belfry were
anxiously awaiting a signal, agreed upon the day before, to start ringing all three of the church bells.

According to Doroquez, the youngsters had gotten their
instructions the previous day and were not supposed to ring the
usual time signal struck by one of the bells on Sunday at 6:00 A.M.,
but were to wait for small arms fire, and then ring all of the bells
including the largest *de ruda* bell which was only rung on special
occasions.

---

224 *Philippine Culture: History-Philippine- American War-Miscellaneous Photos,*
http://www.yonip.com/archives/history/history-000054.html.

Small arms gunfire, however, could mean nothing but war, so Domingo Rebadulla, not wanting to alert the Americans, ordered the signal to start the action by having one of the longshoremen drop an empty kerosene can which would reverberate a signal meaning the Americans had refused an offer to surrender.

According to Doroquez's tale, a courier was dispatched with an envelope containing a surrender demand, although no evidence could be found by this researcher of such a happening. The story continues that when the demand was rejected a thumb-down signal by the courier triggered the fall of the kerosene can which started the whole thing, and *"all hell broke loose."*[225]

Continuing Doroquez's story, some of the rebels were dispatched to the rear of the church to fire their arms in order to decoy the Americans in that direction, while all able bodied men of the town ran to the church to participate in the action even if they were not armed. These natives apparently assisted by pushing bales of abaca/hemp around the convent for the *"militiamen"* to use as shields.

When Sergeant Dusty George heard the hollow drum-like sound of the empty kerosene can being dropped followed by small arms fire at the back of the church, he knew whatever was happening could not be good. He looked over at Sgt. Hall's platoon, who had all stopped in the middle of an "about face" to look up at the church belfry as a cacophony of sound erupted from the tower. He then noted a white clad figure sprinting away from the front of the Convent, the front doors of which were still open as small arms firing continued from the back of the church.

Dusty immediately hollered loud enough for all the troops to hear, "Into the Convent, now! Everybody!"

His command was followed by a mad rush of running soldiers headed for their "barracks" in the Convent. As they ran hundreds of armed insurgents appeared in adjacent streets all headed for the Roman Catholic grounds, some of them firing rifles and their *palteks*, and some brandishing *baids*, the Samurai-like swords. More insurgents could be seen descending in runs down the nearby hills.

---

225 Doroquez, *http://www.samarnews.net/gugma/articles/article29.htm.*

Dusty got to the Convent doors before Hall's platoon, ushered his own troops inside and held the door for the rest. All except four cleared the threshold, Sgt. Hall, who was bringing up the rear, two privates and Dusty who was still guarding the door. All of the soldiers were armed with Krags and cartridge belts and had been so equipped during the morning drills.

As the last three soldiers approached Dusty at the door, a half dozen native rebels attacked, at least one of them armed with a stolen Krag. Jack Hall led the counter attack as the fighting became hand to hand. The four managed to drive off the attackers, but the rebel with the stolen Krag got off one shot at point blank range into Sgt. Hall's midsection, before Hall killed him with return fire.

As he took the first step over the threshold, Hall stumbled and fell forward. He reached Sgt. Dusty George with one hand as he fell and cried, "I'm hit!"

Frothy blood streaked foam trickled from the corners of his mouth as the mortally wounded sergeant collapsed to the floor. Dusty picked him up and carried him into the anteroom of the Convent as one of enlisted men closed and barred the doors.

Corporal Anthony J. (Tony) Carson, the noncom next in charge, stepped forward to help Dusty with his burden. When they got him comfortable on an anteroom couch, Dusty turned to Tony Carson and shook his head indicating Hall was moribund.

"Tony, get the troops spread out and cover all the windows and doors. Have the quartermaster issue all the ammo we have and see that we have enough water to go around. It's going to be a long day!"

"Yes, Sergeant," Tony replied as he turned to comply.

It was indeed a long day. Not only was there constant harassing fire from all around the Convent, but a small cannon was being used from the adjacent church. After nearly two days withstanding a withering fire, with only one KIA, Sgt. Hall, and two wounded, a major break was forced on the besieged when the insurgents set fire to the Convent and the Americans could not control the blaze.

Sgt. Dusty George called a conference with Corporal Tony Carson. No commissioned officers were available since Captain Day had gone to the coast before the attack to meet the re enforcements led by Lieutenant Sweeney and arrange for a riverboat to take them to Catubig. Day was then scheduled to return to regimental HQ to report to Major Allen on the situation in the Catubig Valley before returning with new orders from the Major, who was in charge of all forces on Samar.

"We can't get the fires under control, Tony," said Dusty, "so here's what I'm thinking and we don't have a lot of time. We're surrounded so let's break up into two groups. I'll take one and break out the front door, and fight our way to the docks. You take the other and go out the back and do the same, maybe we'll get lucky and some of us will make it. What do you say?"

"You'll have the tougher fight, Sergeant, so I'll take the two wounded with me. Let us start a covering fire for you before you go through the doors. As soon as you engage hand to hand we'll scoot out the back."

Not realizing the probable truth of such a plan some 100 plus years later, a 21st century blogger[226] describing the events on the internet said this: *"When they reached the outside, the whole regiment (sic) lost all coordination, and broke into two groups: One running for some boats on the river bank, and another for the rear of the barracks. All 15 men running for the boats were killed, either cut down in the streets, or shot in the boats. The others made makeshift trenches, dug with their bayonets, and for another two days kept the guerrillas in check, until a rescue party in the steamer Lao Ang came to their aid in the nick of time. The relief force saved the survivors under a hale (sic) of Mauser bullets, then made it back to their base before the guerrillas could re-group and attack again."[227]*

The blogger was probably parroting the opinions suggested in William Sexton's *Soldier's in the Sun*, which says the detachment *"appears to have become panic-stricken, for it broke into two groups, one rushing for some boats on the river bank and the other for a clump of grass in the rear of the Convent."[228]*

---

226 Richard Johnson, *Reply to a query on the web concerning the Siege of Catubig.* Johnson formerly maintained a website on Fort Drum, http://www.concrete-battleship.org. No longer active.

227 Ibid.

228 Kolb, *"Blaze in the Boondocks, 2002. Fighting on America's Imperial Frontier in the Philippines, 1899-1913,"* 15.

There are other reports perpetuating misinformation about the siege. Doroquez reported that of the thirty-six Americans perceived to be in the garrison fifteen tried to flee and fifteen were burnt alive or otherwise killed. He also called Lt. Sweeney one of the four day survivors, when in fact Sweeney was one of the last day rescuers. Thus, Sweeney's "recollection"of smelling kerosene before the fire must be taken with a grain of salt. The errors are part of the word-of-mouth history, and Doroquez, who performed a great service to history by relating in writing his memorable tale, should not be held responsible for the perpetuity of errors. One other report[229] had twenty-one killed and eight wounded and another nineteen killed and three wounded[230] when in fact there were eighteen KIA and five WIA.[231]

---

229 http://www.enotes.com/topic/Siege_of_Catubig.

230 Kolb, "Blaze in the Boondocks, 2002. Fighting on America's Imperial Frontier in the Philippines, 1899-1913," 15.

231 Annual Reports of the War Department Ending Fiscal Year June 30,1900, Government Printing Office, Washington, DC, 1900. Available on University of Michigan's Library Website, http://books.google.com/.

Artist Richard Hook's SIEGE OF CATUBIG

Richard Hook captured the front door breakout of the Americans on this canvas.

According to Doroquez, the 600 men provided by General Lukban and led by Col. Enrique Villareal-Dagujo did not arrive until early on the third day of the siege, but they already had the information that help for the Americans was on the way via the Catubig River from the soldier's on Lao-Ang. When the rescuers led by Lt. Sweeney arrived on the fourth day, the fight really began in earnest. Richard Kolb described it this way: *"A squad of 12 men, led by 1st Lt. J.T. Sweeney, already on its way to reinforce H Company, arrived just in the nick of time. The steamer Lao Ang 'steamed up to Catubig under a rain of Mauser bullets from both shores.' Landing boats were lowered and the relief party fought its way to the trenches. It was able to rescue 13 men, who were taken back to the steamer and to safety down the river."*[232]

The surviving American hero of the siege, however, was Tony Carson. Captain Day, H Company Commander, later commended the Boston native with these words, which were incorporated into his Medal of Honor citation awarded six years later: "For displaying extraordinary good judgment in the handling of his men, thereby saving the lives of the survivors, and protecting the wounded until relief came."

Corporal Anthony Carson would have been the first to declare that the real heroes of the day were Sergeants Dusty George and Jack Hall and the others who gave their lives so that he and a dozen others could survive. Carson's MOH was awarded by President Roosevelt himself. Later promoted to Sergeant, Carson returned to Massachusetts, where he died in 1943 at age seventy-four. He is buried in Mattapan, MA.

---

232 Kolb, "Blaze in the Boondocks, 2002. Fighting on America's Imperial Frontier in the Philippines, 1899-1913," 152.

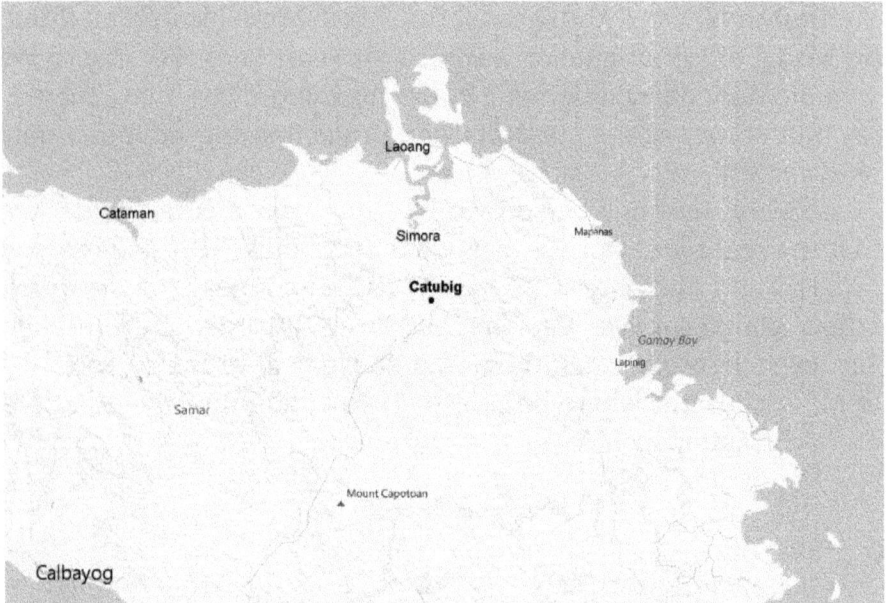

Note Catubig's location in the map above in Samar relative to Manila in Luzon. Catubig could be reached by river boat steamer but was remote compared to coastal ports like Lao Ang.

Corporal Anthony J. Carson, Boston MA, was awarded the MOH for actions April 15-19, 1900, Catubig. Photo[233]

Confirmation of some of the details of some of the actions at Catubig were provided by these two articles from the *New York Times* on May 17 and June 9, 1900, respectively:

THE FIGHT AT CATUBIG.

Gen. MacArthur Confirms the Report of the Attack on the American Garrison.

WASHINGTON, May 16.—The officials of the War Department, after waiting for nearly a week to hear something from Gen. MacArthur, at Manila, confirmatory of the press report of the bloody three days' engagement at Catubig, which resulted in the heaviest loss of life the American Army has sustained in any one engagement in the Philippines, yesterday cabled Gen. MacArthur a request for information.

---

233 Kolb, *"Blaze in the Boondocks, 2002. Fighting on America's Imperial Frontier in the Philippines, 1899-1913,"* 17.

The answer was received to-day, confirming the press reports and adding some interesting details. Gen. MacArthur transmitted a report from Henry T. Allen, a Major of the Forty-third Volunteers, who commanded the United States forces on the Island of Samar.

It appears that this force was divided among several ports on Samar, and, while details are still lacking, it is believed that this particular force, which was besieged at Catubig, was commanded, not by a commissioned officer, but by a Sergeant, either George or Hall, both of whom were killed. Catubig, where the engagement occurred, is a seaport town of nearly 10,000 inhabitants. Gen. MacArthur's cablegram is as follows:

"With reference to your telegram of 14th, the rumored engagement in Samar reported in cablegram of Gen. Otis May 4 has been confirmed by reports recently received from Henry T. Allen, Forty-third Regiment, United States Volunteer Infantry, commanding Samar Island. That detachment of 31 men, stationed at Catubig, was attacked April 15 by 600 men with 200 rifles and 1 cannon. Our men were quartered in a convent, which was fired next day by burning hemp thrown from adjoining church.

"Detachment attempt escape by river. Men getting into boat were killed; remaining men intrenched themselves near river and held out two days longer, facing most adverse circumstances, until rescued by Lieut. Sweeney and ten men.

"Over 200 of attacking party, many of them are reported having come from Luzon Island, reported killed and many wounded. Lieut. Sweeney reports streets covered with dead insurgents.

"Iloilo cable is broken by earthquake. Difficult to procure more definite information."

Published on May 17,1900

A Graphic Tale of American Pluck from the Philippines.

Thirty-one Hold Six Hundred at Bay— "An Example of the Courage of the American Soldier."

WASHINGTON, June 8—The War Department has received reports from Capt. H. M. Day of the Forty-third Volunteer Infantry, and First Lieut. J. T. Sweeney of the same regiment, giving a graphic description of one of the most thrilling and picturesque incidents of the entire Philippine war. The occurrence took place at Catubig, on the Island of Samar, where a party of thirty-one enlisted men of Company H, Forty-third Infantry Volunteers, held at bay a force of some six hundred insurgents during four days of the fiercest fighting, reinforcements arriving just in the nick of time.

According to the reports of Capt. Day and Lieut. Sweeney, who led the relief party, the attack on the garrison at Catubig began without warning on Sunday morning, April 15. From the hills on all sides, from every point of vantage in the town, and from a deserted church directly adjoining came a rifle and cannon fire of terrible intensity. On Tuesday morning handfuls of burning hemp were thrown into the barracks by the insurgents in the church, and soon the soldiers' refuge was on fire. All efforts to subdue the fire failed, and finally the little band made a dash for the river bank.

Some were killed before the bank was reached, others fell dead in a boat in which they were attempting to make the opposite shore, and when a trench was finally dug with bayonets, there were but sixteen of the thirty-one left to man it. Here for two more days Corp. Carson, handling his men with the judgment of a veteran, held out under a terrible fire, until Lieut. Sweeney's command, which had been ordered to supplement the garrison at Catubig and was on its way up the river on the steamer Lao Aug, arrived.

Not until they were within a quarter of a mile of Catubig, says Lieut. Sweeney in his report, did they hear the noise of the engagement. Then he realized that he and his men were sorely needed, and ordered the Captain of the steamer to run his boat at top speed. The Lao Aug steamed up to Catubig under a rain of Mauser bullets from both shores. The small boats were lowered, a landing effected, and the rescuers fought their way through the open to their besieged comrades in the trenches, buried the dead within reach, brought back to the boat the besieged party, numbering now only thirteen men, and then steamed down the river.

Capt. Dey bestows the highest commendation upon Corp. Carson as " displaying extraordinary good judgment in the handling of his men, thereby saving the lives of the survivors, and protecting the wounded until relief came."

To each of the little command and their rescuers he gives the highest praise. " Their zeal and ability," he says, " were a fitting example of the worth and courage of the American soldier."

The New York Times

Published: June 9, 1900

Published on June 9, 1900

As a note of interest, a cursory search of the *New York Times* archives produced no reference to the siege or battle as "horrifying" as reported by some.

CHAPTER SEVENTEEN

Northeast Luzon, Philippines, March 1901

"What is of supreme importance in war is to attack the enemy's strategy."
– Sun Tzu

During the first four months of 1900, 442 engagements by U.S. Forces in the Philippines resulted in 130 American KIA and 325 WIA.[234] Guerrilla ambushes and engagements did not let up with 1026 engagements occurring between American troops and insurgents between May 5, 1900, and June 30, 1901.[235] The War Department reported 873 American casualties during that latter period, 245 of which were KIA's.

The result of nearly 1500 battles in just over a year were no doubt wearing on the Americans, but the cost for the insurgents was much worse with 11,619 casualties of which 3854 were KIA and even more disturbing to the rebel leaders, 23,095 surrendered. By the end of the year 1900, there were more than 70,000 USA armed forces in the Philippines with 69,420 soldiers and the rest including sailors and marines tipping the scale over the 70,000 mark.

---

234 Kolb, "Blaze in the Boondocks, 2002. Fighting on America's Imperial Frontier in the Philippines, 1899-1913," 41.

235 Annual Reports of the War Department Ending Fiscal Year June 30,1900, Government Printing Office, Washington, DC, 1900. Available on University of Michigan's Library Website, http://books.google.com/.

The major turning point of the war occurred in March 1901, under the command of Colonel Frederick Funston, originally of the 20th Kansas Volunteer Infantry Regiment.

Born in 1865 in Iola, Kansas, Funston had the desire to be a soldier as long as he could remember. An adventurer from youth he finally achieved his desire at age thirty-one when he left his job as a botanist for the Department of Agriculture and hooked up with Cuban Rebels in their fight against their Spanish rulers. He carried his wounds, his malaria and his decorations home with him eighteen months after his battle experience in Cuba, with just enough time to heal before the USA answered Spain's Declaration of War with her own. His experience in Cuba was enough to gain him a commission with the 20th Kansas Volunteers and he deployed to the Philippines as a full Colonel.

The 20th Kansas "Jayhawkers" were part of the 1st Brigade, 2nd Division (MacArthur's) in the San Isidro Campaign (see map page 80) on April 26 – 27, 1899, when at the village of Calumet, northwest of Manila the unit *"made history."*[236] Although a fascinating story of itself, the action at Calumet was called by General MacArthur a *"remarkable military achievement"*[237] and resulted in Colonel Funston's promotion to Brig. General of Volunteers and the nickname of "Fighting Fred" as well as Medals of Honor for two of his men and himself.

The event that permitted the turn of events in the war, which was becoming a real political liability at home, was the defection of an insurgent courier who happened to be carrying documents from Aguinaldo's headquarters, which was located in a village called Palanan near the northeast coast of Luzon.[238]

Funston, on going through the documents noted that one of them was a request for additional troops, and now that he knew Aguinaldo's location, came up with a rather ingenious plan. The plan involved the use of Macabebe Scouts who were native Filipinos sympathetic to American plans to provide a safe government for the Philippines. According to historian Arnaldo Dumindin: *"The US*

---

236 Kolb, "Blaze in the Boondocks, 2002. Fighting on America's Imperial Frontier in the Philippines, 1899-1913," 11.
237 Ibid.
238 Ibid.

Army organized special forces officered by Americans but manned by Filipinos. The first unit of this type was experimental, one company of 100 Macabebes enlisted on Sept. 10, 1899, for a term of 3 months and led by 1Lt. Matthew Batson, U.S. Army. It was experimental in the sense that Batson's superiors - including Brig. Gen. Arthur C. MacArthur, Jr. - did not trust any Filipino enough to arm them; Batson had used the Macabebes as guides and interpreters earlier, and was convinced of Macabebe loyalty. The experiment proved successful, with the Macabebes fiercely loyal to their new masters. [The Macabebes were believed to be descendants of Mexican Yaqui Indians who were brought to the Philippines by Spain.]"[239]

Funston composed a "reinforcement company" for Aguinaldo composed of eighty-one Macabebe Scouts and four of his own officers including brothers Lt. Oliver P.M. Hazzard and Capt. Russell Hazzard both from the 11th Volunteer Cavalry, Lt. Burton J. Mitchell of the 40th Vol. Infantry and Capt. Harry W. Newton of the 34th Vol. Infantry. All of these units were part of the promoted Funston's new brigade.

Funston had taken command of his new brigade in December 1899, and, although already famous on an international scale, did not lose his pragmatic experience to egotism. Having fought with guerrillas in Cuba and against them in the Philippines, he surmised his plan to capture Aguinaldo might well end rebel resistance if he could sell it to his boss Maj. General Arthur MacArthur. As part of his "sell plan," he dispatched a native Filipino courier with a message to Aguinaldo written on the captured rebel stationery that help was on the way. He then informed MacArthur of what he had done and explained his plan in detail.

Although skeptical of success, MacArthur approved the plan but according to research provided by Richard Kolb,[240] MacArthur said to him: *"'Funston, this is a desperate undertaking. I feel I shall never see you again.' Funston remarked later, 'It was thoroughly understood we would never be taken alive.'"[241]*

---

239 Dumindin, "Philippine-American War, 1899-1902."
240 Kolb, "Blaze in the Boondocks, 2002. Fighting on America's Imperial Frontier in the Philippines, 1899-1913," 18-19.
241 Ibid.

Macabebe Scouts: Photo published in Harper's Weekly, Dec. 23, 1899. These pro-American Filipinos were nativesof Macabebe, Pampanga Province, in the central plains of Luzon Island. They had originally been loyal to Spain. Note bare feet on some of the Scouts above.[242]

242 Ibid.

It was a significantly long distance for Funston to get his party to Palanan. He shortened the march a little by using a Navy gunboat to land them about a hundred miles south of their target, but the expedition was in trouble from the start because of a lack of food supplies. As Richard Kolb noted:

"Funston's hope of obtaining provisions at a small coastal village proved fruitless. Still, they set off on a difficult, seven-day ordeal with only three days' rations.[243]

By the fifth day, Funston's party was in dire straits from exhaustion and hunger. Keeping up his wily approach to the rebel HQ, which was only about eight miles away, he sent a message to Aguinaldo for help, but under the guise of the rebel leader's requested troops and added an addendum to his message telling Aguinaldo that he had American prisoners. Aguinaldo, not recognizing the ruse, responded as well he should with the requested supplies, and added his own instructions to the relief party to take good care of the American prisoners.

Once Funston and the Macabebes reached the rebel's headquarters and surrounded the place, one volley of rifle fire with only two serious Filipino insurgent casualties was enough to break up the rest of the guards who fled in confusion. Taken completely by surprise Aguinaldo and his staff were flabbergasted. *"Aguinaldo could muster only the feeblest response: Is this not some kind of joke?"*[244] When told of the details of the plan by Funston himself, Aguinaldo said, *"Is there no limit to what you Americans can do?"*[245]

243 Kolb, "Blaze in the Boondocks, 2002. Fighting on America's Imperial Frontier in the Philippines, 1899-1913," 18-19.
244 Ibid,19.
245 Ibid.

The American officers who captured Aguinaldo. Brig.General Funston is 2nd from the right. The two look-alikes behind him are obviously the Hazzard brothers, 1st Lt. Oliver Hazzard in the middle and Capt. Russell Hazzard far right. Capt. Harry Newton is on the far left with 1st Lt. Burton Mitchell front left. Photo taken at Palanan, March 24, 1901.[246]

Filipino Macabebe Scout officers who led capture of Aguinaldo. L to R: Gregorio Cadhit, Cecilio Segismundo, Hilario Tal Placido, Dionisio Bato, and Lazaro Segovia. Photo taken at Palanan, March 24, 1901.[247]

246 Dumindin, "Philippine-American War, 1899-1902."
247 Ibid.

Today, most people would relish tactics of deception in warfare as long as it benefits their side, unlike the author of this Boston Globe article published in 1901.[248]

"Gen. Funston was also criticized for methods used to capture Aguinaldo. A "Boston Post" editorial in May 1902 said: 'When the capture of Aguinaldo by Funston was announced by cable, it was hailed as a great exploit. President McKinley lost no time in making him a brigadier-general. But, as the details have come to light, contempt and disgust have taken the place of admiration. The American people accepted, though not without some qualms of conscience, the forgery, treachery and disguise with which Funston prepared his expedition. But until recently the full infamy of his conduct has not been understood. The historian of his expedition, Edwin Wildman, thus describes the last stage of Funston's march: 'Over the stony declivities and through the thick jungle, across bridgeless streams and up narrow passes, the footsore and bone-racked adventurers tramped, until their food was exhausted and they were too weak to move, though but eight miles from Aguinaldo's rendezvous. A messenger was sent forward to inform Aguinaldo of their position and to beg for food. The rebel chieftain promptly replied by dispatching rice and a letter to the officer in command, instructing him to 'treat the American prisoners well.'

"This incident was passed over lightly in the earlier reports. Its full significance has just begun to dawn upon the American people."[249]

Besides the misleading description by the *Boston Globe* journalist and "historian" Edwin Wildman of Funston's message to Aguinaldo, another obvious error in the above posting is implied by President McKinley's losing no time in making Funston a Brigadier General, when, in fact, he had held that rank for three months before his expedition to pursue Aguinaldo.

Unfortunately, political correctness (read bias) in vilifying our military heroes is just as strong or worse today as it was in 1901. Mark C. Carnes, a professor of history from Barnard College, was quoted in an *American Heritage* publication in September 1998 calling

---

248 *A Virtual Museum of the City of San Francisco, http://www.sfmuseum. org/1906/funston.html.*
    249 *Ibid.*

Funston's actions outrageous and underhanded and implied they were shameful.

On the other hand, Aguinaldo himself *"characterized Funston's plan as 'brilliant' and carried out with 'the greatest cleverness'. He stated: 'It was a bold plan, executed with skill and cleverness In the face of difficulties which, to most men would have seemed insurmountable.' He readily admitted, 'We have been treated with the highest consideration by our captors.'"*[250]

LEFT to RIGHT: Col. Simeon Villa, President Emilio Aguinaldo, Brig. Gen. Frederick Funston, and Dr. Santiago Barcelona. Funston, at 5'4" (162.6 cm), was an inch taller than Aguinaldo (160 cm). Photo taken at Palanan, March 24, 1901.[251]

Other capable researchers like Brian McAllister Linn[252] point out that Funston
- Waged a successful pacification campaign by including key elements of the population in their own defense.
- Although a vocal advocate for severe repression, his actual conduct was characterized by lenient terms of surrender, collaboration rewards, and personal friendships.
- Used large payments or bribes for vital information.

---

250 Kolb, "Blaze in the Boondocks, 2002. Fighting on America's Imperial Frontier in the Philippines, 1899-1913," 19.

251 Dumindin, "Philippine-American War, 1899-1902."

252 Brian McAllister Linn, The U.S. Army and Counterinsurgency in the Philippine.

- Made good use of locally raised Ilocano Scouts, originally recruited by Lyman Kennon, commander of the 34th Infantry.
- Protested the mistreatment of Filipino civilians by US soldiers from other districts.
- By conducting operations that left the native population relatively unaffected but targeted insurgents he was able to pacify the Fourth District in just over a year.

There is no doubt though that Funston, on occasion, used harsh methods. On one occasion, when one of his soldiers was killed by bolo men in front of witnesses who refused to give information, he allowed the burning down of a witness's house. He was also less tolerant of the insurgents themselves or of people he suspected of aiding them.[253] On another occasion he caught insurgents red handed about to murder two of his Macabebe Scouts. He had them hanged on the spot. The problem was that the native population was being intimidated and taxed by the guerrillas who did not hesitate to kill people and destroy property to get their way. The guerrilla commander in NE Luzon that caused the most trouble was General Urbano Lacuna, who, after the failure of multiple attacks on the Americans, resorted to tactics of assassinations and property destruction on his own people. He even attempted the destruction of the entire town of Jaen, whose inhabitants were suspected of aiding the Yanks.

In the long run, however, Funston's approach proved successful; especially after several of the opposition leaders surrendered on Funston's lenient terms both before and especially after Aguinaldo was captured, Aguinaldo then urged the end of hostilities with this statement: *"The country has declared unmistakably in favor of peace; so be it. Enough of blood, enough of tears and desolation. This wish cannot be ignored by the men still in arms if they are animated by no other desire than to serve this noble people which has clearly manifested its will.*

"So also do I respect this will now that it is known to me, and after mature deliberation resolutely proclaim to the world that I cannot refuse to heed the voice of a people longing for peace, nor the lamentations of thousands of families yearning to see their dear ones in the enjoyment of the liberty promised by the generosity of the great American nation.

---

253 *Ibid.*

"By acknowledging and accepting the sovereignty of the United States throughout the entire Archipelago, as I now do without any reservations whatsoever, I believe that I am serving thee, my beloved country. May happiness be thine!"[254]

Aguinaldo lived fairly well in retirement on his family inheritance and continued to pursue his goal of an independent Philippines. In 1935, when the Philippine Commonwealth was established in preparation for independence, he ran for president but was soundly defeated by Manuel L. Quezon. Ironically, the sons of both Funston and Aguinaldo entered the United States Military Academy at West Point at the same time in 1923, although apparently Emilio Aguinaldo, Jr. did not graduate.

Frederick Funston, Jr., son of the general, shakes hands with Emilio Aguinaldo, Jr., son of the first Philippine President, at the United States Military Academy, West Point, New York, 1923.[255]

254 Dumindin, "Philippine-American War, 1899-1902."
255 Ibid.

Historian Dumindin continues: *"After the Americans retook the Philippines in 1945, Aguinaldo (senior) was arrested and accused of collaboration with the Japanese. He was held in Bilibid prison for months until released by presidential amnesty from President Manuel Roxas. In his trial, it was determined that his broadcasts and cooperation were made under great duress (the Japanese had threatened to murder his entire family), and his name was cleared."*[256]

Emilio Aguinaldo Sr. was born in Kawit, Cavite, on March 22, 1869. He lived a long life, actually outliving all the generals he opposed in the Philippine-American war. His first wife died in 1921. He remarried at age sixty-one in 1930. In 1935, when the Philippine Commonwealth was established in preparation for independence, he ran for president but was soundly defeated by Manuel L. Quezon.

He lived to see his goal of independence for the Philippines achieved in 1946 and did not die until February 6, 1964 at the age of ninety-four, outliving his second wife as well. One of his favorite moments occurred when the date of the official Independence Day for the Philippines was changed from July 4th to June 12th, the day he proclaimed independence for his country in 1898. His remains are buried at the Aguinaldo Shrine in Kawit, Cavite Province.

Fighting Fred Funston became a career officer and rose to the rank of Major General. In the early 1900's his subordinates included Lieutenant Dwight D. Eisenhower, Lieutenant George S. Patton, Jr., Captain Douglas MacArthur, and Brigadier General John J. Pershing. In 1917, he was on schedule to command the US Forces and the American Expedition Forces in WW I when he had a massive heart attack and died in San Antonio on February 19, 1917. He is buried in the Presidio's San Francisco National Cemetery. His place in the history of WWI was fulfilled by General John (Black Jack) Pershing.

---

256 *Ibid.*

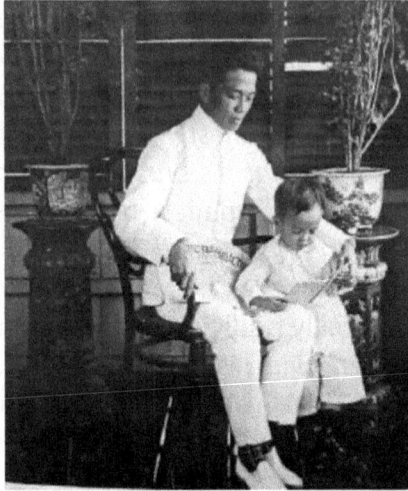

Aguinaldo with his son Emilio Jr. in 1906.[257]

Major General Frederick Funston[258]

257 Dumindin, "Philippine-American War, 1899-1902."
258 Ibid.

CHAPTER EIGHTEEN

Luzon Philippines August 1901

"War is the only game in which it doesn't pay to have the home-court advantage." –Dick Motta

A constabulary is by definition a body of officers of the peace organized on a military basis.[259] The Macabebe Scouts and the Ilocano Scouts so well utilized by General Funston and Colonel Lyman Kennon in Luzon in 1901 became the foundation of a new military police force established on 8 August 1901, by the Philippine Commission. Act number 175 of the Commission established the Philippine Constabulary to maintain law and order in the various provinces of the Philippines and by the end of 1901, 189 officers of the new organization had been commissioned.

The presence of native scout units in the Philippines during the Philippine-American War was nothing new. The *em.esber blog*[260] points out that when the Islands were a Spanish Royal Colony there were some 43,000 Spanish officials, military units, and constabulary forces in the islands along with about 18,000 Spanish soldiers not including additional Filipino recruits in service of King and Country.

Utilization of Native Scout units was not a new phenomenon with the U.S. Army either. Use of American Indian Scouts dates to before the revolution and there are multiple sources to document other use

259 http://dictionary.reference.com/.
260 http://www.army.mil/-news/2010/06/06/40345-macabebes-and-moros.

of indigenous inhabitants in counter insurgency policies throughout the Army's history.

In the Philippine War situation some confusion may exist concerning the Macabebe Scouts, the Ilocano Scouts, the Philippine Scouts, the Philippine Constabulary, the Moro Constabulary, the Philippine Cavalry, and possibly other units.

The Macabebe Scouts were originally hired by the Army as mercenaries in September 1899 on a three month trial basis, with 1st. Lieutenant Matthew Batson as their leader. Batson had proposed the formation of the native force when he realized the natives could navigate the waters of the provinces in their canoes much quicker than could the Americans marching through inhospitable terrain. They soon proved their worth after General Lawton's approval of Batson's proposal, and by October 20th, Batson had formed three additional companies. Four other Macabebe companies were created in the next two years, besides the Ilocano, other tribes including the Cagayano, Boholano, Cebuano, Negrense, and Ilonggo provided companies that were formed and added to the force.

The *Ilocano (also called the Iloco) Scouts* were also natives of northern Luzon who were friendly to the Yanks. They were also easy to recruit because they had an innate disgust with Filipino Tagalogs who dominated Aguinaldo's insurgent forces (the PRG) and who had murdered one of their popular businessmen, Francisco Madrid.

All of the groups were structured like American companies with the additional rank of 3rd lieutenant to accommodate recruited American non-coms and privates who became officers of the new companies. Officers and men alike were paid at half the rate of the American soldiers. Both of the two major groups would evolve into the *Philippine Scouts*, an official auxiliary of the U.S. Army, and personnel from both would also form the foundation of the *Philippine Constabulary*.

Once the success of the *Philippine Constabulary* was established as a rapid response force who could travel light and fast to quell any outlaw uprising, even General Leonard Wood encouraged recruitment of a *Moro Constabulary*, composed of Islamic constables whom he could usurp to supplement his ground forces. Only two *Moro Companies of the Philippine Constabulary* were ever formed.

The Philippine Cavalry was a term used to identify *Philippine Scouts* organized or recruited by dismounted cavalry units, but is also a term used to identify *U.S. Volunteer Cavalry* units who served in the war.

The Army Military-News [261] further clarified the role of the Philippine Constabulary: *"The Civil Governor, William Howard Taft, (approved funds) to maintain the Philippine Constabulary as a paramilitary police force to complete the pacification of the islands. Captain Henry T. Allen of the 6th U.S. Cavalry, a Kentucky-born graduate of West Point (Class 1882) was named as the chief of the force, and was later dubbed as the 'Father of the Philippine Constabulary.' With the help of four other army officers, Captains David Baker, W. Goldsborough, H. Atkinson, and J.S. Garwood, Captain Allen organized the force, trained, equipped and armed the men as best as could be done under the most difficult conditions prevailing at the time. Although (the) bulk of the officers were recruited from among volunteers from among U.S. commissioned and noncommissioned officers, two Filipinos qualified for appointment as 3rd Lieutenants during the first month of the PC, - Jose Velasquez of Nueva Ecija and Felix Llorente of Manila. Llorente retired as Colonel in 1921 while Velasquez retired as Major in 1927."* [262]

---

261 Ibid.
262 Ibid.

1st Lt. Matthew Batson, right, and two of his newly recruited Macabebe Scouts in 1899.[263]

Macabebe Scouts patrolling Rio Grande de Pampanga 1899[264]

263 Dumindin, "Philippine-American War, 1899-1902."
264 Ibid.

Recruiting Macabebes was so popular with the natives that they gathered in crowds like the above to enlist in the Scouts. Original title: "Throng of Macabebes awaiting enlistment into the United States Army, Macabebe, P.I. (photo taken in 1900)."[265]

The Macabebes also had a role in the defeat of the Moro Rebellion. The Moro tribes occupied southern territories comprising over ninety-five occupied islands in Luzon, Visayas, and Mindanao. An article in *Army-Military News* on June 6, 2010, referred to the Islamic Philippine Moros this way:

_____
265 Ibid.

"They were expert in guerilla warfare, and considered the fiercest of all Philippine inhabitants with a tradition of jihad against anyone trying to rule them. The Moros fought with any weapon available – flintlocks, Mausers, Krags, kris, spears, and bolo knives. Relations between Moros and Americans were positive initially, but they eventually deteriorated, and several more skirmishes ensued. Documented accounts describe the Moros as being equipped only with spears and knives which were ineffective against the modern weapons of the Americans. The absence of Moro possession of firearms was due to the successful confiscation of arms by the Macabebe Scouts during previous periods of peace, a task only possible by groups who would not stir ethnic rivalries and had knowledge of the local geography. '...Capt. Batson had told the men that he would publish each month the names of the men who had captured guns or bolos from the insurrectos."'[266]

After the Philippine-American War, the some of the Macabebes were converted or enlisted in the Philippine Scouts an official unit of the U.S. Army and continued to serve with distinction into WWII. Many of the Scouts transferred also into the Philippine Constabulary, and, in 1904, a special subunit of this organization, which was *"the main authority responsible for the day-to-day regional law and order outside of Moroland"*[267] was established in Moro Province. The new subunit was made up of Islamic Constables, some Islamic officers and some Europeans and Americans. Those that stayed loyal to the *Moro Constabulary* would prove to be effective law enforcement officers.

266 http://www.army.mil/-news/2010/06/06/40345-macabebes-and-moros.
267 Fulton, MOROLAND 1899-1906.

Two Philippine Scouts likely from the 51st or 52nd Moro Company. The Photograph most likely taken after 1911, since the headgear was issued after that time –Fulton Personal Correspondence

CHAPTER NINETEEN

The Islands of Mindanao & Samar, Philippines, August 11 – September 30, 1901

"You can't make war against terror. Terror is a technique of battle." –John le Carré

The Island of Mindanao was and is different in population distribution from the rest of the Philippines. The northern islands dominated by Luzon were primarily Christian, and the southern islands (the Sulus) were almost 100% Muslim. Mindanao's population was mixed with Muslims dominating in the west and Christians dominating in the east. Thus, there was support for Aguinaldos's Insurrectionists, the PRG (Philippine Revolutionary Group), in the Christian dominated east, but, when Aguinaldo was captured, just a few days after the principle rebel on Mindanao, General Capistrano, had surrendered, revolutionary activity on Mindanao was essentially ended.

On 29 January 1900, the Americans had their first hostile encounter with Moro thieves. Five members of Company H of the 23rd Infantry were attacked on the Island of Tawi-Tawi during a mapping expedition and some rifles stolen. Ten Moro bandits were caught and executed for that episode

On 29 April 1901, another Moro bandit, Datu (Chief) Amirul and twenty-six of his men got into a firefight with members of the 31st Volunteer Infantry and about 100 Maguindanaos who accompanied the Army. Amirul and all of his men were killed. No American casualties.

On 26 September 1901 at Sugat-Paran-Paran, Mindanao, a patrol of thirty-two men of Company I, 17th Infantry Regiment, was attacked by Moro tribesmen. It was the Americans' third encounter with these fierce warriors and they were lucky to escape without any killed in action. Eleven Moros were reported KIA.[268] Two days later, on September 28th, on the Island of Samar, a battle erupted that would change the whole outlook of the Philippine-American War. It resulted in a huge uproar in the USA, after the public learned of the circumstances of events that killed forty-five Americans and wounded another twenty-two. A series of atrocities on both sides, initiated by the Filipinos, along with a scorched earth policy of revenge by the angry Americans would ruin the careers of commanding officers, escalate events of conflict, prolong the war, and change the political atmosphere at home. It became known as the Balangiga Massacre.

---

268 Kolb, "Blaze in the Boondocks, 2002. Fighting on America's Imperial Frontier in the Philippines, 1899-1913."

It should be made clear that the Balangiga Massacre, however, was not initiated by Moros or radical Islamists, but rather by native

Filipinos. Even though the revolutionist movement was on its last legs, there was still guerrilla activity on Samar, and according to Dumindin two of the revolutionaries, Capt. Eugenio Daza and Sgt. Pedro Duran, Sr., under command of General Lukban, who masterminded the attack at Cubig, were assisting the local police chief, Valeriano Abanador, in a plan to attack the Americans. Lukban, however, was apparently not involved directly, but Prof. Rolando Borrinaga, in reviewing his own book published by the University of the Philippines Manila, 2003, had this to say about Lukban's influence: *"Indeed, it was the very threat of punitive action from Lukban's guerrillas on the Balangiga officials and residents that apparently hastened the end of the peaceful coexistence between Company C and the local community. It triggered an unfortunate series of events that led to the forced detention of the male residents, the confiscation from their houses of all the sharp bolos, and the confiscation and destruction of the stored rice of the local population."*[269]

It is also possible that harsh treatment of natives by one or two Americans may have triggered the violent uprising. Historian Arnaldo Dumindin explains: *"Tensions rose when on September 22, at a tuba (native wine) store, two drunken American soldiers tried to molest the girl tending the store. The girl was rescued by her two brothers, who mauled the soldiers. In retaliation, the Company Commander, Capt. Thomas W. Connell, West Point class of 1894, rounded up 143 male residents for forced labor to clean up the town in preparation for an official visit by his superior officers. They were detained overnight without food under two conical Sibley tents in the town plaza, each of which could only accommodate 16 persons; 78 of the detainees remained the next morning, after 65 others were released due to age and physical infirmity. Finally, Connell ordered the confiscation from their houses of all sharp bolos, and the confiscation and destruction of stored rice. Feeling aggrieved, the townspeople plotted to attack the U.S. Army garrison."*[270]

The viewpoint from the American side differs. Captain Thomas W. Connell, commander of Company C, 9th infantry regiment was concerned about the health hazards of accumulating garbage in the

---

269 Rolando O. Borrinaga, "Revisiting the Balangiga Conflict," *Philippine Daily Inquirer*, 3/15/03.

270 Dumindin, "Philippine-American War, 1899-1902."

village of Balangiga, a town of about 3300 people. He conscripted locals to clean up the mess and intended to hold them in tents until the job was done. Those drafted for the job were said to be tax delinquents and some of those were apparently Daza, the guerrilla leader's men.[271] There is no apparent evidence, in American records at least, of the wine store incident and the conscription of labor *for retaliation* of such an incident is supposition. None the less there is evidence supporting the feelings of nervous tension of both the natives and the American troops.

Balangiga Mayor Pedro Abayan sometime before, probably in the spring about the time of the Catubig siege, had written to the "General-in-Chief of Samar," presumably General Vicente Lukban, and is quoted as follows: *"We have agreed to a fictitious policy with them (the Americans) doing whatever they like, and when the occasion comes the people will strategically rise up against them."*[272]

The Americans, of Company C were veterans, many of them recently returned from China's Boxer rebellion. Others had fought in Cuba and more recently in Luzon. They were aware of the episode at Catubig and were wary of the locals in spite of having socialized and played baseball with them. One of the American sergeants, Frank Betron, and a native woman church leader, Casiana "Geronima" Nacionales, were said to be romantically linked.

The next sequence of events* is not exactly recorded, but is compatible with known records and research by two notable, historians, Bob Couttie,[273] a British writer of impeccable research and Prof. Roland Borrinaga,[274][275] a noted Philippine expert on Balangiga.

When Company C first occupied Balangiga on 11 August 1901, Sgt. Frank Betron was one of the first to notice the attractive lady with

271 Kolb, "Blaze in the Boondocks, 2002. Fighting on America's Imperial Frontier in the Philippines, 1899-1913."

272 Ibid, 21-22.

273 Bob Couttie, Hang The Dogs The True Tragic History of the Balangiga Massacre, New Day Publishers, Quezon City, 2004.

274 Borrinaga, "Revisiting the Balangiga Conflict."

275 Rolando O. Borrinaga, The Human Cost of Wars in Leyte and Samar, Symposium of the College Department of the Sacred Heart Seminary in Palo, Leyte, on 2/25/2000.

the long black hair hanging clothes to dry outside of a bamboo dwelling across the street from his *nipa* (also bamboo with a thatched roof made of leaves from the nipa palm) hut barracks, which had been donated for American troop quarters by the Salazars,* a local wealthy family. Little did he know at that moment of instant attraction how deeply his life would be affected by this vision of loveliness. He shrugged off his feelings of the moment and continued moving his belongings and equipment from the hired pack carabao, to a pile on the ground, where later as the NCO in charge, he would have his men move it into the barracks.

Fate, however, would not let go and he was quickly reminded of the lovely lady when one of his men, Pvt. G. E. Meyers,** a musician bugler who would eventually become a dentist in Chicago, let out a wolf whistle and exclaimed, "Would you look at that!"

Betron couldn't help but look along with everyone else as the beautiful lady demurely glanced their way, smiled and with a flick of her long black hair and a very feminine shift of her hips, grabbed her clothes basket and retreated into her house. Her name was Casiana Nacionales, called *Geronima* a feminine variant of Geronamo or Jerome, meaning a sacred name or a "saint." She had earned the name because of her church work as a Roman Catholic lay prayer leader in the village of Balangiga.

Sgt. Frank Betron, tall dark and handsome with a distinctive widow's peak hairline, was a native of Albany, New York and was orphaned at an early age. He had survived due to the generosity of relatives and an innate desire to succeed. Along the way Betron had also been exposed to a Christian philosophy different than most which would make him stand out amongst all of the other soldiers in the eyes of Geronima.

The romance is fact. The details are not and would likely be more favored by Prof Borrinaga than by Couttie.

**There is some confusion about Meyers' quarters. On pg.115 (Coutie- Hang the Dogs) Meyers is said to be in the Salzar house with Betron and on pg 307 he is with Betron in the Belaez house nipa hut barracks .Chances are the Salazar house is correct. Confusion persists as recorded in Coutie's book, in which later testimony refers to the Betron/Belaez house and the Markley/Salazar house.*

It wasn't long before they met that very afternoon. Just about the time that Betron was finishing up with supervising the unloading and transfer of equipment, he noticed Geronima carrying a load of clothes from her clothesline to her house, and as she struggled to open the door while trying to hold the basket at the same time he rushed to help.

"Here let me help you with that," he said, holding open the door for her.

"Gracias, señor," Geronima replied and then added, "I can speak some English."

"That's good," Betron said, "because except for *como se llama usted and como est`a, Yo hablo muy poco castellano.*" (except for what's your name and how are you I speak very little Spanish).

"That's very good, señor. I understood you. Understand is *entiendo* in Spanish. Perhaps we can teach each other?" she said raising her voice like a question, "and my name is Casiana, but most people call me Geronima."

"I would like that," Betron said, "and *mi llama es Frank.*"

"Ah," she said, "I will call you Francisco." And so it began. In spite of the strict mores of the times and a *no fraternization policy* of the U.S. Army, some days later she would call him *'mi amor'*.

Artist's Impressions of: Sergeant Frank Betron 1901 Casiana Nacionales 1901

Sunday September 1, 1901

Geronima was related to the town chief of police, Valeriano Abanador, through the Salazar family who along with the afore-mentioned guerrillas Capt. Eugenio Daza (also a Salazar relative) and Sgt. Pedro Duran Sr. were to become the major plotters in the *Balangiga Conflict or Encounter*, which are two of the current politi-cally correct terms as proposed by Rolando O. Borrinaga for the bat-tle that occurred that September day in 1901.

Abanador got wind of the passionate romance between the new lovers and immediately thought he might be able to take advantage of it. He didn't know when or how, but he knew the revolution was still alive on Samar, and his two friends Daza and Duran were involved and his sympathies lay in that direction. At the first opportunity Abanador, when he saw his cousin in church, approached her after the Mass.

"Say, Geronima, how's my cousin?" Abanador asked as he approached.

"Well, well, look who's at early mass!" Geronima exclaimed as she turned to him with a broad grin.

"I'm not as much of a heathen as your mother thinks," laughed Abanador, referring to his own mother's sister.

"I'm not so sure," replied Geronima, "but it's good to see you."

"Good to see you, too. Have you got a minute? I want to discuss something with you."

"Anything for my favorite cousin," she replied.

At this point, Abanador was feeling a little trepidation. He didn't want to let on that he knew about his relative's affair, but he wanted to gather some critical intelligence about the American's daily rou-tines because he knew there was going to be a confrontation with the foreign occupiers of his homeland, and he wanted to have the advantage when it happened.

"Walk with me a little and I will tell you a story and of my concerns."

Then, with great care and delicacy, he proceeded to explain his side of the siege of Catubig, which he had no doubt obtained second hand via General Vicente Lukban's subordinates Duran and Daza who were his close friends. He emphasized the part where the Yankees were going to confiscate the rice crop in the Catubig Valley and that the disaster was only prevented by the preemptive attack on the Americans. He elaborated about how the locals in Catubig had prayed fervently for success before they attacked the American soldiers and then said that he had information that Company C was going to get orders to confiscate not only the stored rice reserves, but all weapons in the town and surrounding villages as well. He told Geronima that he and his friends had no intention of starting any trouble but that they felt they had to start stockpiling and hiding weapons just in case. He then asked if she had any suggestions how they could do that without offending the Americans or precipitating trouble.

Although horrified by the possibility of a disaster like Catubig involving people she loved on both sides of a potential conflict, Geronima agreed to find out what she could for her cousin and promised to see him in a day or two.

One anonymous blogger on the internet had this to say: *"Notably, the 1901 Balangiga incident was an unusual historical upheaval for a community generally known to be reserved and peaceable. Understanding the deeper motives and meanings behind this violent phenomenon needs a particular kind of sensitivity to the accumulated history, customs, and conditions arising in Balangiga around this period- a sensitivity that eluded the Americans at that time; and which may have accounted for the people's deadly hostility toward them."*[276]

The author of the above paragraph noted that people of the town *"rallied around the symbols that pertained to their sense of community,"*[277] which included amulets of their religion, their devotion to Saint Miguel, and their sacred church bells. Police chief Valeriano Abanador, Geronima's cousin, was said to have worn an amulet for protection around his neck. According to local legend the amulet, known as an *anting-anting,* had certain restrictions, and Abanador had to swear to remain single or else find someone else who would accept the amulet with that and other apparently secret restrictions. Otherwise, if he wanted to marry, he had to destroy it if he couldn't find someone to accept the limitations.

---

276 *BORONGAN registered blogger, http://www.skyscrapercity.com.*
277 *Ibid.*

Obviously, then, the people of Balangiga and the surrounding villages of Lawaan, Giporlos, and Quinapundan, villages which were also served by the priest from Balangiga were all motivated by similar thinking, so one can imagine the conflicted emotions Geronima must have been feeling after her meeting with her cousin Valeriano. Thus when Betron knocked and entered her family home that Sunday evening he found her weeping in her living room.

Unable to console her or find out what the trouble was, he finally left in frustration and returned to his barracks across the street. It would be several days before he saw her again.

* * *

Friday, September 6, 1901

Valeriano Abanador, Capt. (some sources say Major) Eugenio Daza, Sgt. Pedro Duran, Sr., and Geronima were meeting in the police chief's office; it was about 11:00 AM. Geronima had the floor.

"You promise me, Val, that you fellows are not going to start anything, right?" she said, looking her cousin in the eyes.

"We won't, Geronima, unless they start it first." In his and the others' minds, the Americans had already started it just by being there.

"All right, then. If you want to stockpile your weapons, I will help you. The best place to store them is in the church. I know the cleaning ladies there, and they will put them in some storage closets that the priest never uses. Have each of your people bring one of the smaller weapons that they can hide in their clothes to church next Sunday. I will stand by the door after the service, just have them say 'donde,' ? (where?), and I will tell them where to go. Someone will be there to receive the weapon and put it away."

"What about the the rifles, spears, and big bolos?" asked Pedro Duran. "We can't just walk them into church and the Americans have sentries out at night."

"I can carry some underneath my long skirt. As for the rifles, there is a funeral tomorrow. If you can get some of them to the mortician or coffin maker, they can be hidden easily and carried into the church. You can repeat that every time there is a funeral."

"It's a start," said Capt. Daza.

"Sí, es un comienzo (yes, it's a start)," agreed Valeriano Abanador.

* * *

Sunday, September 22, 1901

Unbeknownst to Geronima back in July, Pedro Abayan, the mayor or *presidente* of Balangiga, had written to the commanding general in Manila (General Adna Chaffee had just relieved MacArthur when the communication was received) requesting protection against *insurrectos* and Moro pirates.[278] The real purpose, however, according to Prof. Reynaldo H. Imperial[279*] of the University of the Philippines, Manila, was to divert their suspicions and keep the plan of an attack secret from the Americans.

Since it was the American's policy to garrison the towns of Samar to prevent insurgency as well as piracy, the request was immediately granted, which was why Company C was there. Geronima had no idea her cousin was actually a pawn of General Lukban's plan to continue the revolution on Samar.

As a result, Geronima's true innocence of any devilish plot against the Americans showed through in dealings with her new love for *Francisco* Betron, and they continued to delight in each other's company. Geronima had heard rumors of piggish behavior by two American soldiers the night before at a local *tuba* (wine) store, and she asked her *amor* about it.

Historical records of interviews differ as to what actually happened. In one instance (Dumindin's version[280]), the soldiers were drunk and tried to molest the store attendant, Catalina Catalon; in another (Imperial's version[281]), the soldiers got angry when Catalina

---

278 Reynaldo H. Imperial, *Balangiga and After UP-CDS Chronicle 3.2, 1998.*

279* Prof Imperial was relating his personal interview on April 7, 1981, with Juliana Abanador, a descendent of the Abanador family. This paper was first presented during the Balangiga Roundtable Conference held on November 27-28, 1998 held at CAP Building, UP Tacloban, co-sponsored by the UP-CIDS, National Commission for Culture and the Arts, and UP Visayas Leyte-Samar Heritage Center.

280 Dumindin, "Philippine-American War, 1899-1902."

281 Imperial, *Balangiga and After.*

laughed at everything they said, thought she was mocking them, although she understood no English, and were about to drag her away when her two brothers intervened. Both versions agreed that the brothers got the best of the soldiers, who returned to the barracks licking their wounds.

Frank Betron told Geronima that he had heard there was trouble involving a couple of the soldiers in Sgt. George Markley's squad who were quartered in the Belaez house, one of the other *nipa* (bamboo) barracks across the street, but he had no details of the incident. There was no doubt, however, that whatever happened at the *tuba* store raised tensions and resentment against the Americans. Feelings and emotions amongst the natives were about to get worse.

Company C's commanding officer was 1894 West Point graduate Captain Thomas Connell. He had been with the 9th Infantry Regiment since Cuba and had also served in China and Luzon. According to Professor Imperial[282] Connell applied McKinley's policy of benevolent assimilation with good intentions at least in the beginning. This benevolent attitude was exemplified by the fact that one of Connell's first acts was to tell his surgeon, Major Richard Groswold, to set up his hospital in the town's municipal building and get ready to serve both the company and the townspeople.

Connell had no idea on that particular Sunday that things would deteriorate to the point that he, Dr. Groswold, and 1st Lieutenant Edward Bumpus, the only other commissioned officers of the garrison, would be among the first to be slaughtered one week to the day. He also had no idea his death would be a certainty once General Chafee's office had approved mayor Pedro Abayan's request for "protection." Neither did Casiana "Geronima" Nacionales.

* * *

Tuesday, September 24, 1901

Captain Connell's major concern when he first saw the town was two-fold. One was the closeness of rainforest-like vegetation so close to the town as to be a security concern for his troops and the second

---

282 *Ibid.*

was the accumulation of garbage both in the streets and under the *nipa* huts.

At first, he ordered that all men over the age of eighteen should help with the clean-up. That went over like a lead balloon and was ignored by the natives, even though the order was posted on every corner.

Next, after he had noted the defiance of the locals and watched them lazily spending time in the local shops, he went to see Valeriano Abanador and asked him to provide a list of delinquents and other assorted lackluster individuals who the chief of police thought might benefit themselves and the town from a work detail. Abanador gave him a few names, but not nearly enough so Connell had his troops round up over 100 of the native men and put them to work under guard. Things definitely went downhill from there. Forced labor and the confinement of the workforce in tents too small to house them comfortably played right into the hands of the guerrillas' desire to work the populace into an angry mob.

The Balangiganons had paid taxes collected by the chief of police and his cohorts, but much of the populace, including Geronima, had no idea that a lot of the money was going directly to guerrilla leader Lukban to support the revolution. It was ironic that those tax dodgers on the list, provided by Abanador, were amongst those confined to the hard labor force to clean up the town. Prof. Imperial indicated the amount paid to the revolutionary government (Aguinaldo-Lukban) for taxes amounted to *"P532.00"*in October 1899.[283]

* * *

Thursday, September 26, 1901

It was after nightfall that evening, and Sgt. Frank Betron was holding the voluptuous Geronima in comforting embrace. She was worried.

"What's going to happen to us, *mi Francisco*?" she asked.

"Nothing bad, I hope," replied Betron. "I'm thinking of getting my discharge here in the Philippines, and maybe settling down. I'm pretty

---

283 *Ibid.*

good with machines and I think I could make a living. Would that be alright with you?"

"Oh, *mi amor*, that would be wonderful!" she said, "but I'm worried. The priest, Father Guimbaolibot, is taking a lot of the women and children over to Leyte tomorrow night."

"What for?" asked Betron.

"He says for a holiday, but I think he knows something and the tension in town is awful. Besides that he is holding a big prayer session tomorrow just for men as far as I can tell."

Geronima couldn't bring herself to tell him about the weapons or her part in hiding them. It would be nearly a day and a half before she would reveal to him what she knew.

Betron thought about it for a while, then reassuring her as best he could, excused himself, and headed out to talk to Lt. Bumpus. After hearing Betron's tale of concern, Bumpus said he would pass the information to Captain Connell. That was the last the sergeant heard of it until he was awakened some thirty-two hours later by the *nipa* hut's guard, **Pvt. George Meyers**. It was close to five in the morning.

* * *

Friday, September 27, 1901

It was the third day of heavy forced labor for the natives. Because of the crowded conditions in the tents where the conscripted laborers were held overnight about half of them had been sent home. A detained labor force of somewhere between seventy and eighty men was held in the tents. The labor force went to work at 6:00 AM after a light breakfast brought by family or loved ones. Ten other prisoners, each accompanied by an American guard, were sent to collect weapons within the town and from the adjacent barrio communities of Sabang, Burabon, **Lawaan, Giporlos**, and Quinapundan.

According to Professor Imperial, four sacks of weapons were collected from Sabang alone, but he didn't elaborate on the size of the sacks. These were apparently taken to the Convent, which was occupied by Company C's three officers and which also served as the company store. U.S guards and quartermaster's kept track of the weapons while cleanup continued in the town.

Geronima was up early and on her way to her cousin's office at police headquarters. A meeting had been called by the local guerrilla leader, Captain Daza, and Geronima had been included. This was the second of two meetings Daza had called. He had previously planned details of the upcoming attack with volunteers from the surrounding barrio communities and started stockpiling the weapons, which were mostly bolo knives newly made by local blacksmiths. Geronima was needed to get the weapons to the church. Under peer pressure from her cousin and the conspirators she could not refuse without arousing their suspicion, but Valeriano Abanador was a step ahead of her.

After they had devised a plan to use one or more real infant corpses in a funeral procession to the church the implications of what was about to happen would be clear to Abanador's cousin Geronima. She would know there were weapons in the caskets. For that reason, Abanador planned to keep her incommunicado for the rest of the day and night to prevent her from warning her Yankee lover. He was partially successful.

The plan was simple but required good timing and deception. The deception started that morning when a column of men dressed as women led a large funeral procession from the edge of town to the church. There were half a dozen coffins in the procession. The participants knew they would be challenged by the American guards, so they made sure there were bodies in the first two coffins. Large homemade dolls covered the weapons in the rest of the coffins, and the dolls were also covered with blankets to which some rotting animal flesh had been had been added. The odor was unmistakable.

When Private Henry W. Manire, who was on guard duty in town center that day, challenged the procession, one of the Filipino men dressed as a woman silently uncovered a body containing casket and said in a high voice, "*cholera.*" The sergeant NCO in charge, Sergeant Scharer, who was closest to the uncovered casket, then waved the rest of the column on. There were enough weapons in the procession to arm half of the 180[284] or so attackers of the next day.

_____
284 *Dumindin says "about 500 men in seven attack units."*

Captain Eugenio Daza [285]

Saturday, September 28, 1901

It was almost 5:00 AM on the feast day of St. Michael the Archangel in 1901, and sunrise wasn't until 5:33 AM. Geronima peeked out from under the thin blanket covering her slender body as she lay on a bunk in a room that served as a jail cell with an open door in her cousin's offices in Balangiga's town center. The Filipino guard was snoring as he slept in his chair near the door. Geronima had waited all night for the guard to relax his vigil so she could slip away without notice and it looked as if this was going to be the opportunity to do so. She had had to promise her cousin not to leave the premises until morning after he let her know that he knew about her affair with Sgt. Betron, and told her that Lukban's guerrillas would kill her if she betrayed them.

285 Dumindin, "Philippine-American War, 1899-1902."

Carrying her slippers in one hand she tiptoed past the guard and out the door. The guard was still snoring when she left. It was just starting to get light when she arrived in front of her house and her *amor's nipa* hut barracks. It was about two minutes to five when she convinced the *nipa* hut guard, Pvt. Meyers, to wake Sgt. Betron. It was another five minutes before Pvt. Meyers returned to his post and another ten minutes after that that Betron appeared fully dressed for the day. The mess was already serving breakfast to the change of guards when the bugler, who was also the *nipa* hut guard, musician George E. Meyers, sounded reveille.

When finally, after Betron had gotten Geronima out of Pvt. Meyers' earshot and had gotten her story out between sobs, it was already a quarter to six and full daylight. He left her house after a quick but passionate kiss and headed for the convent where Captain Connell, Lt. Bumpus, and the surgeon, Major Groswold, were quartered. He moved as fast as he dared without alarming any observers. By the time he had accosted Lieutenant Bumpus and gotten his permission to wake Captain Connell it was almost 6:00 AM. When Betron finally got to talk to Captain Connell, who was trying to awake after a long previous day on a sortie looking for insurgents, he had less than forty-five minutes to convince his commanding officer of the seriousness of what he had learned. He didn't know that at the time, however, since Geronima had not been privy to the attack timetable.

Captain Connell, who besides not having enough sleep was also grumpy due to the fact that news of President McKinley's assassination and death two weeks earlier had finally reached him the night before and he was worried about how that might affect his assignment.

"What's so damn important, Sergeant Betron, that you have to wake me before breakfast?" asked the Captain.

"Sir, we may have a serious problem. I just heard from a native friend of mine that the gugus we have penned up in the tents are going to break out and attack us. They are supposed to have some weapons stockpiled in the church."

"Who did you hear that from, Sergeant? Was it that nice looking lady friend of yours I've been hearing about?"

"Yes, Sir," Betron said, starting to blush because he knew Captain Connell had followed Army policy by posting the non-fraternization rules.

"Well, Sergeant, I think I know you well enough to be concerned if you are," Connell said, switching back to his normal accommodating personality. "We'll talk about your fraternization later. What do you recommend?"

"Sir, I suggest we send a search party to the church to start with, and keep the troops armed at all times."

"Good ideas, Sergeant," said Connell. "Have some breakfast and then make it happen. If they haven't started anything by now, it isn't going to happen this morning. It's already after six and the guards are already lining up the work detail."

"Yes, Sir," replied Betron. "But if you don't mind I think I'll pass the word to get the troops all armed right away."

* * *

When Betron approached the enlisted men's mess tent, he saw Pvt. Adolph Gamlin leaving at the same time. Gamlin was scheduled to take his shift on guard duty and was on his way to relieve the guard on a two hour rotation. As Gamlin was about to take his Krag-Jorgensen from the stack of rifles just outside the tent, Betron called him over and instructed him to pass the word for all the men to keep their arms with them at all times. Gamlin knew better than to ask why when he saw Betron's expression.

There were still quite a few Filipinos confined to the large Sibley tents who had not yet been fed and were awaiting the work detail assignments. Police Chief Valeriano Abanador, whose job it was to provide the workers, was just leaving one of the Sibley tents. He was headed for his office to the right of the enlisted mess tent and waved at Sgt. Betron as he was about to enter the tent where most of the NCO's were already eating and in front of which Gamlin had just spoken with Sgt. Betron.

Betron found a place at one of the long tables in the mess tent in front of the Salazar house. As he ate his breakfast, he passed along

Captain Connell's orders to Corporal Burke one of the NCO's seated next to him. He intended to make the rounds to the other noncoms himself after breakfast. As he was just finishing his meal, Betron noted Pvt. Gamlin approaching the mess tent on his guard rounds from the left front. He also saw Police Chief Abanador coming back from his office. The Chief would pass Gamlin right in front of the mess tent. As Betron started to get up to head for Municipal Hall, Historian Dumindin tells what happened next: *"At 6:45 a.m., on Saturday, September 28, Abanador grabbed Pvt. Adolph Gamlin's rifle from behind and hit him unconscious with its butt. Abanador turned the rifle at the men in the sergeant's mess tent, wounding one."* (Actually he most likely hit two. The first one he hit was Sgt. Frank Betron who had just stood up to leave and he hit him in the thigh. Some said the shot was not a miss and the wound was superficial.[286] The bullet continued through the subcutaneous portion of Betron's leg, mortally wounding the seated Pvt. Cornelius Donahue.)

Dumindin continues: *"He then waved a rattan cane above his head, and yelled: 'Atake, mga Balangigan-on!' (Attack, men of Balangiga!) A bell in the church tower was rung seconds later, to announce that the attack had begun.*

"The guards outside the convent and municipal hall were killed. The Filipinos apparently sealed in the Sibley tents at the front of the municipal hall, having had weapons smuggled to them in water carriers, broke free and entered the municipal hall and made their way to the second floor. The men in the church broke into the convent through a connecting corridor and killed the officers who were billeted there. The mess tent and the two barracks were attacked. Most of the Americans were hacked to death before they could grab their firearms. The few who escaped the main attack fought with kitchen utensils, steak knives, and chairs.

"The convent was successfully occupied and so, initially, was the municipal hall, but the mess tent and barracks attack suffered a fatal flaw - about one hundred men were split into three groups, one of each target but too few attackers had been assigned to ensure success. A

---

286 Rolando O. Borrinaga, *The Human Cost of Wars in Leyte and Samar, Symposium of the College Department of the Sacred Heart Seminary in Palo, Leyte, on 2/25/200.*

number of Co. C. personnel escaped from the mess tent and the bar-
racks and were able to retake the municipal hall, arm themselves and
fight back. Adolph Gamlin recovered consciousness, found a rifle and
caused considerable casualties among the Filipinos. [Gamlin died at age
92 (sic-actually age ninety-one) *in the U.S. in 1969].*

"*Faced with immensely superior firepower and a rapidly degrad-*
ing attack, Abanador ordered a retreat. But with insufficient numbers
and fear that the rebels would re-group and attack again, the surviving
Americans, led by Sgt. Frank Betron, escaped by baroto (native canoes
with outriggers, navigated by using wooden paddles) to Basey, Samar,
about 20 miles away. The townspeople returned to bury their dead, then
abandoned the town."[287]

Other sources confirm Abanador was the commander of the attack and led the main group in the assault, which had three other sections. Capt. Santos Devandera led the first section against the municipal buildings which were quarters for the majority of the troops. Another section was led by police corporal Mariano Valdemor, which attacked the two *nipa* hut squads under Sgts. Betron and Markley across the street from Geronima's place. The third section under another police officer, Corporal Pablo Abejero, covered the town periphery. The group led by Abanador were all residents of the town, and carried the brunt of the attack.

When it started, the American flag had just been raised to a half mast position to honor President McKinley. Some of the troopers were already wearing black arm bands as ordered by their commanding officer.

Geronima, after warning Betron, then headed for the Sibley tents where her brother, Guno, had slept as part of the incarcerated workforce. She was unaware that Guno was part of the conspiracy and was scheduled to lead one of the groups to break out of the tents when the attack started. She did want to warn him though about the upcoming attack and intended to smuggle him a weapon to defend himself and tell him to flee as fast as he could when the fighting broke out. She managed to do this by passing a *punyal*, a small knife hidden in his breakfast rice bowl.

Geronima, after the attack started was reported by some to have "*ran through the streets urging on attackers and pointing out Americans*

---

287 Dumindin, "Philippine-American War, 1899-1902."

shooting."[288] Actually, she was running to the church and waving her rosary. She spent the rest of the battle fervently praying in the church.

After the Americans repulsed the attack, Betron was the most senior NCO who survived. At one point, he was seen firing from a window in Geronima's house.[289]*quoting from James Bertolf's diary part of Jean Wall's collection.*

None of the commissioned officers lived, with both Bumpus and Dr. Groswold hacked to death in their beds. Captain Connell, fighting a brave but futile battle to his death, jumped out a second floor window of the Convent but was run down and cut to pieces on the street below.

Betron, of course, had no idea that Geronima's cousin, Valeriano Abanador, had spared his life at the tearful request of Geronima during her last meeting with her cousin.

It was Sergeant Betron who led the initial thirty-six survivors in a heroic fight through the Filipino attackers to an escape aboard five of the native *bancas*, which were outrigger canoes. The trip to the nearest American outpost, Basey, some twenty plus miles and twelve hours across shark infested waters, was almost as fearful as the massacre the soldiers had just escaped. Shark fins followed the *bancas* the whole way. Some of the soldiers would perish during the trip, either dying of their wounds or beached and killed by following attackers. Others would perish later, some of wounds or complications thereof, or because of the electrolyte imbalance caused by drinking sea water to quench their ravaging thirst. Others were saved by the Tagalog houseboy, Francisco, who wielded a Krag during the firefights. He also, on arrival on shore, climbed trees to fetch coconuts which he split to quench the thirst of some of the survivors.[290]

Initial reports from Balangiga were confusing as to the number of casualties on both sides and some confusion persists to this day. Lieutenants James P. Drouillard and Captain Bookmiller of the Ninth Infantry Regiment, Colonel De Russey of the Eleventh Infantry and General Chaffee were all quoted in this *New York Times* article of October 5, 1901 posted below:

---

288 Couttie, *Hang The Dogs The True Tragic History of the Balangiga Massacre*, 163.
289 ibid-162.
290 ibid 173.

CHAFFEE SENDS NEWS OF THE MASSACRE.

Three Officers and Forty Men Were Killed and More Are Still Missing.

WASHINGTON, Oct. 4.—The War Department to-night received a dispatch from Gen. Chaffee, dated at Manila, Oct. 4, giving further details of the disastrous attack on Company C of the Ninth Infantry, near Balangiga, Samar. The dispatch is as follows:

From those who escaped following:

Manila, Oct. 4.

September 29, while at breakfast 6:45 morning, company was attacked at signal ringing convent bells by about 450 bolomen, 200 from rear of quarters, 200 front. Simultaneously attack officers quarters. Company completely surprised. Force attacking front gained possession arms. Fight ensued forthwith, in which many met death in mess room in rear. Enemy beaten off temporarily by about twenty-five men, who gained their arms.

Sergt. Bettron assumed command, endeavored collect men, leave in boats, reattacked by enemy. Strength command, 3 officers, 72 men. Killed, 3 officers, 40 enlisted men; missing, 6; wounded, 18; present, 13. Party attacking officers in convent entered through church, large numbers led by President. Probably 101 rifles with company; 25 saved, 15 of lost (rifles) bolts drawn; 25,000 ammunition lost.

Ninety-five prisoners outside Cuartel joined in attack at signal. Boat of missing men capsized. Capt. Bookmiller may pick up men.

(Lieut. James P.) DROUILLARD,
(Ninth Infantry.)

Sept. 30.—Have returned Balangiga. Drouillard explains conditions correctly. Landed yesterday. Inhabitants deserted town firing one shot. Buried three officers, twenty-nine men; number bodies burned; quarters buildings fired as we entered. Secured or destroyed most of rations. All ordnance gone. Insurgents secured 57 serviceable rifles, 28,000 cartridges. Forty-eight men of Company C, Ninth Infantry, (and) one hospital corps man killed or missing; 28 men accounted for, found two in boat en route here. Buried dead, burned town, returned to Basey.

(Captain) BOOKMILLER.
(Ninth Infantry.)

De Russey has sent strong company to chastise savages if found.—Hughes. No other details. Names of killed to be determined by elimination of survivors as soon as possible. June muster roll probably latest evidence to be had.

CHAFFEE.

De Russey is the Colonel of the Eleventh Regiment, stationed near the scene of the attack. The muster roll referred to already has been published.

The New York Times

Published: October 5, 1901
Copyright © The New York Times

Things were clarified four days later. See below *NY Times* follow up article. Note that two of the forty-four dead, Corp. John L. Weiss and Pvt. Charles C. McManis were from CO. G and killed earlier on Sept. 1, 1901.

So as of October 8, 1901, American casualties at Balangiga were forty-five KIA including seven missing and presumed dead (many unidentified burned and mutilated bodies). All three officers' remains were recovered.

* * *

THE SAMAR MASSACRE.

Gen. Chaffee Sends List of Casualties Sustained by the Enlisted Men— Forty-four Dead.

WASHINGTON, Oct. 8.—The list of casualties sustained by the rank and file of the ill-fated Company C, Ninth Infantry, in the massacre in the Philippine Island of Samar, is given in the following cablegram from Gen. Chaffee, received at the War Department late this afternoon:

"Manila, Oct. 8.

"Adjutant General, Washington:

"Casualties engagement Balangiga, Samar, Sept. 28. Wounded will be reported as soon as received: Company C, Ninth United States Infantry:

"Killed—Sergt. John F. Martin, Sergt. James N. Randles, Corp. Henry J. Scharer, Privates Joseph L. Godon, James Martin, John W. Aydelotte, Byron Dent, Eli Fitzgerald, Charles E. Sterling, Robert Sproull, John H. Miller, Richard Long, Joseph Turner, Gustav F. Schuytzler, Corp. Frank McCormack, Privates Proal Peters, Leonard F. Schley, Artificer Joseph R. Marr, Privates James F. McDermott, Charles E. Davis, Harry M. Wood, John Wannebo, Joseph O. Kleinhumple, Robert L. Booth, Guy C. Dennis, John D. Armani, Litto Armani, George Bony, John D. Buhrer, James L. Cain, Frank Vobayda, and Charles Powers.

"Died from wounds received in action—Corp. Thomas E. Baird, Privates Chris. F. Recark, and Flyd Shomacker.

"Missing bodies, probably burned when insurgents deserted town—Musician John L. Covington, Privates Patrick J. Robbins, Jerry J. Driscoll, Evans South, August F. Porczeng, Christian S. Williams, Claude C. Wingo; also Harry Wright, Hospital Corps.

"Killed Sept. 1, Basay, Samar, Company G, Ninth Infantry—Corp. John L. Weiss and Private Charles C. McManius."

At the War Department it is said that the names of Joseph L. Godon, Gustav F. Schuytzler, and John Wannebo are subject to correction later. The three-officers killed in the fight are not mentioned in to-day's list, their deaths having been reported in a dispatch sent several days ago.

The New York Times
Published October 9, 1901

This photo has been labeled by some as being the survivors of the massacre, but Sgt. Samuel Whipps, 2nd from left was in the hospital in Manila at the time, and Sgts. Winters and White, probably numbers 8 & 10 are not listed on Couttie's CO C roster, and are likely from Company G.[291] Included in the photo are Sgt. John D. Closson, 1st Sgt. Samuel F. Whipps, Cpl. Arnold Irish, Cpl. James Pickett, bugler Pvt. Geo Meyer, Pvt. Adolf Gamlin, Pvt. Henry Claas, Sgt. Oscar Winters, Francisco (the teen age houseboy who saved lives during the escape), Sgt. John White, Pvt. Henry W. Manire, Cpl. Taylor B. Hickman, Pvt. Case (Carl) Swanson, Pvt. Clifford M. Mumby, Pvt. Charles F. Marak and Sgt. Geo. Markley,. Photo taken with one of the Balangiga Bells in Calbayog, Samar, circa March – April 1902.

There would be many other casualties. Practically all of the American survivors suffered from what we today call PTSD (post-traumatic stress disorder). PTSD symptoms were not limited to the Americans. Professor Rolando O. Borrinaga, quoting research by Prof. Glenda Bonifacio and presented in a paper at the Second Regional Conference on Leyte-Samar History, Ritz Tower de Leyte, Tacloban City, December 16, 1999, described the recurring nightmares experienced by Casiana *Geronima* Nacionales. According to family legend, the attractive Geronima often awoke at night from a disturbed sleep and asked her household relatives if they also saw the white soldier

291 Couttie, *Hang The Dogs The True Tragic History of the Balangiga Massacre*, 298-300.

standing beside the door of her room. According to her relatives, Casiana never married and died a spinster in her old age.

Sergeant Betron did get his discharge in the Philippines. He searched for months to find his lover, but her relatives kept her hidden in fear of American and/or Filipino reprisals. He finally gave up the search and married another Filipino native, Inocente Barrera from Cebu.[292] Betron *"was known to have resided in Batangas, then in Cebu, and finally in Nasipit, Agusan del Norte,"*[293] where a son named Mike was apparently still residing in 1999.

Other American survivors also experienced significant psychic trauma. Private George Meyers, Private George Allen, and Private Adolph Gamlin, who recovered from his bash on the head by Police Chief Abanador to cause considerable damage to the attackers, are all quoted by Professor Imperial describing their ordeals.[294]

Prof. Borrinaga, who was instrumental in inviting Gamlin's daughter, Jean Wall, to be the keynote speaker on a University of the Philippines Symposium on the Balangiga Attack in the late 1990's, also published her remarks from that speech. According to Ms. Wall her father had nightmares his entire life. Even the night before he died at age ninety-one, Gamlin awoke hollering, *"They're coming, they're coming."*[295]

Borrinaga, in a gallant effort toward understanding, and reconciliation, also invited a Filipino descendent counterpart to Jean Wall. He was Engineer Ted Amano, president of the Manila-based An Balangigan-on, Inc. and a great-grandson of Mariano Valdenor.

Valdenor had also inflicted some of the wounds on Pvt. Gamlin. Valdenor, Abanador's second in command, was described in both Filipino and American accounts as armed with a long bolo in one hand and a knife in the other.[296]

After the symposium, Jean Wall and Ted Amano, both descendants on opposite sides of the Balangiga massacre, held a ritual embrace of conciliation. The Balangiga Bells, which were rung at the start of the battle, were taken by and are still in American hands, but that's another story.

---

292 Couttie, *Hang The Dogs The True Tragic History of the Balangiga Massacre*, 223.

293 Borrinaga, *Revisiting the Balangiga Conflict*.

294 Imperial, *Balangiga and After*.

295 Ibid.

296 Ibid.

Valeriano Abanador in old age

Captain Thomas W. Connel

CHAPTER TWENTY

Samar Island, Philippines, September 29, 1901 – April 12, 1902

"The wicked flee when no one pursues." –Proverbs 28-1

When Captain Edwin V. Bookmiller, who was the commander of G Company, received the report of Lieutenant James P. Drouillard, who had just finished debriefing Sergeant Betron on September 29th, he commandeered the SS Pittsburg, a coastal steamboat based in Tacloban, Leyte, and with his Company sailed immediately from Basey to Balangiga. Arriving on September 30th, they found the town deserted except for a lone rifleman who fired one shot at them as he fled.

Bookmiller also found that *"the dead of Company C lay where they fell, many bearing horrible hack wounds. Bookmiller and his men* (after burying 3 officers and 29 men) *burned the town to the ground."*[297]

When newly sworn-in President Theodore Roosevelt heard the details of the Balangiga *Encounter,* he ordered General Chaffee to use *"in no unmistakable terms the most stern measures to pacify Samar."*[298] Thereafter Chaffee told his subordinates that he wanted a "bayonet rule" for the Philippines and encouraged them to do whatever necessary to achieve pacification. Historian Dumindin noted the public's and Chaffee's reaction thus:

---

297 Dumindin, "Philippine-American War, 1899-1902."
298 Ibid.

'The massacre shocked the U.S. public; many newspaper editors noted that it was the worst disaster suffered by the U.S. Army since Custer's last stand at Little Big Horn. An infuriated Maj. Gen. Adna R. Chaffee, military governor for the "unpacified" areas of the Philippines, assured the press that "the situation calls for shot, shells and bayonets as the natives are not to be trusted." He advised newspaper correspondent Joseph Ohl, "If you should hear of a few Filipinos more or less being put away don't grow too sentimental over it." ²⁹⁹

Maj. General of Volunteers Adna Chaffee in 1900

Chaffee was a *mustang* who was born in Ohio in 1842, enlisted in the army during the Civil War and rose through the ranks. After the Peninsular Campaign and the Battle of Antietam Creek, he was commissioned a 2nd Lieutenant in 1863. He served in multiple Indian Wars in western U.S.A. and was on Gen. Leonard Wood's Cuban staff before serving in China during the Boxer Rebellion. He replaced General Arthur MacArthur as the commanding officer in the Philippines in July 1901. He also replaced MacArthur as the Military Governor of the "non-pacified areas" of the Islands at that time.

After the Balangiga affair, Chaffee appointed Brigadier Generals James Franklin Bell to the Batangas and "Howling Jake" also called "Hell Roaring" Smith to Samar. The first appointment, Bell's, was a

299 Ibid.

good choice. The second, Smith's, was a disaster. Smith had earned his nickname when his verbal orders to Marine Major Tony Waller were documented by witnesses at Major Waller's court martial in 1902. No documentation of the infamous circular No. 6, referred to by some and supposedly containing the orders, was ever found.

"I want no prisoners and I wish you to kill and burn; and the more you burn and kill, the better it will please me. Then he tasked his men to reduce Samar into a 'howling wilderness,' to kill anyone 10 years old and above capable of bearing arms."[300]

Rules of engagement (ROE's) were not really written down in black and white in those times. The closest thing to ROE in 1901 was general order Number 100 dated clear back to 1863 , of which Civil War veteran General Chaffee would certainly be familiar. That order stated that if enemy units gave no quarter or became treacherous upon capture, it was lawful to shoot anyone belonging to that unit, captured or not.

Today, our ROE's appear to be highly influenced by politicians in Washington, D.C., which, as Navy SEAL Marcus Luttrell points out, is a long way from a battlefield, where a sniper's bullet can blast your head.[301] Luttrell also elaborates that today's ROE's are so specific that combat participants cannot open fire until the enemy is positively identified and his intentions are clear.

In 1901, the liberal media jumped on the commanders and soldiers who were caught up in this kind of fighting and criticized them much as they do today. Some say one such scapegoat was Marine Major Littleton (Tony) W.T. Waller, whose commanding officer was Army General "Howling Jake" Smith.

Smith commanded one of those special brigades made up on-the-spot, and this one was called the 6th Separate Brigade. As Nathaniel Helms said in a 2008 article[302] Waller's story under "Howling Jake" will likely be vaguely familiar to those reader's familiar with

---

300 Ibid.

301 Marcus Luttrell and Patrick Robinson, <u>Lone Survivor</u>, Little, Brown & Co., New York, 2007, 37.

302 Nathaniel R. Helms, Defend Our Marines http://warchronicle.com/ TheyAreNotKillers/NatHelms/MattisTestimony4June08.htm.

Lt. Col. Jeffrey Chessani, who was charged with dereliction of duty and orders violations for failing to investigate and report an incident on November 19, 2005, when one Marine and twenty-four Iraqis died during an Al Qaeda inspired complex ambush on a squad of Marines.[303]

There are two sides to the Major Waller story, too. One side is told by Texas A&M's history professor and noted military historian, Brian McAllister Linn, who describes Waller as a ruthless, ambitious officer who was fond of the bottle.[304] He goes on to describe Waller's expedition across Samar, after a bloody and suppressive campaign in retaliation of Balangiga, as a disaster of his own making. Linn also denies as plausible the reason Waller gave as a rationale to cross Samar through the jungle, which was to scout a telegraph route between Lanang *(today Lanang is called Llorente)* and Basey. Linn stated there was a telephone line between Basey and Tacloban, so there was no obvious reason for a telegraph line if one could communicate by telephone.

Author and Philippine historian Bob Couttie[305] tends to agree with Brian Linn that Waller was an incompetent commander,[306] but vilification of Waller may have been premature. Couttie, in an interview with *Philippine Newslink,*[307] also had this to say about events after Balanigiga: *"On the orders of General Jacob H. Smith, U.S. troops retaliated against the entire island (600 square miles) of Samar where Balangiga is located. The exchange is known because of two courts-martial: one was of Waller who was later court-martialed for ordering or allowing the execution of a dozen Filipino bearers, and the court-martial of Gen. Jacob H. Smith who was actually court-martialed for giving that order. The jury is out to the extent that order was carried out, because Littleton Waller actually countermanded it to his own men and said '[Captain David] Porter, I've had instructions to kill everyone over ten years old. But we are not making war on women and children, only*

303 Ibid.
304 Linn, The Philippine War, 1899-1902, 315.
305 Couttie, Hang The Dogs The True Tragic History of the Balangiga Massacre.
306 Ibid, 7.
307 http://www.tropmed.ag/material/diagnosis%20and%20control%20of%20 trypanosomosis.pdf.

on men capable of bearing arms. Keep that in mind no matter what other orders you receive.' Undoubtedly, some men did atrocities regardless of Waller's commands."[308]

In addition, The Annual Reports of the Secretary of War of 1901 and 1902 (fiscal years ending June 30th) have this to say about the telephone and telegraph communications on Samar, and the intentions of the brigade commander (Smith): 1901: *"The entire island of Samar is without communication and without any fixed garrison. Nothing can be done here beyond keeping in communication with the coast towns by cables. The greatest land line building will be connections of garrisons too small for telegraph offices by means of radiating telephone lines from the nearest office. Post commanders are willing for their own convenience to put up numerous short lines in their own territory. These lines cost nothing except for material and are a great convenience."[309]*

1902: *"The only towns with telegraph communication were Catbalogan and Calbayog. At the time of installation of cable from Cebu to Ormac a short length of cable was laid across the straits separating Leyte and Samar near Tacloban. In July (1901) this was extended to Basey giving that place a telephone connection to Tacloban. Later a telephone line was constructed from Calbayog to the mouth of the Gandura River.... On November 1, the brigade commander (Smith) submitted an elaborate scheme comprising some several miles of land lines, connecting the interior and east coast garrisons with the cable stations at Calbayog, Catbalogan and Tacloban, and in December the Signal Officer of the Department visited the different stations on both the east and west coasts of the island and equipped four construction parties in command of officers detailed from the line of the army, for the purposes of the brigade commander, with funds and material including 400 miles of wire and 30 telephones. The parties were to work from Basey south to Balangiga, Calbayog north to Laguan; Orus south along the east coast and from Borongon north. The Orus and Borongon parties were unable to get a line up, the insurgents destroying it as fast as it could be put up. The Calbayog party succeeded in getting a line up to Maua, 48 miles north. The Basey*

---

308 *Ibid.*
309 *Annual Reports of the Secretary of War (Princeton's Library) ending fiscal year June 30, 1901, VOL 1, Part 7, 466.*

party constructed a line to Balangiga, 30 miles. Both of these lines passed through swamps and jungles for most of the distance and were cut almost daily (by insurgents)… they were finally abandoned."[310]

The facts show an underwater line across the Straits from Basey to Tacloban, but there was no communication from the Samar interior or from the east coast to Smith's headquarters, and all evidence indicates that Smith did verbally direct Major Waller to scout a route across the southern part of Samar for a communication line to Basey, which could then be relayed to his HQ in Tacloban, Leyte, which was just across the narrow San Juanico Straits near Basey, Samar. According to Waller, he was given freedom to start from either Hernani or Lanang.[311] Robert B. Asprey, in an article originally published in May 1961, had this to say about Waller's trek across Samar:

Brig. General Jacob Smith in 1901

---

310 *Annual Reports of the Secretary of War (Princeton's Library) ending fiscal year, June 30, 1902, Vol. 1. 686.*

311 *Robert B. Asprey, Waller of Samar – Part II, Marine Corps Gazette, May 1961, http://www.mca-marines.org/gazette/waller-samar-part-ii.*

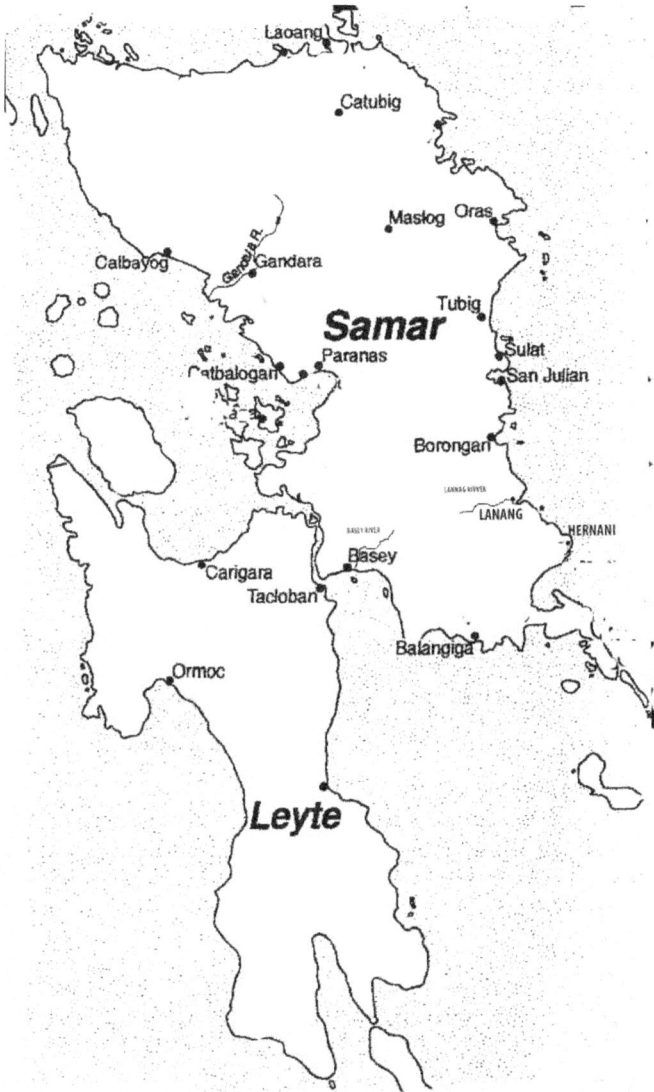

Asprey: *"The exact genesis of what one day would be called the 'March across Samar' is not known, but apparently BGen Smith had favored the notion for some time. Speaking of a conference with Smith in early December, 1901, Waller wrote:*

"'General Smith also asked me again to make the march across the mountain to Hernani, on the east coast. He gave me authority to work from Basey to Balangiga, a distance of about 52 miles by trail, in order that I might either capture or destroy the remnants of the insurrectos, now scattered in small bands and causing much trouble to the other natives. Authority was given me to use my own judgment as to the point of departure from the east coast to cross the mountains; that is to say, either from Hernani or Lanang."'[312]

Other details of Asprey's version of events are supported by testimony from those marines who were involved in the "March Across Samar." Some of that testimony is paraphrased below and can be seen on Arlington Cemetery's website. [313]

Major Waller was considered a good marine officer by those in the Corps. He was said to put his men's welfare first, and had actually countermanded Smith's orders to kill everyone over ten because he didn't want to do it and most likely felt it was unlawful. He knew the natives of Samar were hostile to U.S. authority as demonstrated by both the Catubig and Balangiga massacres, and could not be trusted despite some vocal pretenses and actions to the contrary. He was aware that guerrilla influences by Lukban and his cohorts instilled fear in the natives who were at first more afraid of the revolutionaries than the Yanks. After the suppressive American campaign of late 1901 and early 1902, the reverse was true. It was, however, well known that many of the apparently pro American villagers were members of the *insurrectos* and therefore none could be trusted.

On October 24th, Waller received orders from Smith to find and punish the instigators of the Balangiga attack. Waller's orders to his men were specific, invoking General Order No. 100 of 1863.

"Place no confidence in the natives, and punish treachery immediately with death Allow no man [marine] to go anywhere without his arms or ammunition. All males who have not come in and presented themselves by October 25th will be regarded and treated as enemies. It must be impressed on the men that the natives are treacherous, brave and savage. No trust, no confidence, can be placed in them. The men

---

312 Ibid.
313 http://www.arlingtoncemetery.net/lwwaller.htm.

must be informed of the courage, skill, size and strength of the enemy. We must do our part of the work and with the sure knowledge that we are not to expect quarter."[314]

Waller's initial assault on the insurgents was quick and successful in destroying Lukban's mountain headquarters, although the guerilla leader himself was elsewhere. Lukban would later be captured on February 18, 1902.[315] After weeks of campaigning, Waller then received orders from Smith to scout a telegraph line route across Samar from Lanang on the east coast to Basey on the southwest coast, where the remnants of Company C fled after the Balangiga massacre. Beginning on 28 December 1901, Waller marched his battalion of sixty marines along with thirty-three native bearers and two native scouts and headed through rainforest toward Samar's other coast some thirty-five miles away.

Just a few days into the march, the battalion was already devastated by jungle fevers, blisters, leeches, skin rashes, and sores. Scratches and insect bites became infected and the battalion was running out of food probably due to theft and hoarding or dumping of supplies by the native equipment bearers. By January 3, 1902, Waller decided to split his command, leaving most of them who were unable to continue, with Captain David D. Porter, USMC.

Waller, with fourteen marines and an unknown number of natives set out for Basey arriving there three days later on January 6th. In the meantime Captain Porter chose to return to Lanang with the marines who could still march after a days' rest. Porter left the sick and dying marines with 1st Lt. A.S. Williams, and started back to Lanang with seven marines and six natives. Fighting torrential rains it took him until January 11th to reach safety. Getting those of his party settled, Porter immediately set out to retrieve his own stragglers and rescue Williams and the sick marines.

Waller had also returned to the jungle immediately after getting his party safely to Basey. He searched for Porter for nine days without success.

Williams, meanwhile, realized he and his troops would die if they stayed put, so although nearly dead they began to crawl toward

---

314 *Ibid.*
315 Couttie, *Hang The Dogs The True Tragic History of the Balangiga Massacre,* 210.

Lanang. By the time Porter's relief column reached them, one marine had gone insane and ten had perished. To make things worse, three of the native bearers had attacked Williams with Bolo knives. Although wounded the Lieutenant got things under control probably with his .45 and fought off the attack. These individuals were placed under arrest when Williams reached Lanang and were executed by firing squad on January 20th, on orders of hospitalized Major Waller. Waller's big mistake was not putting the charges of mutiny and attempted murder down on paper.

After the three were executed, Waller, who had been hospitalized with a fever of 105, dug into whoever else was involved and, although there is no record of a formal inquiry, his investigation resulted in eight more native executions before it was over.

When word of the executions got back to Washington, it was all the liberals needed to publicly bad mouth the unpopular campaign. Senator Henry Cabot Lodge started hearings to find out why Waller, now labeled as "the Butcher of Samar," had executed eleven Filipinos "in cold blood." President Roosevelt, who knew and admired Waller from their mutual combat experience in Cuba, was helpless to stop the congressional hearings.

On February 19, 1902, Waller's battalion got orders to return to Cavite, Luzon. Upon arrival ten days later, Waller found himself charged with murder and facing a court martial. On March 17, 1902, Waller's trial began in Manila and lasted until April 12th.

The court consisted of six marine officers and seven from the army. Heading up the court was Army Brig. General William H. Bisbee, another *mustang* from the civil war and a renowned Indian fighter. After the trial, Bisbee would retire with forty-one years of active duty. His first decision of the court martial was to deny Waller's claim that since he had never been detached from the marines an army court had no jurisdiction over him. Later, the Adjutant General would agree with Waller, but, by then, he had already been acquitted.

Waller took full responsibility for the executions, fully believing he was in compliance with General Order No. 100. General Smith was then called to testify concerning the orders he had issued to Waller.

Waller also believed Smith would do the honorable thing and admit to what he had actually ordered, but he was wrong. Smith blamed Waller for everything and lied on the stand, testifying that he had ordered the Marine to treat everyone humanely. Enraged at Smith's lack of honor, Waller retook the stand and repeated what Smith had ordered: *"I want no prisoners. I wish you to kill and burn, and the more you kill and the more you burn the better you will please me… I want all people killed who are capable of bearing arms."*

Waller: "I would like to know the age limit."

Smith: "Ten years." [316]

Waller then produced enough witnesses to convince the court he was innocent. Smith's testimony resulted in his own court martial, which ended his career, and he was forced to retire by President Roosevelt. It was not the first time Smith had been court-martialed. In 1885, he was tried for welching on a poker bet and found guilty of "conduct unbecoming–."[317] A year later, he was court-martialed again, found guilty and was actually sentenced to be expelled from the army. Guess what, he was saved by a politician, President Grover Cleveland. In 1891, he was charged again for using enlisted men as servants, but was never prosecuted and the charges were dropped.

Waller eventually rose to the rank of Major General in the Corps, but was denied his due as Commandant of Marines.

The whole post-Balangiga retribution campaign resulted in an emotional era of anti-imperial and antiwar journalism. Multiple tales of U.S. atrocities emerged in the press, including water torture (water boarding), murder, and beatings, many of which were true. The atrocities committed by the Filipinos on U.S. troops and on their own people by revolutionaries, like Vicente Lukban, were seldom mentioned.

One particular episode where Lukban wrapped a kerosene-soaked towel around an American soldier's head and set it afire was not public knowledge until after the war.[318] As usual, the liberals on

316 Helms, *Defend Our Marines*, http://warchronicle.com/TheyAreNotKillers/NatHelms/MattisTestimony4June08.htm.

317 Bob Couttie, *Hang The Dogs The True Tragic History of the Balangiga Massacre*, New Day Publishers, Quezon City, PI, 2004, 186.

318 http://www.arlingtoncemetery.net/lwwaller.htm.

the homefront had no idea what our troops were up against. The combat soldiers' and marines' difficulty in recognizing true *amigos* from terrorist *insurrectos* was not adequately explained by reporters, even those in the combat zones.

The different opinions of the war persist to this day, and people still have difficulty separating the warriors from the war. As war historian Brian Linn stated (as quoted by Richard Kolb), *"Far from being the bloody-handed butcher of fable, the average soldier in the Philippines was probably as good as or better than any in our nation's history."*[319]

Waller, the Marine Major

---

319 Kolb, *"Blaze in the Boondocks, 2002. Fighting on America's Imperial Frontier in the Philippines, 1899-1913,"* 37, 108.

CHAPTER TWENTY-ONE

March 15 – July 4, 1902

"The pen of the scholar is mightier than the sword of the martyr." –The Prophet Muhammad

The last major fight with the Filipinos occurred at Paranas, Samar, on February 26, when a detachment of the 21st Infantry was attacked by about Eighty Filipinos of the PRG, the last of Lukban's forces. Eighty insurgents were reported KIA, which was apparently the entire force. No U.S. soldiers were killed. Two and one half weeks later, on the ides of March at Paran Paran, Cotabato Provence, Mindanao, the Moro Rebellion began in earnest when seventeen men of the 15th Cavalry were attacked by 200 some Moros in dense jungle. The U.S. had one KIA, and the Moros eight confirmed KIA.[320]

On April 16, 1902, the last major rebel leader, Maj. General Miguel Malvar, who had relentlessly been pursued by Brig. General James Franklin Bell, finely surrendered in Lipa, Batangas Provence, in the southwestern part of Luzon. Malvar acknowledged that Bell's policy of reconcentration of the population into safe villages, removal of accessibility of food supplies outside of these "new" population centers, and the pressure and resultant persecution of the insurgents by the general population were the principle reasons for his surrender.[321]

---

320 Kolb, "Blaze in the Boondocks, 2002. Fighting on America's Imperial Frontier in the Philippines, 1899-1913," 42.

321 Brian McAllister Linn, The U.S. Army and Counterinsurgency in the Philippine, 159.

Malvar's surrender effectively ended the American-Philippine War, which was declared officially over by President Theodore Roosevelt on July 4, 1902. The Moro campaigns, however, were just beginning, and the shooting and loss of life would continue for years to come., and it's not over yet!

To set the stage for the next series of events, we have to back up a year or so to follow what was happening in the southern islands and the archipelago. Captain John J. Pershing, who had finely been promoted to that rank in February 1901 after fifteen years as a lieutenant was already forty years old. His mentor in the Philippines was General William S. Kobbe, who had taken over for the successful negotiator of the Bates Agreement (General John C. Bates), which had resulted in relative peace with the Islamic Moros since the USA had been in force in the Philippines.

Pershing, with a great deal of foresight, anticipated that the small village of Iligan on the north shore of Mindanao, would be pivotal as a trading center between Mindanao, China, and the Visayans, which are the middle islands of the Philippines, and include Leyte and Samar and the smaller islands of Panay, Negros, Cebu, Bohol, Romblon, and Masbate.

When he expressed his thoughts to General Kobbe, Pershing added that the Moros of the Lake Lanao region of northern Mindanao would likely have to be brought under control since they had not been part of the Bates agreement. These particular Islamists were the Maranaos, a tribe of Moros sometimes called the Malanaos, and their leader was the most important *datu* (tribal chief) of the north shore of the lake. He was also a former Sultan of Maydaya, a populated region around the lake, but the title of Sultan was less important to the Maranaos than *Datu,* and he had relinquished the Sultan title to his nephew. His name was *Datu Ahmai Manabilang.* (Ah-my Mana-bee-lang).

Sure enough, when General George W. Davis, who had been the provost martial in Manila, replaced General Kobbe, he had no officer who knew more about the Moros than Captain John J. Pershing. Kobbe had briefed Davis on Pershing's talents and suggestions and, in September 1901, Davis sent the Captain to Iligan with 250 men with instructions to make friends of the Moros.

Pershing took great pains to impress the Datu at their first meeting, which had been agreed to after several invitations had been sent by Pershing. Even thirty-four years later in his personal papers, Pershing was able to describe the event vividly as quoted by excellent researcher and author of *Moroland,* Robert A. Fulton: *"On the appointed day he came in a great state, accompanied by a retinue of about thirty of his people. He was a tall, swarthy, well-built man, past middle age, clean shaven, as most of them were. His jacket was of many colors, his trousers tight fitting, his turban smartly tied and set jauntily to the side of his head. Like all Moros he was barefoot. He rode a fine looking pony, a stallion, and for stirrups used a small rope knotted at the ends which he grasped between the first two toes. On each side of his horse a slave trotted along on foot, one carrying his gold mounted kris (sword), the other his highly polished brass box containing betel nut, buya leaves and lime, kept separate 'til the time for chewing, when, as was their custom, he mixed them in proportions to suit his taste. Leading the procession was a guard carrying a gun and behind this dignitary came another. Then came minor chiefs, relatives, and more slaves, all in their choicest finery. Even in this semi-savage setting the Datu (Pershing spelled it Datoo) was a striking looking man and proved to be very intelligent."*[322]

Pershing waited several months for a return invitation, which finally came after the start of the new year 1902. After several weeks of discussions Pershing gained *Datu Manabilang's* confidence but not quite his trust. He did get permission to rebuild the road and bridges of the Agus River wagon trail, which descended from the north shore of Lake Lanao toward Iligan and which the Spanish had destroyed on their evacuation. The datus of the area, however, hinted at their distrust when they insisted they were the ones that would guard the road to prevent its use for an invasion of their territory.

---

322 Fulton, MOROLAND 1899-1906, 103.

MAP of MINDANAO[323]

General Davis, pleased by Pershing's success, encouraged other commanders to explore Mindanao's interior but with all due caution to avoid confrontations. General Chaffee, however, had assigned one veteran Indian fighter, Colonel Frank D. Baldwin, commander of the 27th Infantry to the area, to back up Davis. Pershing was surprised, upon returning to Iligan, that he no longer reported to Davis, but, instead, to Col. Baldwin. Baldwin, one of only nineteen double recipients of the Medal of Honor, is described by historian Fulton[324] as *"somewhat to the right of the Sherman-Sheridan doctrine of 'the only good Indian is a dead one.'"*[325] Chaffee's choice, although logical in his own mind (he was a veteran Indian fighter, too), was likely a set up for just the confrontations he was trying to avoid.

_____

323 Hook, Map design.
324 Fulton, MOROLAND 1899-1906.
325 Ibid, 106.

The 23rd Infantry, which Baldwin's 27th Infantry Regiment replaced on Mindanao, had orders that its men were not to go into the hinterland or walk about alone. There was no such rule for the 27th.

* * *

March 9 – 12, 1902

A private newly arrived with the 27th, was found dead, his rifle missing. The body was found about a mile from his post at Parang. Three days later, on March 12th, a cavalry patrol, commanded by Lt. Lewis Forsyth, was attacked by Moros with stolen Krags. Forsyth reported one KIA.

* * *

Late March 1902

Later that month two more soldiers were attacked and another soldier was killed. The murderers were later identified as Maranaos from Lake Lanao.[326] Baldwin, showing remarkable restraint, sent for a Muslim cleric, who was a son-in-law of the local chief, *Datu Ali*. He asked the cleric to carry a message to the datus on the south side of the lake demanding the murderers, with the stolen rifles and the abandoned horses be delivered immediately.

* * *

April 9, 1902

The cleric, whose name was Sharif Muhammad Afdal, an immigrant from Afghanistan, returned with the news that Baldwin's demand had been rejected outright. Baldwin then mounted an expedition which initially consisted of seven companies of the 27th Infantry plus the 25th Mountain Battery of artillery, 429 men.[327] By the time his telegraph orders to all posts to assemble the expeditionary force were

---

326 Ibid.
327 Kolb, "Blaze in the Boondocks, 2002. Fighting on America's Imperial Frontier in the Philippines, 1899-1913," 16.

followed, the force had swollen to close to 1000 officers and men.[328] They were also accompanied by about 300 Maguindanaos as *carga-dores* (supply carriers).

* * *

April 11, 1902

Having received copies of all the telegraph communications both Davis and Chaffee were concerned about possible escalation of hostilities and telegraphed Baldwin to arrange an immediate conference with all the datus he could find. Both generals then arrived in Malabang by steamer on April 11th to find that none of the Lake datus had showed up. There were, however, several datus from the south coast and they gave the two generals as Robert Fulton stated *"an earful."*[329]

The problem was a long memory of the coastal Maranaos, who had experienced a loss of some fifteen of their people when these same Maguindanaos, mortal enemies of the Maranaos, had accompanied an American Expedition two years earlier. Now the Americans had showed up again with these same enemies in tow. You can imagine what the Generals were thinking after listening to the diatribes of the disgruntled datus: *"Now what do we do?"*

* * *

April 13, 1902

Had they used the resources available to them, specifically the expertise of Captain Pershing, things might have turned out differently. As it so happened, however, Pershing was left behind in Iligan and despite reservations expressed by Davis, Baldwin convinced Chaffee to issue an ultimatum to the leaders of the tribes of the southern side of the Lake Lanao. Things were almost salvaged when Pershing, having received copies of Chaffee's ultimatum from Davis, with orders to forward it to the datus on the north side of the lake, reworded the document and delayed sending it out, urging General Davis to come to Iligan.

---

328 Fulton, *MOROLAND 1899-1906*, 107.
329 Ibid.

Pershing knew the Moros would expect and would also respect a measured response from the Americans for the assaults, murders, and thefts they had experienced at the hands of the guilty Maranaos. To the Moros way of thinking, the response would be based on "an eye for an eye, tooth for a tooth ancient law." What Baldwin's ultimatum would do would represent an overreaction that would probably unite all of the different tribes against the Americans and start a war with dire consequences. The ultimatum had a deadline (April 27th), and of course here was Baldwin, poised with a thousand troops ready to carry out punishment for any disobedience. The challenge was not misunderstood by the natives.

* * *

April, 17, 1902
After consulting with Davis, who agreed with Pershing's analysis, Pershing headed unarmed and alone to a meeting with Datu Manabi-lang, who had agreed to the meeting if Pershing came without troops. Unfortunately, Baldwin had already left with his expedition and could not be reached. Even a cable from Secretary of War Elihu Root, ordering him to abstain from any aggression, failed to reach him.

* * *

April 21, 1902
Baldwin sent a message to be telegraphed to Zamboanga that he had already captured two *cottas*, which were large bunkers made of logs and mud.

* * *

April 23, 1902
Return orders on April 23rd to halt his column where it was were ignored or not received. President Roosevelt himself sent a message to Chaffee that no expedition against the Moros was to be made until

all efforts to negotiate were exhausted. Chaffee immediately cabled Davis, expressing his concern and dismay.

*　*　*

April 26 – 27, 1902

Davis responded by getting on his horse and personally riding hard for days, finally caught up with Baldwin and *"immediately attached a leash."*[330] What followed was not encouraging. None of the datus showed up for the peace talks that Chaffee wanted, and there was no response to his ultimatum to bring in the murderers. In fact, the Sultan of Bayan sent a threatening letter back rejecting Chaffee's authority. Pershing arrives at Marahui. After the Sultan's response, Pershing was the only hope to avoid war.

*　*　*

April 28, 1902

Captain John Pershing was sitting at a conference table along with his interpreter, Thomas Torres, who spoke Spanish as did Pershing, but Torres also spoke the local Moro dialect. Also at the table were Datu Manabilang, all of the leading datus from the north side of the lake, plus several from the north coast. The atmosphere was sullen if not hostile.

Pershing was addressing the Moros, being careful to look each one in the eyes as he spoke, in Spanish, "You know, señor Datus, that there is difficulty in translating the meanings of General Chaffee's document three times *(meaning from English to Spanish to the local dialect)* into your language, so I will try to cut down the misconceptions," Pershing said, saving his last look for Torres, his own interpreter. He waited for the dialect translation.

"I assure you that the proclamation is directed only to the criminals responsible for the murders of American soldiers and to the three datus, not here today, who harbor those responsible," Pershing

---

330 *Ibid, 110.*

continued, and waited again for the interpreter. The datus maintained sullen expressions.

"The proclamation does, however, claim the right of Americans to travel throughout the islands where we please," Pershing said, and even before Torres started his translation there were angry murmurs from about half of the datus, who obviously understood Spanish. One of them addressed Pershing in Spanish.

"If you Americans come, we will fight!" he said, "and we will all aid the Sultan of Bayan."

Pershing turned to his translator, Torres, and shielding his lips whispered, "Stay calm, do not show alarm or fear."

Historian Fulton tells what happened next: *At the height of the peril, Datu Manabilang openly came to his (Pershing's) aid, speaking in his defense and counseling his fellow datus to adopt a wait-and-see attitude and postpone any assistance to the Sultan of Bayan. After further argument tempers cooled and all but a few pledged they would heed Manabilang's advice and accept Pershing's assurances in good faith. Pershing's calm demeanor and the highly respected elder man's stature and influence carried the day."[331]*

Meanwhile, the 300 Maguindanaos left Baldwin's expedition when they found out they would not be allowed to join the fight against their enemies. The departure of the human packers put a great strain on the soldiers who now had to be tasked with load carrying and hacking out a path through the jungle. Add to that torrential rains, guard duty of the trail, and constant harassing rifle fire from those Moros, especially from the south shore who were not in agreement with Manabilang, and Baldwin's strike force was soon down to half strength. As Chaffee had ordered, General Davis stayed with the expedition to keep a tight leash on Baldwin. With all the setbacks, the column was down to less than a three-day supply of food, sick lists were growing, and mosquitoes were on a rampage.

---

331 *Ibid.*

Captain John Pershing in 1902

Thomas Torres, Pershing's Interpreter

* * *

May 1 – 2, 1902

When Davis got word of Pershing's success in delaying any action by the north shore Moros he felt emboldened enough to send a twenty-four-hour ultimatum to the Sultan of Bayan to give up the murderers. No reply was returned. As Baldwin's column advanced toward the lake, it encountered two large *cottas* which although in reality were like the wood and mud bunkers previously captured, were called Forts by the Yanks. The first one, on higher ground than the second, was called Fort Binadayan. Its Datu was a friend and ally of the Sultan. Lightly defended, the cotta was easily taken by Baldwin's troops at a cost to the Americans of just one wounded. Fulton[332] reported sixteen Moros KIA and Kolbe[333] reported thirty.

The second bunker was called Fort Pandapatan, another old bunker style fort, but which was surrounded by pits filled with sharpened wooden stakes. It was located only about a thousand yards away from Fort Binadayan. It also had ten feet high and ten feet thick earthen walls interwoven with live bamboo trees and a ten feet deep moat filled with sharpened stakes. Baldwin wisely elected to bring up the artillery of four light mountain guns to soften the opposition.

---

332 Ibid, 113.

333 Kolb, "Blaze in the Boondocks, 2002. Fighting on America's Imperial Frontier in the Philippines, 1899-1913," 16.

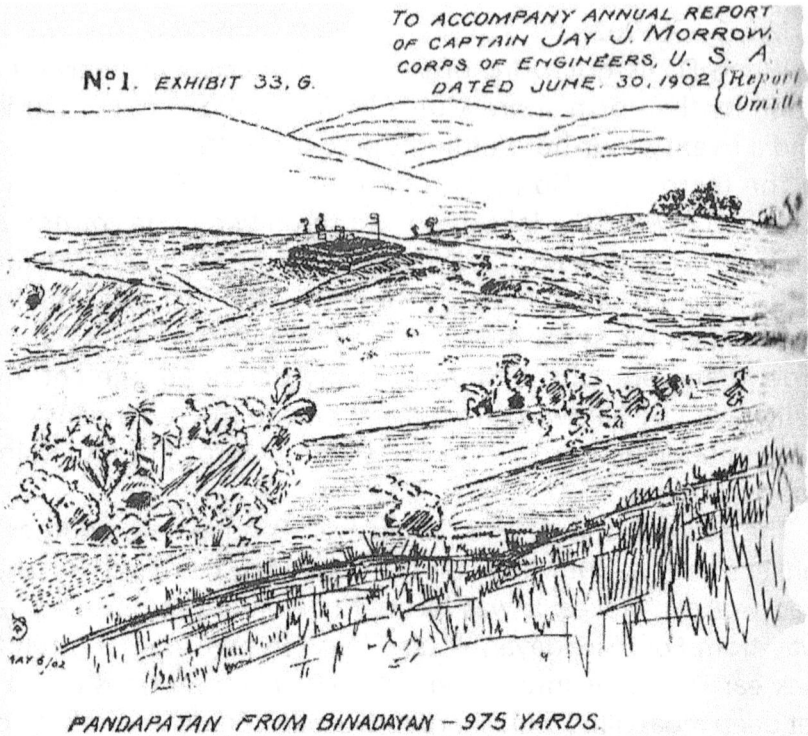

Nº 1. EXHIBIT 33, G.

TO ACCOMPANY ANNUAL REPORT
OF CAPTAIN JAY J. MORROW,
CORPS OF ENGINEERS, U. S. A.
DATED JUNE. 30, 1902 [Report
                        [Omitt

PANDAPATAN FROM BINADAYAN – 975 YARDS.

Drawing published in Moroland[334] courtesy of Robert A. Fulton. The above drawing shows Fort Pandapatan as seen by the artillerymen from the heights of Fort Binadayan.

Following a barrage of the four light mountain guns by the 25th Battery, four companies of the 27th Infantry slowly infiltrated a series of trenches surrounding the Fort. These trenches were occupied by Moro reinforcements which the Americans had watched filling the defenses of Fort Pandapatan.They came from boats across the lake all afternoon. Apparently, Pershing's and Datu Manabilang's success was only partial.

The Americans made slow advances forcing the Moros in the trenches closer to the bunker, some of them retreating into the formidable fort. As light faded, the Moros started shooting down on the trenches from their ten foot advantage, even throwing spears. They

---

334 Fulton, MOROLAND 1899-1906.

also had a number of small muzzle loading cannons called *lantacas* which were deadly at close range. Then the worst thing that could happen, did. Company G, the most forward of the advancing Yankees, ran out of ammo. Despite fixing their bayonets, they were no match for the *kris* wielding Moros who poured out of the *cotta,* viciously attacking in close quarters. Major William (Bill) Scott, Battalion field commander hollered over his shoulder to Lieutenant Thomas (Tom) A. Vicars, commander of Fox Company, which occupied the adjacent trench, "Tom, Tom Give us a hand!"

Vicars did not hesitate. Charging out of his trench, the lieutenant led his men in a charge across the pit filled terrain toward the walls of the cotta. Finding no way to climb the walls, Fox Company soon came under a devastating fusillade from the top of the cotta's parapets. One of the enemy's *lantacas* fired almost point blank in Vicar's face blowing his head clean off.

Continuing the hand-to-hand combat, second in command of F Company, 2nd Lieutenant A. I. Jossman was soon wounded so severely that command was then transferred the senior NCO, 1st Sergeant C. Pederson, who managed to get his battered troops to retreat under cover of a drenching rain and nightfall, leaving some forty-plus wounded soldiers still lying on the battlefield. The rain continued all night.

There were other acts of incredible courage that late May afternoon. Richard Kolb noting that attempting to scale the walls of the cotta was by far the deadliest task elaborates:

"Cpl. John Ward of F Company took the initiative, standing on the shoulders of two fellow infantrymen so he could fire over the walls."[335]

Kolb cites another act of courage that warranted the Medal of Honor: *"1st Lt. Charles G. Bickham was conspicuous enough in his gallantry to rate the Medal of Honor. 'Crossing a fire-swept field,' read his citation, 'in close range of the enemy, he brought a wounded soldier to a place of shelter.'"*[336]

Also during the night, a few unnamed heroes from the 25th Battery crawled through the rain and mud to recover the wounded

---

335 Kolb, "Blaze in the Boondocks, 2002. Fighting on America's Imperial Frontier in the Philippines, 1899-1913," 26.
336 Ibid.

and the remnants of Fox Company, who crawled the 1000 yards to safety.

The next morning, white flags flew over Fort Pandapatan. It turns out that the Sultan of Bayan, the Sultan of Pandapatan, along with Bayan's successor were killed during the battle. Eighty-three Moros surrendered, and later that morning overpowered their guards and escaped. About half of those were cut down by gunfire from nearby troops, eight of them recaptured and the rest escaped.

Losses to the 27th Infantry were ten KIA and forty-one wounded. Estimated Moro killed were between 300 and 400. According to the Americans, it was a victory as the numbers suggest. The Moros, however, as Robert Fulton says *"were using different scorecards for the same game."*[337]

What mattered the most to them was how well they did against the odds and how well they died. To them, they were the victors.

1st Lt. Charles G. Bickham, a native of Dayton, Ohio, and a 1920 graduate of Princeton, was awarded the Medal of Honor for actions at Bayan, Mindanao, Philippines May 2, 1902. Bickham died December 14, 1944, and is buried in Woodland Cemetery and Arboretum Dayton. Lt. Thomas Vicars did not receive any posthumous medals as was Army policy. He did have Camp Vicars, an Army Post, named in his honor near the battleground where he died. Capt. Pershing is inspecting a Company of 27th Infantry at Camp Vicars, above left. Photo courtesy of Robert Fulton.

337 Fulton, MOROLAND 1899-1906, 117.

CHAPTER TWENTY-TWO

July 4, 1902 – May 11, 1903

"The only principle for which they (some Moros) fought was the right to pillage and murder without molestation from the government." –Captain John .J Pershing

President Teddy Roosevelt's declaration of July 4, 1902, that officially ended the Philippine war was much like George W. Bush's "Mission Accomplished" concerning the Iraq war of the early 21st century. There was never a formal surrender, nor a peace treaty, but simply a political statement. It did differ, however, in that there was a qualification in Roosevelt's cable to General Chaffee in which he referred to *"provincial civil governments having been established throughout the ...archipelago not inhabited by Moro tribes."*[338]

In other words, Roosevelt was admitting there was still not any civil control over Moroland. Under Roosevelt's administration, the islands of Mindanao, Basilan, and the Sulu were now consolidated into a Moro Province, which he hoped could be controlled by a force of less than 5000 American soldiers. Fortunately for him, the Yanks were supplemented by the Philippine Scouts, the Philippine Constabulary mentioned earlier, and four gunboats of the U.S. Navy. He also had the genius of Captain John Pershing, who had been given far more authority by Chaffee and Davis than an officer of his rank should technically have. Pershing was soon to be the sole commander of the new Army post of Camp Vicars.

---

338 Fulton, MOROLAND 1899-1906, 121.

The new Philippine bill passed by congress and signed on July 1st, three days earlier than Roosevelt's declaration of the end of the Philippine war, terminated the office of military governor, thus relieving General Chaffee of those duties. William Howard Taft, the presiding officer of the Philippine Commission, was to be the new Governor General of the Philippines.

Changes in the military hierarchy were also forthcoming. Brig General Davis was promoted to Major General and would replace General Chaffee on October 1, 1902. Colonel Baldwin was promoted to Brig. General and reassigned as Commander of the Visayans. Davis's replacement was Brig. General Samuel S. Sumner, whose father, Edwin, Commanded a division of the Union Army at Antietam Creek. Captain Pershing was given "temporary" command of Camp Vicars, which included three companies of the 27th Infantry, the 25th Battery, and two troops of the 15th cavalry, a total of 700 some men and larger than an average battalion in size. Chaffee and Davis had manipulated the assignments so that their protégé, Captain Pershing, would have a free reign in the upcoming campaigns against the Lake Lanao Moros. Both of the generals knew a response to the continuing harassment of their troops by the Moros was a necessity.

Pershing, though, showing the patience of a saint, knew he had to build a solid base camp at Vicars before undertaking any action against the Moros, in spite of the almost daily attacks against the horse and mule-led supply trains from Malabang. Within a couple of months, the Army had lost nearly two dozen rifles and several belts of ammunition to the raiders.

The first indication of how tough and yet fair Pershing was going to be with robbers and murderers occurred when one of his soldiers was killed and his rifle stolen. Having been tipped off by a friendly native, Pershing promptly arrested the Sultan who had possession of the stolen Krag. Within hours, Pershing had a visit from a datu whom he thought was unfriendly, who told him that the Sultan had just bought the rifle from a bandit named Bugulung, and the Sultan was not guilty of theft or murder. Pershing challenged the datu, whose name was Datu Adtu, to prove it. The next morning, three bodies were lying in front of Pershing's tent, and one of them was the bandit Bugulung.

From that day Datu Adta was one of Pershing's best sources of information.[339]

From the fall of 1902 through the spring of 1903, there were several minor skirmishes around the lake. Pershing, knowing he could not be successful if he had to fight all of the datus and tribes, chose his targets with care and reason. He first had to find out who was friendly and who was not. As Robert Fulton so ably points out, *"...he (Pershing) knew from his close association with Ahmai Manabilang that real power in the datu system came not from force or wealth but from being wise and reasonable, but still tough and nobody's fool."[340]*

Minor clashes included an action on August 11, 1902 when twenty Bacolod Maranaos, trying to free the Sultan of Binidayan, who had been arrested as the responsible party for attacks on the supply trains, attacked a Camp Vicars outpost killing two and wounding two other American soldiers. On August 13th, two nights later, the attack was repeated with about thirty or so Maranaos from nearby Maciu (today spelled Masiu). The captive Sultan, hearing the disturbance, fashioned a club from his bunk and hit his guard over the head. The soldier, who was the sergeant of the guard, recovered from the blow, drew his revolver, and shot and killed the Sultan.

Pershing, using remarkable ingenuity, honored the departed Sultan, with a military formation and an appropriate artillery salute when the Sultan's people came to retrieve the body, thus averting an expected major attack. The ceremony, however, did not help to lessen the number of attacks on the supply trains from Malabang, nor on the nightly rifle fire from the jungle on the camp.

Besides the innumerable minor clashes, there were six major battles fought around Lake Lanao. The first of these was Bayan, already described, on May 2 – 3, 1902. There were two more that autumn before weather and disease called a halt to battle action. There was an encounter near the tiny thread-like Lake Butig (to the left of the town of Butig in the right lower part of the map on the next page) on September 18th, and the campaign at Masui (Macui) that lasted from September 29 – October 2, 1902.

---

339 *Ibid,119.*
340 *Ibid, 125.*

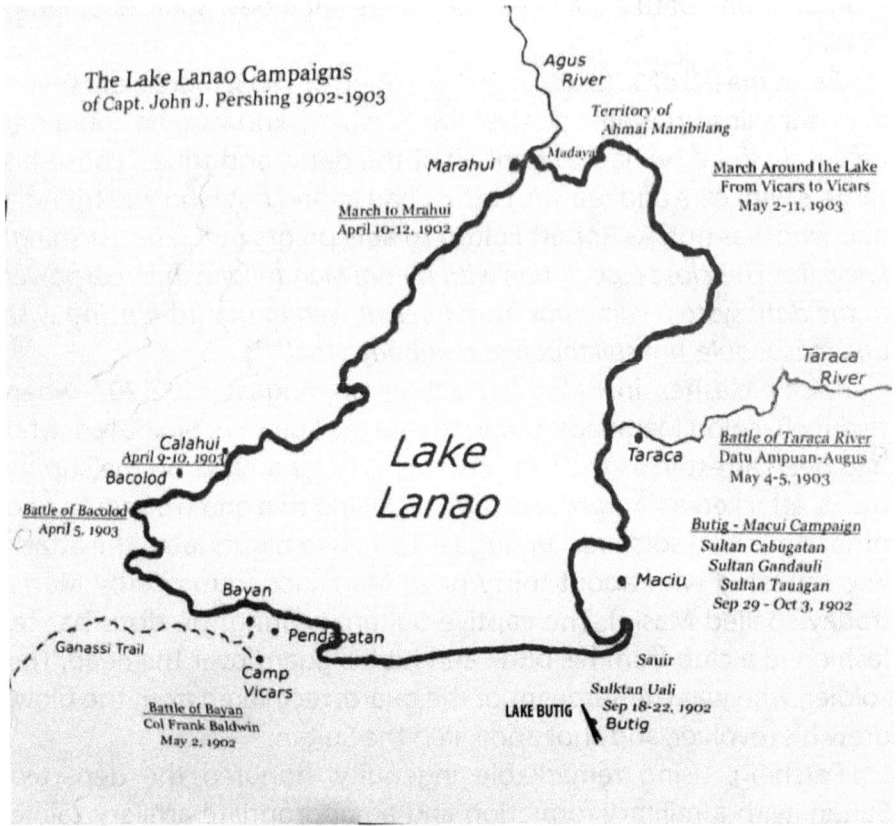

The Lake Lanao Campaigns
of Capt. John J. Pershing 1902-1903

Agus
River

Territory of
Ahmai Manibilang

Madaya

Marahui

March Around the Lake
From Vicars to Vicars
May 2-11, 1903

March to Mrahui
April 10-12, 1902

Lake
Lanao

Taraca
River

Calahui
April 9-10, 1903
Bacolod

Battle of Bacolod
April 5, 1903

Taraca

Battle of Taraca River
Datu Ampuan-Augus
May 4-5, 1903

Butig - Macui Campaign
Sultan Cabugatan
Sultan Gandauli
Maciu   Sultan Tauagan
Sep 29 - Oct 3, 1902

Bayan

Ganassi Trail

Pendapatan

Camp
Vicars

Battle of Bayan
Col Frank Baldwin
May 2, 1902

LAKE BUTIG

Sauir

Sulktan Uali
Sep 18-22, 1902
Butig

Map (modified by author) courtesy of Robert A. Fulton author of
Moroland

The first episode in September was an authorized expedition of forces from Camp Vicars issued by orders from Chaffee to Sumner against bandits and snipers from the southeast side of Lake Lanao. Two Sultans, one from the Butig Lake area called Sultan Uali and another from further north along the east coast of the lake, the Sultan of Maciu, were the targets. Sumner wanted to use a large force to solve the problem, but Chaffee, having learned a lot from Captain Pershing, insisted on a small force, to make the point that the Americans could destroy their cottas effectively while limiting loss of life on both sides. To accomplish this, he wisely put Pershing in command of the small attack force and held Sumner in reserve.

The result was three captured and destroyed cottas, no Americans casualties and few killed or wounded amongst the Moros during the assault on Butig. The next objective, Macui, took a little more effort. Two more cottas blocked the trail from Butig to Macui and besides that the trail was flooded by recent heavy rain. Using the same tactics of artillery barrage to soften the defenses and sharpshooters to pick off the enemy snipers, Pershing soon had the additional cottas plus two more under control and abandoned by the Moros. Attempts to advance further toward Macui were thwarted by mud, so Pershing elected to return to Camp Vicars and await better conditions. Although frustrated, Pershing's men had to endure derisive comments and gestures from the belligerent Moros as they left the area. Pershing had to promise them they would be back soon to prevent a spontaneous uprising from his angry soldiers. When he got back to Camp Vicars, Pershing sent some of Sumner's reserves to destroy the captured cottas.

On September 28, 1902, a week after his return, Pershing started out again, this time with a two pronged attack force. One by land was an engineering company of twenty-one men who built in two days a passable trail over the mud. The other was a small amphibious force traveling by a catamaran along the shore.

When the road was complete, the attack force was reinforced by elements of the 27th Infantry, so that the total force was now just under 600 men. On September 30, the reinforced company started towards Macui.

Over the next two days Pershing, using his now proven tactics, *"captured almost a dozen cottas manned by a total of 400 or more hostile Maranaos. The only tense moment occurred when 2nd Lt. Loring made his way with ten men to the entry gate of the largest cotta with the intent of setting it on fire and was almost trapped. But instead of trying to fight it out, Loring withdrew quickly under intense fire and got all his men back to safety, with only one man wounded."*[341]

During the remainder of the fall and winter of 1902 – 1903 a hiatus of hostilities ensued because of incessant monsoon rains and a cholera epidemic, which devastated the Maranaos population with at least 1000 deaths. Livestock, including the post's horses and mules, were infected by surra, which is a chronic wasting disease caused by

_____

341 Fulton, *MOROLAND 1899-1906*, 129.

trypanosomes, which are single-celled blood parasites related to the organisms that cause sleeping sickness. The disease, which is spread by biting flies, is most severe in horses, donkeys, and mules and is usually fatal. It was not known to affect humans in 1903, but a recent report from India suggested a possible endemic human source in that country.[342]

In addition to that, locusts attacked the native crops near Camp Vicars and rinderpest, a viral disease of cattle, added a plague involving the local carabao and cows. The natives and some of the soldiers must have thought their god(s) were angry.

By March, things were looking up. The cholera epidemic had subsided, the locusts had disappeared, and what animals were still alive appeared relatively healthy.

Pershing had proposed a "march around the lake" to find out who was still friendly to the USA, map the lake, and to demonstrate the Army's ability to travel where they pleased. Sumner and Davis both approved the proposal, Chaffee having already returned to the states.

Pershing's first objective of the march was to challenge the strongest known bad guy in the area, the Sultan of Bacolod. Bacolod was a community on the Southwest part of Lake Lanao. Pershing left Camp Vicars on April 5, 1903, with a force of over 500 men and about 100 mules carrying supplies and light artillery. On the first night, they were fired upon resulting in two American wounded.

A subsequent three-day siege at Bacolod killed 120 Moros[343]. Extension of the assault to Calahui, a cotta just three miles away from Bacolod, and which had fired on some of the troops trying to encircle Bacolod, accounted for twenty-three additional Moro KIA's. The Moros at Bacolod refused to surrender even after Pershing gave them more than three chances and allowed their women and children to escape. About half of the warriors fled with the women and children. The rest fought to their deaths.

342 http://www.tropmed.ag/material/diagnosis%20and%20control%20of%20trypanosomosis.pdf.

343 Kolb, "Blaze in the Boondocks, 2002. Fighting on America's Imperial Frontier in the Philippines, 1899-1913," 31.

The datu from Calhui, Datu Ampuan, surrendered the next day with several dozen of his men. He informed the Americans that most of the warriors who fled came from the east side of the lake to help. They were from Taraca, which was north of Macui, which Pershing's troops had bested the previous fall.

Pershing also required and obtained an oath of allegiance from Datu Ampuan, which he swore on a copy of the Qur'an, which according to historian Fulton,[344] Pershing kept for just that purpose.

On April 12, 1903, Pershing resumed his march north on the west side of the lake after four of his troops, escorting wounded were attacked by Moros wielding *kampilans* which were two-handed double-edged swords. Although the odds were even of four against four, and the Yanks were able to fight off the attackers and protect the wounded, they came off the worst for wear with all four severely wounded and one who died later. Pershing's expedition reached the Agus River on the same day and returned to Camp Vicars by the same route on the 16th with no further incidents. The west lake shore was now secure and mapped.

On May 2, Pershing started out again with a similar sized force supplemented by a number of friendly Datu-provided interpreters. The expedition was preceded by requests that friendly Datus would fly white flags and those opposed to the Americans would fly red ones. Surprisingly, as Robert Fultan stated, "many obliged."[345]

On the march towards Taraca, the 27th Infantry ran into multiple episodes of sniper fire, but no red flags until they reached the Taraca River, where the cotta of Datu of Ampuan-Agaus (not the Ampuan of the west shore) was completely covered in red.

Two companies of the 27th Infantry formed a skirmish line and advanced toward the red flagged cotta, while it was being bombarded by the artillery's mountain guns. One small cotta, not previously detected, sent irritating fire from the left flank of the skirmish line. It was quickly captured and destroyed. Then, there was suddenly significant resistance encountered by Company C led by 1st Lt. George C. Shaw. With additional reinforcements by two more companies of

---

344 Fulton, MOROLAND 1899-1906, 137.
345 Fulton, MOROLAND 1899-1906, 138.

the 27th and troop G of the 15th Cavalry, the skirmish line made an advance of about a mile and ran into another previously undetected cotta named Pitacus, also covered with red flags. Author Robert A. Fulton tells what happened next: *"At first there was little resistance.... from the Pitacus cotta and Shaw, believing it to be lightly defended, attempted to scale its eastern wall. Meanwhile, Lt. W. B Gracie approached the fort from the opposite side of the river. Shaw and two of his men reached the top of the parapet but were immediately hit with withering fire from within, knocking and badly wounding the two soldiers from the parapet. Shaw stood alone on top of a bamboo ladder, coolly and single-handedly shooting back with his .45-caliber revolver. When he ran out of ammunition, Shaw had his men pass him up rifle after rifle. Lt. Gracie, hearing the battle, immediately crossed the river and led his men in scaling the south wall, Shaw and Gracie pouring in a deadly cross-fire as one by one, others of Company C joined Shaw atop the parapet of the east wall. It was a brief but vicious battle, ending in hand to hand fighting but American fire power prevailed."*[346]

After the fight at Pitacus, the soldiers of the expedition had the cotta at Ampuan-Agaus, their initial objective, surrounded, but it was getting dark. The next morning, a white flag was flying above the cotta, and the datu and his ally the *Cali* of Maciu surrendered. Two days later, Pershing's expedition reached Marahui, at the headwaters of the Agus River. Awaiting them were General Sumner and many Islamic leaders and datus from the north shore of the lake. One of them, the *Pandita of Nuzca*, was *"the acknowledged religious leader of the Islamic faith for all of Lake Lanao."*[347]

The presence of the *Pandita* as a coup alone was a significant one, which might have brought peace to the Islands, except for a monkey wrench thrown into the mix by President Theodore Roosevelt. That wrench was the appointment, by Roosevelt, of Harvard trained physician turned line officer, Brig. General Leonard Wood, as the Governor General of the newly designated Moro Province.

For his part in the battle, Lt. Shaw, was awarded the Medal of Honor.

---

346 *Ibid, 139.*
347 *Ibid, 139.*

348*

George Clymer Shaw was born in Pontiac, Michigan on March 6, 1866. A career officer, Shaw rose to the rank of Brig General. He died in February 1960 and was buried with full military honors in Section 3 of Arlington National Cemetery. His wife, Ida Adams Shaw (August 24, 1867 – February 13, 1946), is buried with him.

348* Photo cropped from a larger one provided courtesy of Moroland author, Robert A. Fulton

CHAPTER TWENTY-THREE

July 9, 1903 – February 1, 1904

"Juramentado definition, a Muslim, esp. a Moro, bound by an oath to be killed fighting against Christians and other infidels." –Dictionary .com

For a fascinating discussion of the pre-presidential election politics of 1903, the reader is referred to Robert A. Fulton's *Moroland* pgs 150 – 160. The bottom line is that the decisions of 1903 were not in the best interests of the USA or the Moros. They were made in the words of historian Fulton *"jointly to further the ambitions of three men, Theodore Roosevelt, William Howard Taft, and Leonard Wood."*[349]

From the publicity given to Captain Pershing in the USA and around the world, particularly after he was made an honorary *datu* by a prominent Islamic religious leader, an unheard of event for an infidel, inevitably stirred up jealousy amongst the regular Army officers, extending far up the ranks to include Brig General Leonard Wood. The public climax of the situation was illustrated by an editorial that appeared in the *New York Sun* on May 15, 1903, which suggested that Pershing needed a well-connected journalist like General Wood had in the flamboyant Edgar Bellairs, to promote his interests. After the editorial appeared, General Wood *"viewed the lowly Captain as a dangerous rival."*[350]

Some month's later, the *NY Sun* exposed Edgar Bellairs as an ex-convict and con man who had changed his name, which left

---

349 Fulton, MOROLAND 1899-1906, 158.
350 Ibid, 160.

Leonard Wood even more infuriated. Fortunately, Pershing had left the Philippines on a new assignment six weeks before Leonard Wood and his entourage arrived on July 9, 1903, which quieted the rivalry for the moment.

A prolific volume of history and literature has been written about Leonard Wood, probably the most enlightening is a biography by Texas Christian University's Jack McCallum, MD, PhD. Another biographer, Jack Lane, author of *Armed Progressive*, written earlier is also very informing. Both researchers paint Woods as a very complicated personality who was known for his intelligence, athleticism, charm, self-confidence, and energy. He was also described as a self-serving, arrogant, overly ambitious *(jackass?)* who would resort to cruelty and possibly even murder to get his way.[351]

Wood graduated from Harvard Medical School with an MD degree following an internship at Boston City Hospital in 1884. He started a private practice in Boston, but soon quit to take a contract as a civilian surgeon for the Army. He was sent to Fort Huachuca, Arizona Territory in the summer of 1885. There, he made friends with our hero of earlier chapters, Captain (later General) Henry Lawton. To make a long story short, Wood spent the next several months as Lawton's surgeon on an expedition to capture or kill the infamous Chiracaua Apache, Geronimo.

When it was over, Wood, who had sought and been offered a commission in the Army Medical Corps, had gained fame as one of the heroes that captured Geronimo, and had gained the confidence and trust of senior officers like Lawton, and General Nelson Miles. General Miles was the one who promoted Wood's and Lawton's heroism, for whatever political reasons, over the officers who actually did all the work, General George Crook and 1st. Lt. Charles Gatewood. The reason Geronimo surrendered was primarily due to the trust he placed in his friend, Lieutenant Charles Gatewood.

Transferred to San Francisco in 1890, Wood married Louise Smith, a daughter of a politically prominent family, which helped him get a transfer to Washington, DC. There he became ingratiated with the prominent military brass and politicians of the day and soon found

---

351 *Ibid, 168.*

himself appointed as the personal physician to the first lady, Ida Saxton McKinley in 1897.

At a White House function, Wood met Theodore Roosevelt, who was enamored to meet one of the men involved in the capture of Geronimo. The then assistant secretary of the Navy, Roosevelt soon became fast friends with Wood. In April 1898, just before Congress declared war on Spain, Wood was awarded the Medal of Honor for his role in the pursuit of Geronimo in 1886. The award, given more than ten years after the events, would later become a scandalous controversy since the man who allegedly recommended it (Lawton) was dead and the person who signed it (Secretary Alger) was supposedly suffering from dementia.

When Roosevelt was offered command of a volunteer regiment to go to Cuba, he declined, saying he would take second in command if his friend, the Indian fighter and Medal of Honor recipient, Leonard Wood would take the offered command instead. Secretary of War Russell Alexander Alger, for whose family Leonard Wood, MD, was the physician as well as he was for Mrs. McKinley, agreed and thus were born the Rough Riders, with Colonel of Volunteers (physician and Regular Medical Corps Army Captain), Leonard Wood in command.

After the Spanish surrendered, Wood was first appointed Military Governor of Santiago Provence, and later of all of Cuba, courtesy of President McKinley. As his volunteer commission was about to expire, McKinley then promoted him to Brigadier General of Volunteers and made the promotion permanent in 1901. Talk about politics in action! Wood was advanced over more than 500 officers.

So now there is a new Governor General of Moro Province, who is also about to replace the retiring General Miles as Military Commander of the Department of Mindanao and Jolo and whose combat experience was limited to a half day's fight in Cuba. He is also a General who wore the Medal of Honor for a long hard ride in the western USA, certainly not above and beyond the call of duty. Even General Miles, who had initially promoted Wood's heroics concerning Geronimo, remarked publically that he had never recommended Wood for anything more than a commendation and *"wondered aloud how this could happen."*[352]

---

352 *Ibid, 176.*

Taft, hearing all the controversy and rumors of Wood's unlimited ambition, was concerned that Wood's aggression would place his own position as Governor General of the Philippines in jeopardy.

In spite of the all the hullabaloo, Wood overcame Taft's concerns and they became friends. In truth Wood did not want Taft's position, but instead had his eye on the Roosevelt-promised promotion to Major General and thus become Department of the Philippines Commander. It was easy for Wood to agree to Taft's suggestion that if Wood would allow Taft and Roosevelt flexibility in the timing of his promotion, he could manage Moro Province with a free hand.

When Wood took over the Army Departments of Mindanao and Jolo on August 6, 1903, it was just three days later that Roosevelt announced his appointment to become a Major General. Ohio Senator Marcus Alonzo Hanna, was viciously opposed to Wood's advancement for one reason anyway, because he (Wood) had been involved or at least charged with obtaining public works contracts for his brother while he was Military Governor in Cuba. Hanna probably had other reasons as well, but the bottom line was that Wood's promotion was going to run into considerable opposition in the senate. It would not deter that there was a new "sheriff" (Leonard Wood) in town, a new hard line approach to criminal activity by the Moros, and damn the consequences that was about to happen.

Leonard Wood

William Howard Taft

Theodore Roosevelt

1903 Political Power Players

* * *

August 24 – 31, 1903

One of the first indications of how Wood would handle his new power happened during his self-proclaimed *First Sulu Expedition*, which was a journey across Jolo with three companies of the 23rd Infantry, two more companies of the 17th Infantry, three troops of the 15th Calvary and two mountain guns of artillery. The show of force was larger than anything Pershing had used in the lake country of Mindanao, but it was Wood's intention to show his power after three incidents of unprovoked attacks by Jolo Moros resulted in three deaths, only one of which was an American. Colonel William Wallace, the district commander, thought the incidents might be a renewal of *juramentados*, the 19th century equivalent of today's suicide bombers, and, although he was apparently wrong according to a later investigation by General Davis, the thought fit General Wood's preconceived notion of deliberate provocations, especially since the American soldier's death was caused by an unprovoked assailant who was shot and killed during the attack.

In spite of Wood's good-for-me, good-for-the-USA-intentions, the First Sulu Expedition resulted in:

- Surprise visits to each datu's territory with forced summons of the leaders.
- Public embarrassment of the Rajah Muda, brother of the Sultan. Muda had pleaded illness to avoid the meeting, but was pronounced fit by an Army doctor, was hauled in forcibly on the back of a slave and scolded publically by General Wood.
- Loss of confidence amongst Wood's own officers some of whom knew the Rajah was a direct lineal descendant of the Prophet Mohammed. As author Fulton said, *"Wood might as well have publicly burned the Sultan's flag or spit on the Qur'an."*[353]
- Insulted previously friendly Datus Joakanian, Opau, Indanan, and Panglima Hassan who was a powerful war leader.
- Wood being perceived by the above Islamic leaders as a bully and a coward who refused a challenge by Datu Indanan to do

353 Ibid, 183.

battle with an equal number of warriors and soldiers which was the normal Moro way of settling a dispute. (George Patton of WWII fame would have loved that!)

- Wood's detractors labeling the First Sulu Expedition as the Great Promenade.
- The appointment by Wood of his trusted subordinate, Major Hugh Scott, as Governor of the Sulu District.

Historian Dumindin gives additional information about Panglima Hassan: *Hassan was the district commander of Luuk, Sulu, under the Sulu Sultanate. He was the first Tausug leader to defy the sultan's order that, in the interest of peace, the people should acknowledge American sovereignty. As an Imam (roughly translates to "prayer leader"), Panglima Hassan looked at the intrusive American "infidels" as threats to Islam and Moro society . The Tausug Moros had allowed the Spaniards to build a garrison in Siasi and a church in Jolo by virtue of the 1878 peace pact, but that was all. After 300 years of almost continuous warfare, the Spanish had known better than to try and impose their authority over the fiercely independent Sulu people. But the Americans - backed by utterly lethal modern weapons – had no such reservations."[354]*

---

354 Dumindin, "Philippine-American War, 1899-1902."

Panglima Hassan (Central figure), a former friendly datu, was killed in action against the Americans on March 4, 1904, at Bud Bagsak ("Mount Bagsak"). See later text.

* * *

September 8 – September 20, 1903

On September 8, 1903, a major problem for the Moros was born, which was Act No. 8 of the Legislative Council of the Philippine Commission (of which Wood was a member), which established slave holding or hunting as a crime punishable by up to twenty years in prison and a fine of 10,000 pesos.

Slavery as a problem, which had previously been virtually ignored by the Bates Agreement, was now on the agenda of enforcement.

Another of the major problems as the Moros saw it was the implementation of a *cedula* or head of household tax on each family, which, although originally instituted by the Spanish, had never been enforced on the Moros. This tax had been approved by the Philippine Commission, the War Department, the President, and the U.S. Congress, all of whom had apparently forgotten about the openly negotiated monetary settlement to end slavery, which was going to be accepted by the Moros.

Now here come the Yankees with a "new" tax and a law to eliminate a slave system that worked well for both groups, slaves and owners,[355] no compensation for either, and a policy that was set in secret which would override Sharia and Moro Law. Aside from the fact that the Bates Agreement was still technically in force, the announcements of the new policies which included a threat of enforcement by the Yankees under General Wood, amounted to, in the eyes of the Moros, *"a military dictatorship by a foreign power."*[356].

It was Major Hugh Scott who found himself in the middle of one of the first confrontations involving slavery. The four Schuck brothers lived on a Jolo Island plantation and were sons of a German emigrant who had married a Muslim woman. Eddie Schuck, the oldest, was a multi-linguist who interpreted for the Americans, asked Major Scott to help with a problem. One of the Schuck plantation inhabitants was the father of a young woman who was indentured to another and after mistreatment had fled home to her father. Biroa, the son of a datu, had killed a man on the Schuck plantation while recovering the runaway. Biroa was under the protection of the local Sultan,

355 Bob Couttie, *Chew the Bones.*
356 Fulton, *MOROLAND 1899-1906,* 186.

who was away. The Rajah Muda, who General Wood had publically embarrassed, was still acting as the Sultan, when Wood, hearing of the problem, issued a warrant for Biroa's arrest and gave Rajha Muda five days to produce the wanted man.

Now Scott was in a pickle because he was obligated to carry out the Woods-issued warrant, which he knew would not hold any legal authority with the Moros. The only solution, he thought, was to have the Moros themselves bring in the killer. He finally convinced the Rajah to intervene, who in turn gave the job to Datu Indanan, the man who had challenged Wood to do battle with his soldiers against his Moro warriors but had been refused.

Datu Indanan managed to recover the girl, but refused to spend his men's lives assaulting a fortified 500 foot mountain top to which Biroa and his father had retreated. The acting Sultan then appealed to the most powerful datu, Panglima Hussan *(Panglima, a title meaning war chief[357])* to complete the arrest. After many weeks of negotiations, threats, and posturing by both sides Biroa finally turned himself in after Wood agreed to allow him to be processed by a Moro court, which fined him $25 Mexican and dismissed the criminal charges.

* * *

October – November 1903

The records of events for October and November are confusing due to discrepancies in official reports, meetings and correspondence as well as memoirs and various biographies. But as historian and author Fulton says: *"The facts…. are less important than the outcome."[358]*

Suffice it to say that the principals, Wood and Scott for the Americans, and Hassan and his allies for the Moros continued their posturing even after the Biroa affair was over.

In early November, Brig. General Leonard Wood put together an immense expeditionary force of fourteen companies of infantry, two troops of cavalry, and a battery of field artillery, plus all of the necessary supply train animals and human *cargadores* and started on his

---

357 Fulton, *MOROLAND 1899-1906*, 193.
358 Ibid.

2nd Sulu Expedition, this time following Pershing's trail around the west side of Lake Lanao.

Despite torrential rains the expedition made the Agus River in two days, but during the crossing on small boats called *vintas* (manned by soldiers who followed the expedition along the lakeshore), three of the boats capsized in high winds with the loss of one life, countless rounds of ammo, a couple of dozen rifles, and five to six days of rations. Just as Wood was dealing with this small disaster, he received a message, sent by Major Scott, that an American Army surveying party on Jolo had been attacked by Moros who had been supplied with modern rifles by Panglima Hassan.

Later documents and diaries contradicted the urgency with which Wood reacted. He turned the entire force around and did a forced march back down the west coast, had them board transports, stopped at Zamboanga, where Gatling guns, more ammo and his entire staff including Captains George Langhorne and Frank McCoy were loaded on board and set out for Hassan's territory near Esseo Bay. The force was joined by a battalion of Engineers, two Navy gunboats, and two additional transports.

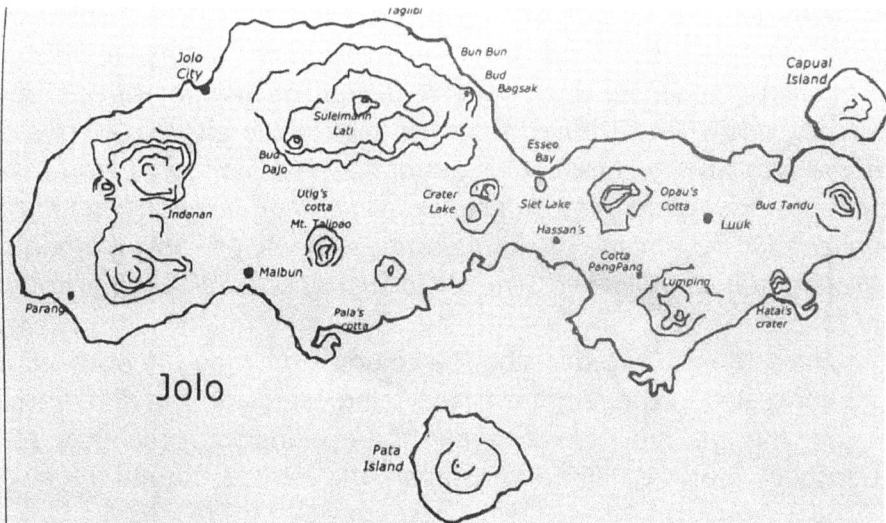

Jolo Map courtesy of Robert A. Fulton author of Moroland.

While Wood's "invasion fleet" anchored in Esso bay, his ship continued west to Jolo City where, according to Fulton, he caught Major Scott completely by surprise, particularly when Wood informed him that his forces, the "2nd Sulu Expedition" would land at Esso Bay before dawn.[359]

Unlike Pershing, the headstrong General Leonard Wood didn't believe in coddling the Moros or negotiating further, or even finding and punishing the real culprits of the ambush. And even though Scott had already learned who the culprits were and that they had lied to Panglima Hassan to get the rifles used in the ambush, he couldn't convince Wood otherwise. The invasion, whose purpose was to kill or capture Hassan was a go.

There are several versions of what happened next. One is Dumindin's: *"In early November 1903, Hassan and about 3,000 to 4,000 warriors besieged the American garrison in Jolo. Armed only with krises (wavy-edged swords) and some old rifles, they bottled up the Americans for a week before being forced to withdraw. Following a battle, Hassan was captured while bathing near his camp at Lake Seit in late November 1903, but he soon escaped."[360]*

Robert A. Fulton's version is better documented: *"Wood noted in his diary 'Little opposition to our landing.' The command was split into three columns, Wood in the center with the main contingent, Bullard (Battalion commander Major. Robert L. Bullard) on the right with his 28th Infantry, and when he arrived Scott was to be on the left with two troops of the 14th cavalry, three companies of the 17th Infantry and the 18th Field battery. Wood's reconstituted expedition had now swollen to just under 1,250 fighting men with supporting staff and two navy gunboats, the largest military force assembled in Sulu since the Spanish invasion of 1878."[361]*

Fulton goes on to describe the columns drawing fire from snipers concealed in the rainforests and tall grasses and the differences in training and firepower between the opponents. Arriving by sea transport, Scott's cavalry didn't debark the transports until the next

359 Ibid, 199.
360 Dumindin, "Philippine-American War, 1899-1902."
361 Fulton, MOROLAND 1899-1906, 199.

morning; they had to swim their horses ashore and were several hours behind the infantry, who had already started towards Hassan's luxury home, which was closer to the south coast. On their way to catch up with the infantry, Scott's cavalry noted an increasing number of Moro bodies and burned out dwellings the closer they got.

When the American's reached Hassan's mansion he had vanished. Scott, knowing how proud the Panglima was of his home and possessions, ordered the most valuable furnishings and possessions put under guard. The next morning, Scott, Charlie Schuck, and a troop of cavalry went looking for him. They found him with the information obtained from a captured Moro and persuaded him to give himself up. On the return, as they neared Hassan's home, they found General Wood in one of Hassan's priceless rocking chairs watching the mansion burn to the ground.

Wood then ordered Scott to take the prisoner back to Jolo City and left to rejoin his expedition. On the way, Hassan persuaded Scott to pick up his wife and family at a location only he could find. Otherwise, Hassan argued, they would hide in the swamp where Hassan's enemies would find and kill them.

Fulton continues the tale, using as a source one of Scott's letters to his wife: *"As they crossed through a bamboo thicket, Hassan suddenly bolted. Using both hands, Scott brought up his revolver and took a bead on Hassan,* (he had previously warned him he would shoot to kill if he tried to escape) *but before he could fire a shot rang out and the gun was knocked out of his hands. When he stooped to retrieve it, a volley of bullets whizzed over his arched back. Unable to pick up the pistol, Scott realized that both of his hands had been nearly blown apart by the bullet."*[362]

Scott managed to get back to a place of safety, and stop the cavalry from charging the thicket because he didn't know the size of the opposition. Luckily they had an Army doctor with them who stopped Scott's bleeding and got him sedated. He awoke in a hospital in Jolo.

On Sunday, November 15, 1903, word of Hassan's escape and Major Scott's wounds triggered emotions for revenge, not only by General Wood, but by most of the troops who felt Hassan had deliberately led Scott into a trap. Wood set out with his expedition again,

---

362 Ibid.

and managed to stir up a fight in a swamp where most of the Moros were located. They then marched west from Luuk and by the time they were done the body count ranged from 1000 to 1500 with an untold number of cottas destroyed. The Americans had one KIA, Pvt. Martin Brennan, 14th U.S Cavalry, and seventeen WIA.

* * *

December 1903 – January 1904

At Taft's request after the action of the 2nd Sulu Expedition Wood traveled to Manila just before Christmas to meet with the Philippine Commission. Taft had been appointed Secretary of War to replace Elihu Root and was about to start out after the holidays on the five week journey to the states. Taft still led the Philippine Commission, however, and he wanted Wood's to present to the Commission his (Wood's) recommendations on the Bates agreement.

Wood not only recommended abrogation, but he added his intentions of establishing a new code of laws modeled after those in the USA. The Commission spent little time discussing the findings and initially passed a resolution to proceed with the Wood recommendations without dissent. The Moros had no input whatsoever.

Later, when he had time to read the documents outlining the abrogation, which included stopping payments to the Tausug[363] [364] Moros, Moro Legislative Council member Najeeb Saleeby, a Christian physician who had interned in New York, went carefully over the Bates Agreement and found wording that upset him. In order to make a point, he wound up filing a lawsuit against Eddie Schuck,

---

363 Dumindin, "Philippine-American War, 1899-1902."

364 Historian Dumindin clarifies: There are at least ten Moro ethno-linguistic subgroups, all descended from the same Malayan stock that populated the rest of the Philippines. Three of these groups make up the majority of the Moro. They are the Maguindanaos of North Cotabato, Sultan Kudarat, and Maguindanao provinces; the Maranaw of the two Lanao provinces; and the Tausug of the Sulu Archipelago. Smaller groups include the Banguigui, Samal, Badjao, Yakan, Ilanon, Sangir, Malabugnan, and the Jama Mapun.

They are not closely knit and lack solidarity. Each group is proud of their culture, identity, and language, including their variation of Islam.

the interpreter of the Agreement. It was Saleeby's contention that if the Americans stopped the payments, the Sultanate and datus had a legitimate claim to reclaim property that the Americans had in effect leased.

Fulton feels that *"The dispute seems to explain why Taft quietly took Wood's report and recommendations with him back to Washington, rather than cabling Roosevelt for a rubber stamp approval,"*[365] because if there were a political embarrassment, no doubt Taft and Wood would be blamed. The delay in delivery proved to be an astute political move by Taft. By the time he arrived in Washington, D.C., on February 1, an Army Board of Inquiry had obtained a second opinion on the wording and found no discrepancy.

U.S. Army headquarters on Jolo, early 1900's. One of the properties the USA paid "lease fees" to the Tausug Moros before abrogation of the Bates Agreement.

---

365 *Ibid, 209.*

CHAPTER TWENTY-FOUR

January 1904 – October 15, 1905

"The greatest griefs are those we cause ourselves." –Sophocles

Even though Major Hugh Scott's hands were like mincemeat and he was hospitalized for two months, he clearly wanted to establish a dialogue with the fugitive Hussan. As he began to explore ways to do so his talks with the friendly datus (that he knew) revealed another more serious problem of the backlash that was occurring as the search for Hassan by the Army got more intense.

More than one datu told him that if the searches continued without regard for native property rights that the natives would soon not only be hostile to the Americans, but would solidly back up Hassan and the two outlaws, Maharajah Andung and Datu Tallu, who had been responsible for the initial sniper attacks that started the whole thing on Jolo in the first place.

After some resistance from his boss, General Wood, Scott managed to convince him that he could take charge of the search for Hassan despite his current disability. With both hands in one sling, he spent the next month recruiting a force of Muslims numbering almost 2000, to search for the fugitive Hassan. Like Pershing, Scott had the natural ability to communicate with the Moros with mutual respect.

On the 6th of February the search and pressure got through to one of the outlaws, the Maharajah Andung, who surrendered in Jolo

City. *"Scott exiled him to a southern island, he mended his ways and never was a problem again."[366]*

Just over two weeks later, having finally heard that Hassan was secluded not far from his burned down mansion at a cotta called Pang Pang (see map page 291). Major Scott, with a troop of 14th Cavalry, four companies of the 17th Infantry and a battery of artillery headed for Pang Pang accompanied by two of the Schuck brothers as interpreters. Also on the expedition were a number of Moro datus including Datu Indanan and their men. After several hours of fighting, at least three requests for surrender by the Schucks, and enduring a crossfire from Indanan's men, who were supposed to be the point of the attack, Scott's assault was successful killing 226 of the enemy and sustaining only seven American and one faithful Moro WIA. Once again, Hassan managed to escape. Somehow the treachery of Indanan's men failed to deter Scott from using Moro allies any further.

On March 3, 1904, following another tip, Scott with four troops of the 14th Cavalry surrounded Mount (Mount is *Bud* in Tausug language) Bagsak, and awaited the appearance of the fugitive. He was surprised by the appearance of another Maharajah named Opau, along with about a thousand of his men. Although reluctant to let the Moros participate, Scott had them circle the mountain some distance back while he and about 400 of his troopers advanced up the mountain in the middle of the night.

At dawn on the 4th, Hassan with two companions appeared from a *nipa* hut near the top of the mountain. Before Scott saw him, two shots rang out. Both of Hassan's companions went down immediately, but Hassan himself fired his rifle and hit one soldier in the hip. He then drew his *kris (Fulton says barong)* and charged the Cavalry sergeant, who had shot the rifle out of his hands. *"Hassan had 17 wounds in his body, but died game, crawling with his kris in his mouth toward the nearest wounded American soldier when the last bullet dispatched him."[367]*

Fulton describes it a little differently and is likely more accurate, a kris was longer than a barong but both would be difficult to carry in one's teeth:

366 Fulton, MOROLAND 1899-1906, 214.
367 Dumindin, "Philippine-American War, 1899-1902."

"Hassan drew his barong and charged towards the sergeant across the open ground. Thirty two Krag bullets hit Hassan before a last bullet from the sergeant's .45 revolver plugged him dead between the eyes."[368]

For the entire pursuit, lasting nearly a month, Major Scott had no use of his hands. He was never commended nor given a medal by General Wood. He did, however, gain his place of respect among his men and among the Moros, both the friendly ones and the hostile.

* * *

March 5 – 17, 1904

On Mindanao, Muslim leader Datu Ali had openly voiced his opposition to the new legislation as word of it spread throughout the Maguindanao population.

Datu Ali was the leader who had rejected the demand sent by Col. Frank Baldwin via Ali's son-in-law, the cleric Sharif Muhammad Afdal, to deliver the murderers and thieves who had attacked soldiers in March 1902 (See page 161). The rejection of Col. Baldwin's demand was a little surprising since the culprits were Maranaos and Ali was a Maguindanao, a mortal enemy.

Ali was also the son-in-law of Datu Piang, one of the wealthiest of the leaders on the island. He was also another of those Muslim leaders who traced his lineage back to the Prophet Mohammed. There seemed to be a lot of those in Moroland.

Ali was building a large cotta along with a number of his Maguindanao allies in the Cotabato Valley, and it was rumored that the new fortress would be manned by warriors as soon as it was ready. Ali intended to fight.

From Richard Kolb: *"Ali had pledged: 'I will try to kill all the people who are friends of the Americans.' Wood had placed a $500 reward on his head-dead or alive. That was a tidy sum for the time and place, and helped in the manhunt."*[369] Kolb's statement referred to a manhunt which Wood later instituted.

---

368 Fulton, MOROLAND 1899-1906, 215.
369 Kolb, "Blaze in the Boondocks, 2002. Fighting on America's Imperial Frontier in the Philippines, 1899-1913," 31.

On 5 March, Wood started out on his "1st Rio Grande Expedition" headed for *Siranaya* (Fulton spells it *Seranaya*) the site of the new cotta in the Cotabato Valley. His intent was a show of force to *"over-awe this incipient uprising."*[370].

From March 7 – 11, 1904 Wood's force, numbering about a thousand traveling overland but which included some sailors and marines traveling up the Taraca River, reached Siranaya, and after a fierce firefight, started an artillery bombardment on the 10th, and were scheduled to assault the cotta the next morning. At daybreak, there was a white flag flying over the cotta and Ali and his warriors had vanished.

The Expedition against Datu Ali and the Sultan of Taraca resulted in 130 cottas destroyed or captured along the Taraca River, about 100 Moros KIA, and enough mosquitoes slapped that as reported by General Wood, *"The men were almost crazy."*[371]

When he got back to his headquarters on March 17th in Zamboanga, Wood found on his desk the Roosevelt-signed order abrogating the Bates agreement. The next day, he finally received his long awaited promotion to Major General.

* * *

---

370 *Fulton, MOROLAND 1899-1906, 218.*
371 *Ibid.*

Datu Ali, a son, and one of his 3 wives circa 1900. Photo courtesy Robert A. Fulton, www.morolandhistory.com

May 8 – November 15, 1904

The Cotabato Valley was on the south coast of Mindanao, south of the coastal towns of Malabang and Parang (see map page 260). The Rio Grande (Grand River) flowed southeast from the town of Cotabato past Datu Piang's estate, and through the Litguasan swamps. Just north of the swamps was Lake Simpetan and there on May 8, 1904, thirty-six men of Company F of the 17th Infantry Regiment in pursuit of Datu Ali, were ambushed by about 160 Moros[372] (Fulton says no more than fifty Moros[373]) losing fifteen KIA, six WIA, and two captured. The captured Yanks were released four days later. The pursuit of Ali continued for months.

General Wood had been instrumental in forming provisional companies for special assignments. These were likely the forerunners of our special forces today. In the early 1900's, they were called "Provo's"

---

372 Kolb, "Blaze in the Boondocks, 2002. Fighting on America's Imperial Frontier in the Philippines, 1899-1913," 31.

373 Fulton, MOROLAND 1899-1906, 226.

and were created especially to track down Datu Ali. A month after the Cotabato Valley Ambush, Wood was back in the valley with one of these units and although they could not find Ali, his troops got into a firefight that killed twenty-six Moros. He continued sending Provo units throughout Mindanao looking for the elusive datu without success all summer. The forceful, destructive policy, however, took its toll with the indiscriminate loss of life including women and children, the interruption of commerce, and the destruction of property.

By fall, even Ali's relatives including his father-in-law, Datu Piang, had had enough and were ready to turn him in. The Moros on Mindanao were about to be given a break, however, for three reasons. The first was an acceleration of troublemaking on the Island of Jolo, and the second was the deteriorating health of Major General Leonard Wood.

Wood's health problem was the presence of a large benign brain tumor called a meningioma, which was causing intermittent episodes of paralysis and seizures. In spite of his health, Wood mounted another large expedition to quiet the unrest on Jolo. The troublemaker was a rebellious datu named Perika Utig who was raiding his neighbors. On the very day Wood landed with his new expedition, Utig had attacked Major Scott and killed three of his men,[374] but Wood did not hear of it until the next day.

On landing, Wood's soldiers had their hands full in firefights in which they killed about fifty Moros with the loss of one of their own. When he heard about Scott's losses Wood' joined him in surrounding the cotta where Utig had taken refuge. At dawn the next morning his artillery reduced the cotta to rubble and when the Moros in the adjacent village refused to surrender they were overrun by the Americans. The Americans had seven KIA. All the Moros were killed, including women and a few children. The women were reported armed. Another cotta was destroyed the next day with similar Moro loss of life.

Wood returned to Zamboanga after the last cotta was destroyed and another captured with the aid of intimidation by a U.S. Navy destroyer's searchlight. It was his last expedition for a while.

The third reason the Moros were given a break was that Wood was called to Manila to assume temporary command of the

---

374 Jack McCallum, Leonard Wood Biography, New York U Press, NY, 2006, 223.

Department of the Philippines, the post he had wanted all along. Although he had been severely upset with Roosevelt when the President appointed General Henry Corbin to the post he had been promised, he was glad to fill-in until Corbin could get there. Corbin arrived on November 11th, and Wood was back in Zamboanga on the 15th. Roosevelt had been reelected the previous week,

Moroland historian Fulton speculated that General Wade, the lame duck Commander of the Department of the Philippines, had been ordered back to the USA before the election so that Wood could be sent to Manila in order to prevent a potential Philippine-Moro crisis during the Presidential election period which Wood was prone to commit, if he remained in Moroland.

* * *

November 15, 1904 – November 15, 1905.

When Wood formed his first Provo units, he handpicked each officer and man from the regular line regiments at Camp Vicars, which included the 14th Cavalry and the 17th, 22nd, and 23rd Infantry Regiments. The Provo's were larger than usual companies, were around 140 men each, and were strenuously physically trained much like today's special forces. Wood also tapped a Moro Constabulary Unit to serve in the Cotabato region of north central Mindanao, which was Datu Piang's and Datu Ali's territory.

These units were tough, fast, and highly mobile. They were the outfits that brought havoc down on the lawless Moros albeit at a high price for the innocents of the population. The scourge and scorched earth policy continued into the winter of 1905 when Wood finally abandoned the concept, sent the Provo's back to their regular regiments and extended Datu Ali's deadline to surrender. His deteriorating health may have had something to do with it too.

Finally, Wood relented to the doctors' recommendations and left Manila on May 26, 1905, to obtain the neurological consultation they had advised. He underwent surgery in Boston on July 7 and would not return to Zamboanga until late October. His surgery today would be labeled incomplete or at best palliative, but it did relieve the pressure on his brain and his symptoms improved, for a time. The tumor was not removed. According to neurosurgeon Jack McCallum, MD, PhD, author of *Leonard Wood*, Dr. Arthur Cabot, Boston's premier surgeon, removed and scraped the bone flap over the tumor but never recognized the bony invasion by the meningioma nor did he even see the tumor.[375]

While he was on Medical leave, Wood had ordered a halt to any active campaigns against the Moros until his return. He had also talked General Corbin out of sending in a temporary replacement for himself while he was gone. Captain George Langehorne, who had been on Wood's general staff, was appointed acting governor of Moro Provence in his absence. Into Langehorne's lap fell Datu Ali's first offer of surrender in late July 1905. Wood had demanded an unconditional surrender from Ali but the fugitive would have none of it and stated he would fight to the death, if not granted a pardon or parole.

Although encouraged to accept it by fellow members of the Moro Legislative Council, Dr. Saleeby and Captain Van Horn, who was the District of Cotabato Governor, Langhorne vetoed the surrender but allowed he would forward the proposal to General Wood. Langhorne's letter never reached the recuperating and traveling Wood. It was a moot point, however, since Corbin, when he heard of Wood's delayed recovery, had passed temporary command of Moro Provence to General James Buchanan of the Department of the Visayas.

Buchanan, in a staff meeting, let it be known that he did not want another massive campaign to capture Ali and asked for suggestions. Captain Frank McCoy had one.

375 McCallum, *Leonard Wood Biography*, 224.

Captain (later Major General) Frank Ross McCoy 1905 Photo courtesy Robert A. Fulton, Morolandhistory.com[376]

McCoy was another one of Wood's general staff officers. Ali's location had been tipped to McCoy by Datu Piang, Ali's father-in-law, and confirmed by Ali's son-in-law, the cleric Sharif Afdal. Both relatives were disgusted by Ali's stubbornness, which had wrought devastation on his family and death to many of Piang's followers.

McCoy had previously been a part of an exploration party which traveled the headwaters of the Rio Grande area nearly a mile high

[376] Robert A. Fulton, Morolandhistory.com.

above the Davao Gulf. There, he knew of a trail where a small force could get to Ali's hideout discretely from behind without detection. Historian Robert Fulton continues the tale: *"Of equal importance, Datu Inuk, a sworn enemy of Ali and Tomas Torres, the long-time head scout (and Pershing's interpreter) for the Americans in Mindanao, volunteered to accompany and guide McCoy to Ali's location, then identify him in person (the few Americans who could recognize him at sight were no longer stationed in the Philippines).*

"In secret, McCoy assembled a 100-man provisional company from the 22nd Infantry Regiment, stationed at Camp Keithley in Lanao; so as not to alert the residents of Cotabato that an operation was underway. They sailed October 11 from Iligan to the small town of Digos on the Davao Gulf with a short stopover in Zamboanga. Picking up two squads of Philippine Scouts, McCoy's party force-marched fifty miles across the high route he had traveled the year before, skirting the flanks of the impressive Mt. Apo, the highest mountain in the Philippines. As they descended into the valley, it was decided to leave the lame and exhausted behind, reducing the expedition to 77 men.

"Four days after leaving Digos and just after dawn, the advance guard, led by 2nd Lt. Philip Remington broke out into a clearing where a house lay. Inuk and Torres spotted Datu Ali, sitting on the porch of the house, with ten of his warriors and shouted out to Remington who ordered an immediate charge. As his men disappeared into the house, Ali stood in the doorway, shouldered a Spanish Mauser rifle and fired almost point blank at the charging Remington, but instead hit and killed Pvt. L. W. Bobbs running beside him. Remington paused, leveled and fired his revolver at Ali, bringing him to his knees but still grasping his rifle. Raising back up to his feet Ali died in a hail of gunfire from at least a dozen of the attackers Krag rifles. As the rest of the column closed in on the house, a gunfight followed. Before long at least fifteen men inside, including one of Ali's sons, were dead, and another four or five wounded. Around twenty women and children were also wounded in the firefight, including Mingka, Piang's daughter and one of Ali's three

wives. Two Americans were killed and three severely wounded. The long hunt was over."[377]

BUD APO WHERE DATU ALI'S HIDEOUT WAS LOCATED

---

377 Ibid.

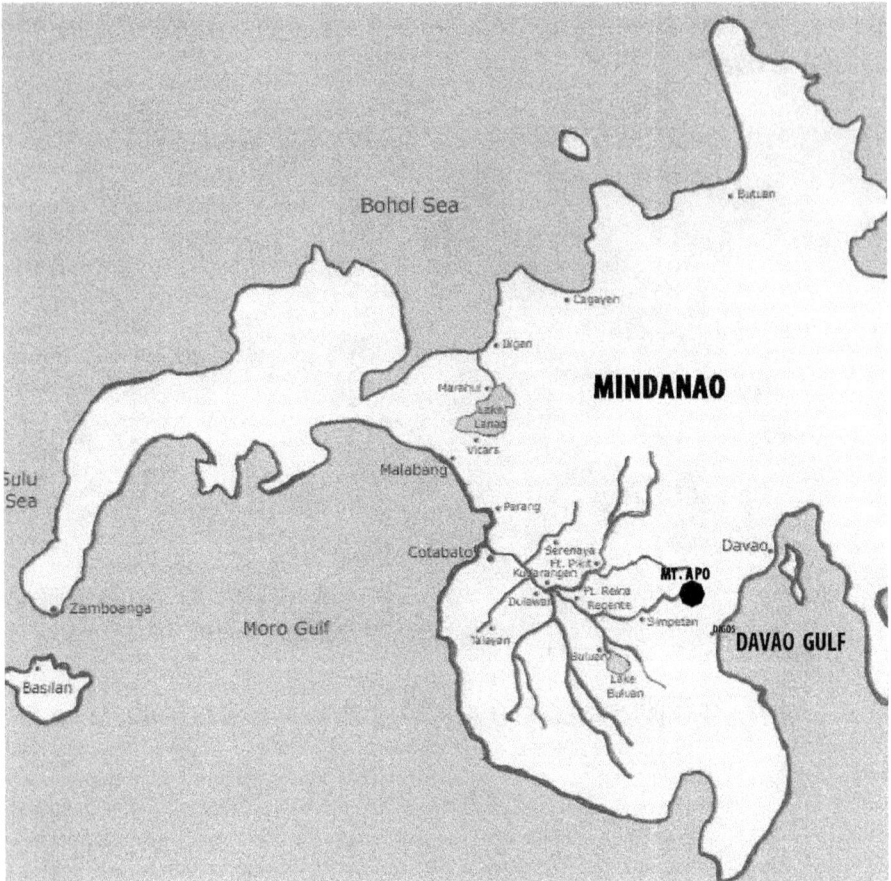

Site of (Mount) Bud Apo where Datu Ali met his end. Map courtesy of moroland.com originator Robert A. Fulton, modified by author.

CHAPTER TWENTY-FIVE

November 19, 1905 – January 31, 1907

"To capture a man who prefers death is almost an impossible feat." –Rowland Thomas, Boston Transcript

SETTING THE STAGE: THE BATTLE OF BUD DAJO

All during the time that Wood was on Medical leave Major Hugh Scott was having his problems with Wood's general staff, particularly the acting governor Captain George Langhorne. At one point, he had to threaten Langhorne with public embarrassment if he would not provide rice from the Army's stores for the starving population in his District. Langhorne relented and supplied the rice.

Wood, on his return to duty, was actually pleased about Datu Ali's death and did not raise the question of why his pre-departure order of no actions against the outlaw had been ignored. Shortly after his return, General Corbin became ill and left the Philippines for a recuperative period. He would not return. Wood was ordered to Manila to take his place, with the post to become permanent February 1, 1906. He had finally achieved his goal of Commander of the District of the Philippines. General Tasker Bliss would replace Wood as Commander of Moro Provence.

In the winter and spring months before he had left for his medical consultations in May 1905 and subsequent surgery, Wood had sent his 3rd Sulu Expedition to revisit the Island of Jolo, where Datu Hassan had met his fate the previous year. The purpose was to collect the *cedulas* head tax, but the end result was the migration of the families, datus and their followers to the top of a volcanic mountain a little over six miles from Jolo City. In addition, there were numerous small battles with the destruction of property and loss of life and destruction of crops during the time the Expedition was tramping around the Island of Jolo.

By the summer solstice of 1905, there were over 600 people living on Bud Dajo (today spelled Dahu) and included amongst the rebels was the treacherous Datu Indanan, whose warriors had fired on Scott's men as they assaulted Hassan's cotta at Pang Pang. There were actually three settlements on the mountain, the largest near the top end of the east trail. The two others were near the ends of the west and south trails respectively. Major Scott, during Wood's absence, recognized that tensions were building between the isolated rebels and their former datus and leaders as well as his own tax collectors and forces. Therefore, he negotiated a temporary agreement that he would hold off on the tax collections if the rebels would return to their homes, and rebuild the villages that had been destroyed during Expedition 3.

The rebels agreed and the relaxation of tensions came just in time before the official state visit of Alice Roosevelt, the President's feisty and free-spirited daughter. All went well during the visit with the exception of a close scare for Major Scott when a U.S. Senator borrowed an Army ambulance, loaded his wife on board, and set out to tour Jolo Island. Scott brought the grumbling Senator back assuring him he was lucky not to be brought back in pieces.

Things remained quiet through Wood's return in late October and transfer to Manila in November. Scott left for the States on a long awaited medical leave in January, leaving as Acting District Governor, Captain James R. Reeves. Then, on January 31, 1906, a hut on the U.S. Army rifle range was burned down.

* * *

February 1 – 19, 1906
Investigation by Reeves implicated the Bud Dajo Moros, who were also implicated in cattle rustling. Captains Reeves and

Langhorne then got together and found out that two of the cattle thieves had sought sanctuary on the mountain, along with a gang of bandits responsible for a local crime spree. The two captains then got their informants to agree to help the Americans in exchange for a full amnesty along with exemption from the cedula for one year. A cash bribe was also involved. Langhorne informed General Wood of the proceedings in a letter dated February 9, 1906 adding that the *"Moros on Dajo are violating their alleged agreement, harboring Cattle thieves and other outlaws and giving trouble. They will probably have to be exterminated."*[378]

Wood agreed. Despite a letter from Roosevelt expressing concern for his health and demanding a reason why he should not be recalled for further medical treatment, Wood ignored the request and proceeded along with his two captains to plan for the attack on Bud Dajo.

* * *

February 21 – March 1, 1906

Wood, before leaving Manila for Zamboanga, ordered two battalions of the 6th Infantry to leave their station on Leyte, one to go immediately to Jolo City and the other to Zamboanga, the headquarters of the Army in Moro Provence on the southern tip of Mindanao. General Tasker Bliss, who had already arrived in the Philippines, was told to accompany Captain Halstead Dorey, one of Wood's general staff, to Jolo for orientation. No mention of the pending action on Jolo was made.

They arrived in Zamboanga on February 28th. The next day, March 1, as he stepped off the Army transport ship at a Jolo dock, General Bliss met Major Elon Wilcox, commander of a 4th Cavalry squadron, and Captain Reeves. Both Reeves and Wilcox were expecting General Wood, not General Bliss. When the confusion was straightened out and Reeves showed Bliss the paperwork authorizing the Bud Dajo cleanup, all three officers,

---

378 Fulton, *MOROLAND 1899-1906,* 265.

at Capt. Dorey's suggestion, wrote letters (the cable was out) to Zamboanga HQ asking for clarification of their responsibilities. The letters reached HQ that evening on the transport's return trip. Another SNAFU.

* * *

March 2, 1906

By the time Wood read the letters (he was not pleased), he had already started things in motion having sent for the 6th Infantry's commander, Colonel Joseph Duncan, and informed him to send two of his Zamboanga Companies to Jolo immediately with *"nothing but blanket rolls, field mess outfit, 200 rounds per man, (and) 7 days field rations."*[379]

He had also called Colonel William S. Scott, commanding officer of the Moro Constabulary, and informed him of an armed rebellion underway on Jolo and asked him to send a company of his Moro Constabulary to help. Although all of his Constabulary Companies were already deployed on missions to suppress the rampant criminal activities in the Sulu, Scott agreed to put together a provisional force of as many as he could find and lead it himself.

One of the popular Constabulary officers was a red haired Brit, who had almost as colorful a history as the legendary William H. Young of earlier chapters. His name was Captain John R. White. Historian and author Robert A. Fulton describes him best: *"White was tall and slim, but with an athletic build. Because of his hair, his friends called him 'Red.' Personable, well-liked and intelligent, White was easily identified by his accent; only twenty-six, he had been born in England in 1879 to a relatively affluent, upper middle-class family....Belying his boyish countenance, he was tough as nails, one of the most combat-tested in the Constabulary, and a dead shot with a pistol. A bachelor, he worked, played and drank hard."*[380]

---

379 *Ibid*, 269.
380 *Ibid*, 270.

Fulton goes on to reveal an impressive life of adventure for such a young soldier. White ran off to join the Greek Foreign Legion right out of college prep school and got into combat with the Ottoman Turks and was wounded. After going home, he heard about the Alaskan and Klondike Gold Rush and set off for the Yukon Territory, where he ran out of money, but learned to work with dynamite for the Canadian Pacific Railroad. In 1898, he joined the American Army and fought in the Philippines for the next two years. Although he had worked his way up the enlisted ranks to sergeant, he wanted to become an officer, but, because he was not a U.S. citizen, he was not eligible…until Act 175 of the Philippine Commission created the Philippine Constabulary. From October 1901, when he was first commissioned a 3rd Lieutenant, he was promoted in less than two years through three ranks to Captain and was picked to assist in organizing the Moro Constabulary. After a convalescent medical leave because of cholera and malaria, he returned to Moroland in October 1905, just after the climactic pursuit of Datu Ali.

Col. William Scott tapped Captain "Red" White to help him put together the provisional Moro Company for the attack on Bud Dajo, and he responded by gathering twenty-nine men from the 1st Sulu Company who were all Muslims. He also garnered twenty additional constables from the 3rd Zamboanga Company who were all Christians.

Captain "Red" White, left and Lieutenant Leonard Furlong, right were two legendary officers of the Moro Constabulary. The Filipino seated on the floor was not identified but is probably Celedonio, the babbaylan boy that White captured on Negros who served him for ten years.[381] Photo courtesy of Robert A. Fulton, morolandhistory.com

Somewhat of a romantic, Red tore a picture of Alice Roosevelt, who he had seen on her state visit, out of a magazine the night before they left Zamboanga for Jolo, and stuck it in his shirt pocket.[382]

* * *

_____

381 J.R. White, *Bullets and Bolos*, The Century Co, New York, 1928, 309.
382 Fultan-Moroland, 271n.

March 3, 1906

On March 3, 1906, at the Jolo pier, the provisional Moro Constabulary Company led by Col. William Scott, two companies of the 6th Infantry led by Col. Duncan and five men of the Army Signal Corps debarked the Army transport ship *Wright*. Major Elon Wilcox and some of his 4th Cavalry and two additional companies of infantry were already on Jolo and would not arrive at the assembly area until later due to their escort assignment of General Bliss. Also later to arrive from Malabang on the south coast of Mindanao below Camp Vickers was the Coast Guard Cutter *Busuanga* carrying two companies of the 19th Infantry and two more troops of the 4th Cavalry.

Inexplicably, General Wood decided to go bird hunting and would miss the first two and a half days of the upcoming battle.

Two incidents of subsequent import happened while Captain Red White was supervising unloading of men and equipment that day. One was the appearance of a an ex sergeant of the Constabulary named Eduardo Fernandez, who White knew and liked, but who had been kicked out after the powers that be had suffered too many embarrassments for his debauchery and gambling. The straw that broke the camel's back was Fernandez having one too many wives. Fernandez wanted in on the fight in order to get back into the Constabulary fold and had actually made a reconnaissance on his own of the mountain top. White issued him a cartridge belt and a rifle. The move likely saved his life.

The second incident was not known to any of the principals on the American side, but likely affected the attitude of the rebels on the mountain and converted most of them to become, or at least act like, *juramentados*, those fierce Islamic warriors who would fight to the death if they could kill the infidels.

What happened was that two of the spies and conspirators, with whom Lt. James Reeves had been negotiating to betray the "evil doers" on the mountain, had witnesses who had seen the massive amphibious force of Americans and Moro Constabulary unloading at Jolo City. They were Datu Janarin and Adam, who historian Fulton describes as a minor headman or leader of the group at the top of the south trail. Reeves had told them that only the Jolo units would be involved in the operation to get them down from the mountain, so when Adam heard about the size of the force being assembled he figured the Americans were going to kill all of them anyway. The two were on the way to meet Reeves when the witnesses reported. Adam turned around and went back, and when Datu Janarin met Reeves without him, Reeves knew the deal was caput.

General Bliss had arrived back in Zamboanga, Mindanao, earlier that Saturday. General Wood invited him aboard the ship *Sabah* for another day of duck hunting.

* * *

Sunday, March 4, 1906

The trail out of Jolo City toward Bud Dajo ran for about two miles to the Schuck Plantation where it split in two, into a trail that circum-navigated the base of the volcanic mountain, one part going south-east and the other northwest. From this elliptical trail, three separate paths originated heading for the crater on top. These were known as the South Trail, the steepest, most difficult climb and had the least cover; the West Trail, which was the longest; and the East Trail, which was fortified the best.

On this Sunday, Colonel Duncan, the force commander, ordered a reconnaissance in force. The section that turned to the right at the Schuck Plantation got lost when the little used trail became confus-ing and split into several different paths. They turned around and re-traced their steps back to Jolo City.

Similar confusion was encountered by the northwest bound reconnaissance column, but they too managed to get back to their assembly point without other difficulty.

Colonel Duncan, knowing he would have better luck with some-one who had been there before, assigned the South trail to Captain Red White's Moro Constabulary with Eduardo Fernandez and another experienced constable, Corporal Sayary on point, for the next day's action. Major Omar Bundy, with three companies of the 6th Infantry, would follow and be in command.

* * *

Monday, March 5, 1906
Colonel Duncan, in command of the expedition, did not leave until the next day Tuesday at 0200. He took with him the mobile reserve force and his headquarters along with Colonel William Scott of the Moro Constabulary, no doubt the latter for his local knowledge and expertise. Major Wilcox would stay in Jolo City as another reserve along with the hospital and reserve supplies. The mobile reserves were the last to depart.

The first of the three attack columns, to reach their trailhead (having left at 0400 this Monday) and come under fire, was Captain Edward P. Lawton's improvised battalion consisting of two companies, B and D, of his own 19th Infantry, and Company G of the 6th Infantry. Along for the assault were a surgeon and two hospital corpsmen. Lawton's battalion also took the first American casualty, a private who was shot in the leg.

Major Bundy, in the late afternoon, ordered Captain White to explore a way to advance up the steep South Trail. So taking Eduardo Fernandez and Corporal Sayary, Captain "Red" White and his two companions with about twenty-five Constables trailing *"scouted the ground ahead in a nerve wracking, tedious, inch-by-inch climb, either scrambling on all fours or crawling on their bellies. Sodden with perspiration from the heat and humidity, the three were continually scratched by thorns and swarmed by biting insects."*[383]

After about three hours of this painful belly-crawling advance, Corporal Sayary, who was in the lead, crawled back to White and whispered:

"Captain Red, I heard voices up ahead. Can't see anything!"

"They sound like Tausugs?" whispered White in his distinctive British accent.

---

383 *Ibid, 279.*

"Yes, Sir."

"Don't move a muscle. Let Eduardo know. I'll crawl back and stop the troops. Be back soon."

With that, White crawled off and Sayary motioned Fernandez over. White, in contact with his constables, sent a messenger back to inform Major Bundy, and after the messenger returned with orders for them to stay put, White crawled back to the point. He and his men stayed in place, silent and relatively motionless for twelve hours. Their sleep was disturbed intermittently by war chants, loud gongs, and drums from the rebels, and multiple insect bites.

Meanwhile, communications were a mess. The signal corps was ineffective due to the terrain, and messengers dispatched from either the columns or from Duncan's Headquarters were slow for the same reason, sometimes up to several hours delay. All columns were stalled by nightfall.

* * *

Tuesday, March 6, 1906

On the South Trail, Captain "Red" White with his outfit now supplemented by four Army sharpshooters, supplied by Captain Sam Schindel of the 6th Infantry, resumed his careful belly-crawling trip up the slope shortly after dawn. Passing the point where Corporal Sayar had heard the voices, he and his point men found a trench that was empty, but they soon came under fire from a high point about 200 to 300 yards up the slope. The U.S. Army sharpshooters began to pick off the enemy snipers, whose rifle fire at that distance had been ineffective.

White, along with an all Moro squad of twelve, continued the advance under fire and soon ran into an *"abattis, a hedgehog-like, impassable fence made from sharpened tree logs, spanning the entire width of the hogback ridge and presenting no easy way around it."*[384]

One of his Moro Constables, Pvt. Diukson, was shot and killed as he tried to crawl over the barrier. Another, Pvt. Usama, was badly wounded. After about two hours of trying to get over or around the

---

384 *Ibid*, 280.

barrier, White's Constabulary troops became the victims of short artillery rounds fired from the U.S. mountain guns. White sent an impolite message back to Major Bundy and Captain Schindel after having to withdraw his troops to safety.

Duncan, who could not see the sharpened-log *abattis* barrier through his binoculars, then decided to order a simultaneous attack, by all three columns on the summit. The problem was that communications were still SNAFU, so critical good timing was almost impossible. Duncan did, however, order up from Jolo City, the Army's new light weight machine gun, the forerunner of the famous BAR (Browning Automatic Rifle) of WWII fame.

On the West Trail, the force was commanded by 4th Cavalry Officer Captain Tyree Rivers. The force included an additional company of 6th infantry and was led by Captain Lewis Koehler, after Captain Rivers was wounded by rebel rifle fire. Koehler's men worked to within about seventy-five yards of a blockhouse cotta sustaining only a few wounded in spite of dense foliage protecting the enemy from being seen. Believing they were in a good position to overrun the blockhouse after a couple of failed attempts and appropriate messages had been sent to Duncan, Koehler put his men at rest while he awaited approval to proceed. Because of the fouled up communications, he never got such a message and his troops spent the night on the trail without blankets.

The East Trail Force was commanded by Captain Edward P. Lawton, who had sent a scouting party of two companies under Captain A. M Wetherill up the slope. They got within seventy-five yards of the summit before being challenged by a Tausig sentry, whom Wetherill dispatched with his scattergun (shotgun). Lawton sent an urgent message to Duncan asking permission to take the summit, but due to the message delays nightfall came before any reply was received. Once again, all three attack units spent the night on the slopes, listening to war cries, gongs, and fighting insects.

* * *

Wednesday, March 7, 1906—The third day under fire

Captain Red White and his barefoot company of mixed Moro and Philippine Constabulary advancing at dawn made it back to the *abattis* barrier from where they had been forced to retreat by the friendly fire of the Yankee artillery. This time they slowly cut a few man-sized holes in the obstructing fence with their bolos and barongs while being protected by the Army sharpshooters. As White sent his men one by one through the openings, *"it seemed they were killed or wounded as fast as I could push then through"*[385]

Red was the last one through and saw his top kick, Sergeant Arasid, take a blast from one of those small hand held cannons called *lantakas*, through his right arm. The force of the blast spun the sergeant 180 degrees before he collapsed. He did survive.

Approaching the cotta, the Constabulary force found themselves in a close-quarters fight. The Moros were throwing everything they could find including rocks and spears at the attackers and they were singing their "death song" while they were doing it.

The cotta walls had bamboo loopholes sticking through from which the defenders could look or poke a rifle through the hollow center to fire at the attackers. Red plugged one of these with a block of wood, so he could gather enough people to go over the wall all at once without warning to the defenders. Earlier, one of his men had been shot through the eye while peeping through the hollow bamboo.

Just after Red had blocked up one of bamboo firing holes a Moro Tausig defender fired through it. The blast caught Red by surprise, and he actually recalled later seeing the splinters fly as the bullet passed through his left thigh just above the knee.[386]

---

385 Ibid, 285.
386 Fulton, MOROLAND 1899-1906, 286.

Inside of a cotta wall on Bud Dajo showing the bamboo firing holes through which the Moros fired, one of which was used to wound Capt. "Red" White.

Eduardo Fernandez, the ex-Constabulary civilian was close by when White was hit. He hollered at another constable that he knew from the old days, Supply Sergeant Arcadio Alga, "Me dan alguna ayuda, Cady! (Give me some help, Cady)."

"Estoy en el camino (I'm on the way)," Alga yelled back.

Together, the two of them half carried and rolled their agonizing British leader down the slope out of range of the fanatic defenders. White swore in his distinct British accent all the way down. They plopped him in a shallow trench with some other wounded, slapped a field dressing around his leg, and when the hospital corpsman was in attendance, returned to the battle. Later Arcadio Alga would be decorated for his actions. Eduardo Fernandez reenlisted after the fight and was not heard from again until some years later when John R. (Red) White found him in the guardhouse for throwing a wild party and, after that, in prison for rape. White managed to get him to a trustee's post until his sentence of seventeen years was over.[387]

---

387 White, *Bullets and Bolos*, 303.

Shortly after White was hit, the Moro Rebels charged with their bolos and barongs. Adam, the Moro leader of the South Trail who was supposed to help the Americans but returned to his village on the mountain when he heard of the size of the force, was said to have charged over the top of the cotta wall with a baby in one arm and his weapon in the other. One participant reported that Adam was hit by a dozen bullets before he hit the ground.[388]

Hearing the melee in progress was Lt. Gordon Johnston of the Army Signal Corps. Johnston was supposed to be running the communications for the attack, but had been thwarted by the impossible terrain and had run toward the noisy fight on the South Trail. As he passed the wounded near the bottom of the South Trail, Captain "Red" White tossed him his scattergun which he carried into the battle. One witness later, said Johnston, was shot by a woman Tausig Moro as he was trying to climb the steep cotta walls.

Captain John "Red" White is on the second stretcher with his face turned away and his hat askew on his head. He wrote on the bottom of the picture: "1. 6th Infantry corporal who died AM after. 2. Myself 3. Packard-cut across the loins with kris. 4. 6th Infantry private shot with slugs-" Photo from White's personal papers archived at the University of Oregon, courtesy of Robert A. Fulton.

388 Ibid, 286.

Johnston soon joined Captain White on a nearby stretcher and the two of them along with one other wounded officer sere soon aboard mules and on their way to the hospital.

Historian Fulton noted that all of the charging Tausig Moros were killed and there was only light resistance the rest of the way to the summit, which the South Force reached by 0730.

Captain Schindel then called for a cease fire, concerned that Captain Lawton's East trail Force might soon be coming over the top.

Meanwhile on the West Trail, Koehler's outfit took the same block-house cotta that had given them trouble the previous day. Just as they were about to assault the summit, Duncan's day-late messenger finally arrived with instructions to withdraw a short distance and await further orders. Koehler reluctantly obeyed thinking the orders were current and not knowing they were a day old.

Of course, the same thing had happened to Lawton who was still awaiting permission to attack the summit.

General Wood on arrival at the base camp, asked for a status briefing. Trailed by his staff, General Bliss and two reporters with a cameraman Wood nearly had a conniption when he discovered the communications mess and lack of coordination.

Confiscating copies of Duncan's delayed delivery orders and Lawton's request which had just arrived, Wood wrote out orders for an immediate assault of the summit by Lawton, and sent it along with a U.S. Navy gun crew toting two light weight Colt automatic machine guns and 4500 rounds of ammo to Lawton at the East Trail-head location.

To add to General Wood's distress, as he watched a number of wounded on their way to the hospital in Jolo City, he spotted an acquaintance and fellow Rough Rider veteran, Lt. Gordon Johnston.[*]

By early afternoon, Lawton's East Trail Force was augmented by the Navy guns from the USS Pampanga and was poised for a charge over the top. When Captain Lawton ordered the charge and

_____

Some months later, Wood would be the right in the center of a controversy surrounding Johnston when he was awarded the Medal of Honor. The controversy was not helped by the fact that the Princeton graduate was a friend of Roosevelt's.

his bugler sounded it, all hell broke loose. Most of the damage was caused by the two Navy machine guns as they raked the Moros from an elevated position about twelve to fifteen steps away. Return fire from the Tausugs was not without its toll. Almost a third of the attackers were casualties with ten KIA and twenty-five WIA. A quick count of the Moro dead, before General Wood ordered them covered with dirt, was in the neighborhood of 400. A cameraman accompanying the reporters took the picture below, not published until several months later.

On January 25, 1907, almost eleven months after the battle, a cropped, black and white copy of the above photograph accompanied an editorial that appeared in the Johnstown (Pennsylvania) Weekly Democrat. Photo is from the National Archives, courtesy of Robert A. Fulton.

A short version of the battle was written by Captain McCoy, who although he did not actually observe any of the action on the 7th, was able pass on this observation as recorded by Richard Kolb: *"It was the most remarkable the fierce dying of the Moros. At every cotta efforts were made to get them to surrender or to send out their women but for an answer a rush of shrieking men and women would come cutting the air and dash amongst the soldiers like mad dogs."*[389]

General Wood himself later recalled of Bud Dajo: *"women are garbed like the men and, in the melee are indistinguishable from them. They advance with their husbands in intrepid rushes, leaping down from the parapets into the attacking force, clutching a soldier in a death grapple and rolling with him down the slope."*[390]

Casualties from the South Trail Battle of March 7 being evacuated by mules. Photo courtesy of Robert A. Fulton.

* * *

---

389 Kolb, "Blaze in the Boondocks, 2002. Fighting on America's Imperial Frontier in the Philippines, 1899-1913," 33.
390 Ibid.

Thursday, March 8, 1906

The next morning, there was only one cotta left, whose occupants had spent their night completely surrounded. As Captain Lawton's party advanced, the Tausugs opened fire from about 150 yards. This time there was no effort to ask for surrender. No such orders had come from below.

At the first volley, one of the Navy gunners, Ensign Cook, was hit. He was replaced by another officer, but the automatic gun ran out of ammunition. A firefight followed by a "bolo rush" ensued with a large number of Tausugs killed. Lt. Bissell of the 19th Infantry, saved the man beside him from being decapitated by one of the bolo men during the rush. He shot the charging man in the head with his revolver.

Even though it was quiet after the bolo rushers had been killed, Lt. Bissell was cautious about entering the cotta. A call for a volunteer by Lawton brought wounded Seaman Joseph Fitz limping forward. He stuck a pistol in his belt, and, with a couple of boxes of cartridges, climbed a tree to peer down into the cotta from his advantage point. What followed was an old-fashioned pistol shootout between Fitz and the defenders down below. The observers could see only Fitz, but they could see the bullets hitting the tree he was in fired from the cotta. After several minutes and several reloads by Fitz, he hollered down that they were all dead.

Rushing through the cotta gate, the attackers found sixty-seven dead bodies. Lawton ordered them cremated. General Wood on his arrival ordered everyone out after they had covered the non-cremated bodies with dirt. They were to expedite the evacuation of the mountain without an accurate body count or damage assessment.

Historian Fulton noted there were at least twenty-four survivors, possibly more. Three women and four children were captured at the South Trail, and twelve to fourteen men escaped but later surrendered through their datus. Apparently, four or five remained defiant including one of the original cattle rustlers.[391]

* * *

---

391 Fulton, MOROLAND 1899-1906, 195.

March 8, 1906 – January 31, 1907

When the fighting was over, somewhere between 600 and 1000 Moro Tausugs had perished. The Yankees had fifteen KIA and fifty-two WIA. The Constabulary Force had six KIA and twenty-one WIA.[392] I believe it's safe to say that the aftermath in the States was a media frenzy using a modern term. Charges of wonton slaughter of women and children versus General Wood's attempted spin of events made for a real newspaper circus that lasted for weeks, finally abated only by news of the great earthquake in San Francisco on April 18, 1906.

Then, in January 1907, the controversy got new life when the photo on page 324 was published with a blistering editorial in a Johnstown, PA newspaper, the *Democrat*. The controversy did not last long, however, and was not sustained. People were reminded that the Philippines were not yet pacified and often asked, "What are we still doing there?" History, as it were, moved on.

392 Kolb, "Blaze in the Boondocks, 2002. Fighting on America's Imperial Frontier in the Philippines, 1899-1913," 33.

CHAPTER TWENTY-SIX

April 28, 1907 – October 24, 1913

"Outnumbered, Always; Outfought, Never." –Motto of the Philippine Constabulary

In the early 20th century, a warfare that would be called unique to the southern Philippines was described by many historians. It was called *"running or going juramentado."* Derived from the Spanish word *juramentar*, and previously described under the title of Chapter Twenty-three, a juramentado referred to a warrior or individual who had sworn an oath to kill infidels. As Richard Kolb points out: *"With hair cropped, eyebrows shaved and arteries and genitals bound to slow the flow of blood, the juramentado waged a personal jihad: Killing Christians assured one's place in Paradise."*[393]

Personal attacks and suicide bombings by jihadists are no strangers to the world today, but in the early 1900's tales of such happenings were tales of legend. Although such stories were told around U.S. campfires for years and dismissed by most as just stories, things began to change when the reality of the *"jittery business"*[394] struck home in the Philippines. The actions of Datu Ali at Bud Apo and the Tausug Moros at Bud Dajo added to the legends. Tales of juramentado fortitude and invincibility grew with each telling of various episodes. One lieutenant wrote the following: *"As I reflected that there might be months and months of this-with every night a possibility of*

---

393 *Ibid, 33.*
394 *Ibid.*

night attacks from juramentados, it cracked my nerves more than I care to admit."[395]

For months after the Bud Dajo battles, General Bliss had been requesting budget help from Wood, without success. The only peace-keeping force he had as Moro Province Governor was the Constabulary Force which was also budget-strained and now the Army wanted the officers loaned to the Constabulary and the civil government returned to their regiments, which put further strain on the police and therefore the peace-keeping functions of the Governor. There was further strain between Bliss and Wood when Bliss's Annual Report to the War department was published in the Congressional Record, basically criticizing Wood's policies.

One of the solutions to the problem was posed to Bliss by Colonel Scott, who urged Bliss to turn over pursuit of some of the criminals wanted by the Army to him as Chief Inspector of the Constabulary. It worked because the Constabulary was a highly mobile, lightly equipped force that could travel much faster and cheaper than an army expedition. From Robert Fulton: *"In early 1907 more than a dozen such small scale successful actions took place in both the Buldung region and on the always turbulent eastern shore of Lake Lanao.....The total men employed and cost had been minimal. There had been less than a dozen Moro deaths, and all those clearly guilty parties. There had been zero Constabulary casualties and the civilian population had been left unmolested and unaffected."*[396]

Although the Constabulary was involved in pursing many of the criminal activities, juramentados were responsible for others, and the Army had to deal with them. In April 1907, juramentados attacked and killed three men of the 4th Cavalry on Jolo. Across the water on Mindanao in the Taraca Valley that same month on April 28, a Constabulary patrol, led by a tall Constabulary 2nd Lt. James (nicknamed Redwood) Wood, was ambushed by "kris wielding" Moros. A private in the patrol was killed, but actions by a close detachment rescued the rest. Corporal Malaco became the first enlisted Moro Constabulary

---

395 *Ibid.*
396 Fulton, *MOROLAND 1899-1906*, 329.

member to win their highest award, the Medal of Valor, in the ensuing action.[397]

* * *

May 1, 1909 – July 4, 1909

In May, two soldiers of H Company, 18th Infantry Regiment, were
attacked and killed by juramentados at Camp Ramain, Mindanao.[398]

On July 4, a juramentado-like attack by the infamous brigand and
former bodyguard of the Sultan of Sulu, Jikiri, in the Sulu Archipelago
occurred as the notorious pirate and his band of cutthroats were found
holed up in a cave on the Island of Patian by troops of the 6th Cavalry.

Actually, Jikiri, tired of being chased by authorities, had left word
where he would be and even sent one of his fathers-in-law (he had
more than one wife) to guide the pursuing Americans to his location.
He also let it be known that he intended to fight to the death as a
Juramentado, an honorable way to go for an Islamic warrior.

Jikiri had been raiding small craft throughout the Sulu for years
and recently had been seeking prey on Borneo as well as numerous
small islands in the archipelago. The British Governor on Borneo had
actually put a large bounty on Jikiri's head, but the bounty hunters pursuing him were captured by Jikiri's men who *"cut off their ears and fingers and sent the hapless and illicit posse (they had crossed international
boundaries without permission) back to the mortified British Governor."*[399]

The first Americans to reach Jikiri's home island of Patian was
Lt. Archie Miller's company of thirty riflemen of dismounted 6th
cavalry along with a machine gun crew and interpreter Charlie Schuck.
They arrived on July 2nd and were promptly led to Jikiri's cave by his
father-in-law.

What happened over the next couple of days was analogous to an
episode of *Keystone Cops* were it not so bloody and tragic. On the day
of arrival, interpreter Schuck verified Jikiri's presence and urged him

---

397 *Ibid.*

398 Kolb, "Blaze in the Boondocks, 2002. Fighting on America's Imperial Frontier in
the Philippines, 1899-1913," 33.

399 Fulton, MOROLAND 1899-1906, 351.

to send out the women and children. Two women, three children, and one old man appeared and surrendered. Then, before the machine gunner could get off a shot, he was killed by a single shot from the cave, and a replacement shooter was wounded.

After a few bursts from the machine gun point blank into the cave from a distance of just a few yards, return fire from the cave destroyed the wooden tri-pod of the gun which slid backward down a slope with Yankee gunners and riflemen in pursuit. A jury-rigged support stand made from tree branches was rejected as unstable by the experienced gunners who refused to man the weapon.

The angry Lt. Archie Miller had one of his rifleman fire the weapon which resulted in a few wild shots and repeated jams. Fortunately the commander of the expedition, Captain Bryam, had followed Miller and showed up just before dark. He ordered the firing stopped and had his troops form a semi-circle under cover in front of the cave and await daylight.

On 3 July 1909, additional American forces from two Navy gunboats and the Army ship Nashville, showed up during a heavy rainfall. Jikiri's sharpshooters had kept the encircled soldiers' heads down all day. Capt. Bryam accepted an offer from the Navy to set up two of the Colt Automatic Rifles, and a small cannon, and, from the Army ship, a thousand pound, three-inch mountain gun. By the time they were set up it was dark.

The next morning on this U.S. Independence Day in 1909 was unique in that about 4000 Moros from other islands, principally Jolo, and which included the war chief of other Moro episodes, the Datu (and Panglima) Indanan and also the Sultan of Sulu, arrived to watch the proceedings. The Sultan had apparently decided that if the Americans did not kill Jikiri, then they would since the pirate's actions were bad for business.

Shortly after sunrise, the mountain gun under the command of Lt. R. S. (Polly) Parrott was first fired at the cave from about fifty feet away, its crew protected by firing from the dismounted Cavalry rifles and the Navy machine guns. After ten rounds, Polly Parrott decided to move his thousand pound gun close, to within thirty feet of the cave's entrance. Before his gunner could fire at the close range one of Jikiri's men stepped out of the cave and fired a shotgun into the gun crew, mortally wounding one of the three he knocked down.

Parrott then ran to the gun and pulled the lanyard which resulted in recoil of the weapon which sent it backward over a four foot drop to a resting position on its side.

While Polly and his crew were recovering and repositioning the gun from this latest disaster, Bryam sent Charlie Schuck to repeat his offer of surrender. The defiant reply:

"Come and get us, Jikiri will never surrender."[400]

Subsequent chanting and singing by the Moro pirates were interpreted by Charlie Schuck as *"they were singing their death song."*[401]

Suddenly, the cut-off and isolated pirates came charging out of the cave without further warning. Jikiri and only six of his juramentados killed one U.S. Soldier and wounded another fifteen in vicious hand to hand combat in a matter of seconds. Before it was over and all of the juramentados were dead, four U.S. Medals of Honor were earned by the U.S. combatants. Not counting his years of piracy it was determined that just recently Jikiri had been responsible for nine American deaths, including American civilians, and had injured another twenty-six.[402]

Robert Fulton, in his meticulous research, quoted a personal letter of Polly Parrott's to his friend, Bill: *"For a week afterward I had nightmares and saw the whole thing in my dreams. Every officer who was there said the same thing. Baer said he scarcely closed his eyes for a week without seeing it. Every jump it seemed to me they went three feet in the air and covered about ten feet, first to one side and then the other, and with each jump the barongs would come down with all a man's weight behind it. Wilson was right beside the door and caught the first slash in the back of the neck, making a cut a foot long and very deep along the side of the neck, under the jaw and down the back. John Kennedy got the*

400 *Ibid, 355.*

401 *Ibid, 356.*

402 Kolb, *"Blaze in the Boondocks, 2002. Fighting on America's Imperial Frontier in the Philippines, 1899-1913,"* 33.

next- a slanting blow across the back of the head and neck. Miller caught the flat of a barong on the kidneys, which laid him up for a week. If it had been the edge he would have been cut in two. One man's hand was sliced off and several others cut more or less seriously, before the Moros were all killed. I don't suppose the whole thing lasted more than ten seconds, but I never want to see another ten like it."[403]

Fulton's casualty assessment was also more detailed than quoted by some. Two Americans killed, twenty two wounded including two sailors. Besides the seven juramentados, three women were shot as they exited the cave after the melee. One fell on her infant who survived. There was controversy as to how many of them were armed. Some of the wounded Americans were disabled for life.

* * *

September 24 – December 31, 1911

More than two years passed with numerous episodes of piracy, rape, kidnapping, and other assorted crimes challenging the Constabulary and the U.S. Army. Gunboats of the U.S. Navy made a big difference in suppressing high seas piracy, and episodes of heroism and daring established the Philippine and Moro Constabularies reputation as an effective police force for the Philippine Islands. Two more episodes for this period are noteworthy.

The first was an attack on a shore party of twenty-one sailors from the USS Pampanga, the same vessel that supplied the machine gun crews for Bud Dajo. This time the location was on Basilan Island near the town of Mundang.

---

403 Fulton- Moroland 357.

Basilan Island

Mundang
(Mangan Plantation)

Ambushed by about twenty Moros, the sailors lost one KIA and seven WIA. Five sailors were awarded the Medal of Honor in the fierce hand to hand battle.

In late December 1911, the second battle of Bud Dajo occurred when around a thousand U.S. soldiers surrounded about 800 Moros who were again holed up in the Bud Dajo crater trying to avoid starvation, the crippling *cedulas* head tax, assaults by their neighboring datus, and to avoid the recent disarmament order issued by General Pershing.

* * *

SETTING THE STAGE: THE SECOND BATTLE OF BUD DAJO
A number of significant events occurred prior to the second battle which allowed for the event to occur and almost all were political in one form or another. The events:
- Pershing returned to the Philippines Nov. 1909, now a Brig. General
- Lt. Col. John "Red" White is selected to manage the Moro Province Fair, late 1910

- Pershing stages the Moro Province Fair, February 1911
- Major General James Franklin Bell replaces Major General Leonard Wood.
- Political infighting between the U.S. Army Philippine Scouts & the Constabulary.
- 1st Lt. Walter Rodney is killed by a juramentado on Jolo. April 16, 1911
- Capt. Furlong, the legendary member of the Moro Constabulary, is a suicide, July 11, 1911
- Gen. Bell supports Pershing's Executive Order # 24 to disarm the Moros, Sept. 8, 1911
- Both the Scouts and Constabulary object to Order # 24.
- Gen. Wood, now Army Chief of Staff, is aware of Order #24, Fall of 1911
- Desertions occur in the Moro Constabulary, join the outlaws. October and November 1911
- Outlaws and others reoccupy Bud Dajo, defy authorities. Dec. 1911

On reviewing the above list, it becomes obvious that events were spiraling out of control in Moroland. Budgetary restrictions on both the Philippine Scouts, who sacrificed about one-third of their manpower, and the Constabulary were significant enough to hamper law enforcement in the southern islands to the point of near anarchy at times. No place was entirely safe.

Pershing had staged the Moro Province Fair to garner political favor of Lt. Col. "Red" White, and others, since he didn't have the manpower to use from his own forces to suppress the out of control Moro outlaws. He gave the management of the Fair to White, who did a magnificent job, relished the honors he received because of it and became a friend of Pershing's whom he had initially disliked. It didn't hurt that Pershing recommended him for a commission in the U.S. Army.

Likewise, General Bell, our hero of previous chapters, was skeptical of the young General Pershing, no doubt influenced by the departing General Leonard Wood. Pershing won him over, too.

When young 1st. Lt. Walter H. Rodney was attacked and killed by a juramentado, while walking with his daughter just outside of the garrison compound on Jolo, the outrage among witnesses and the garrison troops and wives was almost too much for Pershing, who for the first time realized that his policies of reasonableness with the Moros was not going to work like it had in the past.

The political infighting between the Scouts led by Major C. C. Smith and Captain Leonard Furlong of the Constabulary was aggravated by Furlong's successes and Smith's failures, the latter no doubt at least partially due to the bureaucracy, cost, and slowness of moving the Scouts around as compared to the fast, mobile, and less expensive Constabulary. Although both were instructed by Pershing to cooperate, neither would speak to the other. A major mistake was made when General Bell, now acting as the Commander of all the Philippines, rebuked Pershing and his request to transfer Smith out of the area to dampen the problem. Pershing had no choice but to then put a request in to have Furlong transferred even though he favored him over Smith. When Furlong was ordered to Manila for medical evaluation by his Constabulary superiors, he took it as a reprimand and wound up committing suicide. The whole of the Constabulary took it badly and became demoralized.

Although Pershing had requested and General Bell had approved a six month leave back to the States, the situation now required something else, particularly after Bell had transferred one Philippine Scout Battalion out of the province. Not getting any help from the demoralized Constabulary, Pershing changed his tactics and decided to issue Executive Order No. 24, the disarming of the Moros.

Neither the Scouts nor the Constabulary, whose jobs it was going to be, were happy about enforcing an almost impossible task. Most were savvy enough to know that a few weapons might be turned in but most would be hidden. The actual response by the Moros, that of fleeing to Bud Dajo again on Jolo, shouldn't have been too surprising, but the desertions by Moros from the Constabulary was. Army Chief of Staff General Leonard Wood was probably licking his chops in anticipation of vindication of his previous heavy handed policies.

Pershing had placed a deadline of compliance on his Order No. 24 of December 2nd. On November 28, before the deadline, *"waves of Tausugs charged the Taglibi encampment (of U.S. forces on Jolo) but were thrown back, hung up on the barbed wire" (ordered placed around the camps by a prudent Pershing).*[404]

Patrols sent out after the deadline sighted a few bands of Moros, who quickly scattered before they could be challenged. Meanwhile, back in the States, General Wood was cautioning members of the Taft administration about his concerns that disarming the Moros might trigger renewed fighting in the Islands, that last thing Taft would want just prior to the upcoming Presidential election year in 1912. No doubt Wood was laying the groundwork for his own Presidential bid later. The result was the appearance of Newton Gilbert, the ailing Governor General Forbes' right hand man, in Jolo to meet with Pershing. It was a surprise visit.

Gilbert had gotten wind of Pershing's intent to launch a major enforcement of the new disarmament order on the Moros holed up on Bud Dajo. After the visit it was obvious that Pershing had agreed to avoid significant bloodshed. The result of Leonard Wood's agitation was most likely just the opposite of what he wanted. Instead of Pershing getting involved in a bloody massacre, he laid siege to the Moros holed up on Bud Dajo for over a week. On December 19th, twenty of the culprits surrendered their weapons and for the next few days a *"steady stream came down off the mountain, particularly women and children."*[405]

By Christmas Day, only a few holdouts were still on the mountain. From Richard Kolb: *"Timely maneuvering prevented excessive bloodshed; the crater was cleared at a cost of only three soldiers wounded and only 12 Moros killed."*[406]

---

404 Fulton, MOROLAND 1899-1906, 423.

405 Ibid, 427.

406 Kolb, "Blaze in the Boondocks, 2002. Fighting on America's Imperial Frontier in the Philippines, 1899-1913," 33.

CHAPTER TWENTY-SEVEN

January 1, 1912 – December 31, 1913

"None but the dead are permitted to tell the truth." –Mark Twain

SETTING THE STAGE: THE BATTLE OF BUD BAGSAK

Except for presidential politics, the year 1912 passed relatively peacefully. Woodrow Wilson easily gained for his Democratic Party the Presidency, basically handed over by the Republican (Taft)—Bull Moose Party (Roosevelt) split. Wilson was *"indifferent to the (Philippine) islands and had given it little thought."*[407]

The Philippine Constabulary, including its two Moro Companies, had regained its strength led by one of its dominant personalities, the Prussian emigrant Captain Oscar Preuss. Preuss had replaced Furlong, as the most respected hero and officer.

Moro resistance in the Sulu was quiet after the second battle of Bud Dajo, but had not disappeared and was still active, particularly on Jolo, led by Datu Naquib Amil. In December, Pershing picked up the dormant unfinished business of disarming the Moros, which he hoped would be more successful since there was a new generation of Moro leaders. It actually fanned the flames of a new resistance. Civil agents sent by the District Governor to Datu Amil's stronghold near Taglibi on the north coast of Jolo (see map page 177) were rebuffed when they asked for weapons. Fulton reports that a curt message was sent back: *"Tell your soldiers to come on and fight!"*[408]

---

407 Fulton, MOROLAND 1899-1906, 431.
408 Ibid, 433.

Datu Amil shows a defiant war painted face at one of the bicharas (peace talks) prior to the battle at Bud Bagsak. He told one of the Civil Agents "Tell your soldiers to come on and fight"! Library of Congress photo courtesy of Robert Fulton.

That was the first incident in the sequence of events that led to the bloodiest battle of the Moro Campaigns. The incidents included:

- Datu Amil defies order to disarm. December 1912.
- Philippine Scouts led by Capt. Patrick McNally and assisted by a Moro Constabulary Company approached Datu Amil's cotta, were fired upon, although bearing a white flag, and lost ten KIA and twenty-three WIA in the ensuing battle. January 12, 1913.

- Juramentados attack detachments of 8th Cavalry and Constabulary at Camp Severs near Taglibi, Jolo, two KIA and four WIA. Mid-January 1913. Pershing evacuates American civilians.
- Between six and ten thousand Moros leave their homes to occupy Bud Bagsak, ten miles east of Jolo City. Pershing asks Sultan of Sulu to negotiate return of Moros to their homes.
- Moros continue attacks and sniping at Camp Severs. Jan – Feb 1913.
- Unrest among Filipino Christians in Zamboanga, Mindanao. Possible resurgence of Philippine Revolution. Rumors of unrest on Jolo reach Manila Press. February 27.
- Governor General Forbes approves increase in Constabulary Force by 40% (700 men).[409]
- Datu Amil offered amnesty if he turned in the guns, most of which were modern weapons purchased in Borneo or China. Nothing was said about bladed weapons.
- The rebel datus reject peace meetings aboard an Army vessel. May 1913. Sultan's peace efforts fall short, stopped by Datu Mandi, one of the rebels.
- Pershing fearing imminent attack by the Bud Bagsak Moros arranges preemptive strike, June 11, 1913.

Richard Kolb continues the story: *"About 1200[410*] troops, mostly Philippine Scouts, led by now-Brig General Pershing marched against Datu Amil's followers. U.S. units included M. CO., 8th Infantry; H Troop, 8th Cav; and the 40th Mountain Artillery Battery. It took four days of bloody combat to overrun all of the crater's five forts. To the cry of 'mak sabil' (to the sword) those 'dressed up to die' repeatedly charged American lines; not one made it past the U.S. perimeter. More than 500[411**] Moros died defending the volcanic fortress."[412]*

On the last day of fighting, June 15, 1913, the exhausted American and Constabulary troops fought against the entrenched Moros

---

409 Ibid, 440.
410* Fulton's count was 883.
411** Fulton estimates 200-300.
412 Kolb, "Blaze in the Boondocks, 2002. Fighting on America's Imperial Frontier in the Philippines, 1899-1913," 33.

for over nine hours, and sustained nearly half of all their casualties. Besides those units listed above by Kolb, included in the three attack columns led by Pershing were seven companies of Philippine Scouts and three hospital corps units, a total of 883 officers and men.[413] The Americans lost fifteen KIA and twenty-nine WIA, Scouts and Constabulary included.[414]

Although the war was not over, it was winding down. On 24 October, the last major battle of the Moro Campaigns was fought by Philippine Scouts at Bud Talipao. People in Talipao municipality on island of Jolo refused to pay road tax. They fortified themselves in Mt. Talipao on Jolo Island and on Oct. 22, 1913, were engaged by a unit of Philippine Scouts, who lost six KIA and forty WIA[415] (Fulton says nine WIA[416]) in a battle lasting two days. By the end of 1913, American combat units had been withdrawn from the field.

---

413 Fulton, MOROLAND 1899-1906, 442.

414 Ibid, 449.

415 Kolb, "Blaze in the Boondocks, 2002. Fighting on America's Imperial Frontier in the Philippines, 1899-1913."

416 Fulton, MOROLAND 1899-1906, 477.

EPILOGUE

Former President Teddy Roosevelt had told General Leonard Wood that if he could not run for President in 1920, that he wanted Wood to do it. Roosevelt died in his sleep on January 6, 1919. His doctors blamed it on a probable pulmonary embolus (blood clot traveling to the lung) from thrombophlebitis, from which he had suffered just three weeks earlier. Leonard Wood did run for the Presidency and nearly won the Republican nomination, which was secured by Harding. His biographer, Jack McCallum, MD, PhD,[417] indicated he probably would have secured the nomination and been elected except for a manipulation of parliamentary procedures and bribery used by his opponents. Leonard Wood died in surgery in 1927 during a third operation on his recurrent meningioma, which had grown to a massive size and invaded critical blood vessels in the brain. He had been prevented from an active command in Europe during WWI by his old nemeses, Generals Pershing and Bliss. Except for the Army training base at Fort Leonard Wood, MO, there are few memorials to the dynamic General who has been called the "Architect of American Imperialism."[418]

Colonel John R. White, the red headed leader of the Philippine Constabulary, recovered from his wounds, although left with a stiff knee for life. After several months in various hospitals, he accepted a position as warden of the Iwahig Penal Colony on the Island of Palawan. He later served as a Lt. Col. in the U.S. Army in 1918 under Pershing. His administrative office of the 202nd Military Police Battalion was in Paris at the end of the war. Thereafter, he settled back in the States, became superintendent of Sequoia National Park, where he served for nearly twenty-five years before his death. White has personal papers archived at the University of Oregon, Knight Library,

---

417 McCallum, Leonard Wood Biography, 298.
418 McCallum, Leonard Wood Biography.

Special Collections. He is also the author of *Bullets and Bolos, Fifteen Years in the Philippine Islands.*

The Philippine Constabulary served alongside American troops in WWII. It was the oldest of the independent nation's armed forces established in 1901. It became a nucleus of the Commonwealth Army in 1936, and its Military Police Division in 1946. In 1959, it was again renamed the Philippine Constabulary. Then, in 1975, it was reorganized again following creation of the Integrated National Police and operated under a joint command until 1991, when it became the Philippine National Police. At that time, its responsibilities included (besides policing the nation) fire and jail services, counterterrorism, and counterinsurgency operations.

Today, the Philippine Government has its hands full in trying to maintain peace amongst several factions still agitating for Moroland independence. The Moro Islamic Liberation Front (MILF) and the Moro National Liberation Front (MNLF) are populist movements easily confused by officials and others with terrorist outfits like the Abu Sayyaf Group (ASG). As historian Fulton points out, not many of us are aware that Moroland today is an active front on the now (Obama Administration) politically incorrect "War on Terror." Although the Moros even today have never been subdued, the hope is that if they can control their own radicalized members to respect human rights and the laws of their nation, whether it is the Philippines or someday an independent one, perhaps they can learn to live together with the rest of the human race. Otherwise, the world will eventually find a way to destroy any group no matter their religion or origin that preys on the innocent or helpless.

END

APPENDIX I

A Squad is the smallest unit of the army, typically nine to ten soldiers, and usually a "noncom," meaning non-commissioned officer (NCO) (i.e., a corporal or sergeant is in charge). Today, with highly trained specialists, we have a much more complicated organization, but, in 1899, it was not so complicated. Privates were privates without a stripe. Prior to 1919, the insignia of private first class consisted of the insignia of the branch of service without any arcs or chevrons. The Secretary of War approved "an arc of one bar" for privates first class on 22 July 1919. In 1898, corporals had two stripes and sergeants had three or more.

A Platoon consisted of two or more squads, usually twelve soldiers minimum, at the turn of the 19th century, but very flexible, particularly in the volunteers. Today, a platoon at full strength can be sixteen to forty-four soldiers and two to four squads. The platoons are rarely at full strength and usually commanded by a lieutenant with an NCO as second in command.

A Company in today's army would be 62 to 190 soldiers. In 1898, a company commander, usually a captain or major, would be lucky to have thirty plus soldiers in three or more platoons, especially in the volunteers.

A Battalion consists of 300 to 1000 soldiers in four to six companies usually commanded by a Lt. Colonel or Colonel. In 1899, a battalion was more commonly commanded by a major. Battalions today are about the same size. When my Army Reserve Hospital was recalled in 1990-91 for Desert Storm, we were battalion size with some twenty-four doctors and over 400 personnel.

A Regiment is composed of two or more battalions, usually at least three. When the 1st North Dakota Volunteer Regiment was activated in May 1898, it was undersized with just seven companies in two battalions. It later filled out with eleven companies.

A Brigade is composed of two to five Battalions of 3000 to 5000 soldiers and usually commanded by (you guessed it!) a Brigadier General. In 1898, provisional brigades were often created on the spot as combat missions required. These creative units are frequently mentioned in the text of this story and were real, active combat units (e.g., Wheaton's Brigade).

A Division is 10,000 to 15,000 soldiers in three or more brigades and is commanded by a two star Major General.

A Corp 30,000 to 60,000 soldiers in two or more divisions and is commanded by a three star Lieutenant General.

INDEX

ABOUT THE AUTHOR

William Franklin Hook, MD, a graduate of Stanford University and the Jefferson Medical College of Jefferson University, Philadelphia, PA, is a retired physician radiologist, ex associate professor of radiology U of North Dakota School of Medicine, and author. He currently lives in Hot Springs, SD. Some of his work can be seen on UND's Radiology website: http://www.med.und.edu/radiology/xrayreading.html

Dr. Hook has a long and distinguished military career. Besides his three year active duty Navy time, he was a reserve Army officer. Col. Hook commanded the 311th Evacuation Hospital during its deployment to the Middle East during the First Persian Gulf War (Desert Storm). His military awards include the National Defense Medal with clusters, Armed Forces Reserve Medal, Army Service Ribbon, Army Reserve Component Medal, Overseas Service Ribbon, Armed Forces Expedition Medal (Cuba), Meritorious Service Medal, Army

Commendation Medal (Desert Storm), Liberation of Kuwait Medal (Saudi Government), and the Kuwait Liberation Medal. Col. Hook belongs to the American Legion and is a lifetime member of the VFW.

His publications include:

"Common Sense and Modern First Aid." Bismark Medical Foundation, 1966.

"Complications of Cardiac Catheterization and Angiography." *The Journal Lencet 88*. June 1968. 135.

"Anterior Mediastinal Teratoids." *Minnesota Medicine*. 1972, 55-238.

"Pulmonary Embolism, Diagnosis & Management." *Reports of the Q&R Clinic 4.3*, 1984.

"Acute Tubular Necrosis. *Reports of the Q&R Clinic 4.3*, 1984.

"Four Phase Bone Scan." *Reports of the Q&R Clinic 5.3*, 1985.

"False Positive GI Bleed Scan." *Reports of the Q&R Clinic 6.3*, 1986.

X-Ray Film Reading Made Easy, CD-ROM (2001).

www.ingramcontent.com/pod-product-compliance
Lightning Source LLC
Chambersburg PA
CBHW071404090426
42737CB00011B/1339